THE HISTORY
OF TORTURE IN ENGLAND

PATTERSON SMITH SERIES IN
CRIMINOLOGY, LAW ENFORCEMENT, AND SOCIAL PROBLEMS

A listing of publications in the SERIES *will be found at rear of volume*

PUBLICATION NO. 180: PATTERSON SMITH SERIES IN
CRIMINOLOGY, LAW ENFORCEMENT, AND SOCIAL PROBLEMS

THE HISTORY OF TORTURE IN ENGLAND

By

L. A. PARRY

M.D., B.S., F.R.C.S.

Reprinted with the addition of
an Introduction by Sawyer F. Sylvester, Jr.,
and an Index

PATTERSON SMITH

Montclair, N. J.

First published London 1934 by
Sampson Low. Marston & Co., Ltd.

Reprinted 1975 by
Patterson Smith Publishing Corporation
Montclair, New Jersey 07042

New material copyright © 1975 by
Patterson Smith Publishing Corporation

Library of Congress Cataloging in Publication Data

Parry, Leonard Arthur.
    The history of torture in England.

    (Patterson Smith series in criminology, law enforce-
ment, and social problems. Publication no. 180)
    Reprint of the 1934 ed. with addition of introduction
and index.
    Bibliography: p.
    1. Torture—England—History. I. Title.
HV8599.G8P3   1975   364.6'7'0942   74–172590
            ISBN 0–87585–180–0

This book is printed on permanent/durable paper

INTRODUCTION TO THE REPRINT EDITION

AT a time when we can look on torture as a relic of a brutal and unenlightened past, we tend to forget that a legal system such as ours, with its emphasis on rational proof, evidentiary data, and a sense of balance between protection of the accused and of the public, is a luxury achieved after centuries of ideological and scientific ferment. Even now, the temptation to force the criminal to damn himself out of his own mouth still lurks in the shadows of our refined jurisprudence. How much more powerful must have been that temptation when legal systems could not call upon the techniques of scientific proof or when the systems themselves were threatened by conspiracies they could not penetrate. Yet, it is noteworthy that within the history of judicial torture there is also a history of attempts—some successful, some not—to limit its use.

Picture, if you will, the court of a District Magistrate in traditional China. The headman and constables with their whips and clubs were frequently called upon to produce confessions from reluctant defendants. Even considerably later, the Ch'ing Code allowed the torture of both principals and witnesses for the purpose of extracting confessions and evidence as a normal part of judicial procedure. The forms of torture included beating, twisting the ears, and the use of thumbscrews. In addition, it was possible to aggravate the death penalty—usually carried out by strangulation or by decapitation—by the horrible "death by slicing." Even in those days, however, these procedures could

[v]

only be called upon in certain preestablished cases and used within prescribed limits.[1]

In the judicial procedure of ancient Greece, the application of torture was generally limited to slaves; though, if his offense touched upon political conspiracy or the like, the free citizen might also be subject to it. The torture of slaves might, at first glance, seem to open up a rather limited source of information, until one realizes the pervasiveness of slavery in Greece and the positions of importance which slaves often occupied. Lea notes among the methods of torture "the wheel . . . , the ladder or rack . . . , the comb with sharp teeth . . . , the low vault . . . , in which the unfortunate witness was thrust and bent double, the burning tiles . . . , the heavy hogskin whip . . . , and the injection of vinegar into the nostrils."[2]

In ancient Rome, slaves were also subject to torture, and to an almost limitless extent. As in Greece, their occupation of numerous positions of commercial importance and trust made them an available source of information in both civil and criminal matters. Slaves who were condemned in capital cases might, as in China, suffer aggravation of the death penalty. At various times in Roman history, laws regulating the use of torture in judicial proceedings were enacted. A slave could not be tortured, for example, to implicate his master; the plaintiff in an action wherein the defendant was tortured could himself be tortured if he failed to sustain his charges; no free citizen of Rome was supposed to be liable to torture. And yet by the time of the later Empire all of these limitations had been gradually breached. When republicanism changed to Caesarism and the philosophy of "Senatus Populusque Romanus" to the cult of the Emperor, the crime which became the threat to those at the apex of legal

1. Bodde, D., and Morris, C., *Law in Imperial China* (Cambridge, Mass.: Harvard University Press, 1967), pp. 91–8.
2. Lea, Henry C., *Superstition and Force* (New York: Haskell House, 1971), p. 326.

power was *crimen laesae majestatis*. Under this accusation, citizens were permitted to be tortured, and slaves tortured to implicate their masters. The scope of *majestas* under some emperors became widely extended, and, with it, the legitimate use of torture. The sanctioning of such practices in Rome through the concept of *majestas* is important, since in later times this idea in its more modern guises of treason and heresy would more often than not be the prime excuse for the resort to torture.

Among the barbarian tribes of Europe, on the other hand—much as with the early Saxons of England—the concept of "crime," as thought of today, was unknown. The wrongs which one might do another were considered private matters for which one took private vengeance or sought private recompense. If there were any conception of a community's being offended by an individual's act, it was not that the state was offended, for such did not exist. In those cases where the injured party could not seek his own satisfaction—as in homicide—the collectivity which bore his injury was the one closest to him, his family; and the resort to feud was not at all uncommon.

In those times, the law—what little there was of it—inhibited only very slightly a man's right to exact his own retribution. Later on, it could insist that the injured party accept a money payment in place of blood; but the substitution had to be fair and accepted and made widely public. Courts were held in the open air. Judges had no great power, but applied the customs of the people, the common law. Any arbitrary decision would have been scoffed at and disobeyed, and the court would have lost what little hard-won ability it had to keep the peace. Under this sort of system, the torture of a litigant would have been inconceivable. His appeal was not to his judges for proof of his cause, but to God. He would wage his law by oath or sustain the ordeal or render himself subject to divine choice in trial by battle.

Torture, therefore, was virtually unknown among the primitive peoples of early Europe. What factors cause it then to be so pervasive in many jurisdictions of the Continent in later years? Two have been cited: one, the revival of Roman law and with it the memory of the widespread use of torture in the later Empire; and, second, the Holy Office of the Inquisition. Either of these alone might have been sufficient to introduce torture into the criminal procedure of those countries influenced, but the combination and interaction of them both made it irresistible.

The breakown of feudalism, with its roughly independent governmental units and its interdependence of governor and governed, and the gradual coalescence of power in the hands of the Crown brought about a fundamental change in the nature of the legal systems themselves. The great—now anonymous—mass of citizenry on the one hand and the increasingly bureaucratic state on the other were more polarized entities than the more integrated units of feudalism had been. The law, heretofore the crystalized custom indigenous to the people it governed, changed to a positive law, legislated from a remote central office and enforced by a body of strangers. Law came to be more rationalized and more instrumental, i.e., it was increasingly a tool for implementing the policy of governmental bureaucracy rather than an embodiment of the visible mores of a self-governing people.

In France, for example, in the thirteenth century, the Crown had greatly extended the royal prerogative, aided in its efforts by the growing hosts of civil lawyers which would come to be the backbone of so many burgeoning governments. These servants of the Crown had trained for their tasks in the universities, where interest in the Roman law was newly revived. This system of law and administration which had governed an empire before seemed meet to govern one again; and the Roman law not only had sanctioned torture but had a procedural and evidentiary system congenial to its use.

While the nation-states of Europe were in the process of development, another bureaucratic government—already rich in power—was mounting a major campaign against its internal enemies. The Church, having suppressed with considerable effectiveness those who openly resisted its supremacy, now faced the far more troublesome problem of heresy. For a while, it was more than equal to the task, for it invented what was perhaps the most formidable engine for the crushing of dissidents known to Western Christendom—the Inquisition.

The main features of the Inquisition could not have been better designed for the introduction of torture. First of all, one must not underrate the magnitude of the threat which heresy presented to a Christian world at all times. Just as *crimen laesae majestatis* was seen to threaten the very foundations of the Roman Empire, and treason to question the very right to exist of any government, so heresy disputed the ideological foundations of the Roman Catholic world and, perhaps of more practical importance, it questioned the legitimacy of the functionaries of the Church and the system of authority which supported them. The feverish attempts to extirpate witchcraft in the Middle Ages cease to be puzzling when it is realized that the prime danger which the Church saw in witchcraft was that it was heretical.

To war against such fearsome enemies, the Inquisition used its most effective weapons. It enlisted the aid of the secular arm of the law, threatening uncooperative governments with interdiction and individuals with excommunication. It pursued the suspected heretic relentlessly on the merest breath of suspicion. The poor wretch thus accused was assumed to be guilty, and even his own attempts to exonerate himself—whose ineffectiveness was aggravated by the absence of counsel—were frequently themselves condemned as punishable obstinacy. All the efforts of his inquisitors were bent on sustaining the legitimacy of their original accusation. In the pursuit of heresy and witchcraft, the flitting shades of opinion, supposition, reputation, and rumor were deemed probative evidence. In a sense, it could not be otherwise with offenses which would be unlikely to leave any material trace. The ultimate confirmation of the prisoner's heresy could therefore only be found in his agreement with his inquisitors. He must confess. And herein lay the genius of the Inquisition: secret trials of limitless duration; constant imprisonment of the accused; unhindered treachery of the interrogators in making false promises of leniency and mercy but very real promises of torture and death; starvation to the point of physical and spiritual collapse—and torture. The rack, the wheel, the pincers, the strappado—all were used with increasing abandon. The accused must confess, witnesses must testify, the condemned must implicate others, and then they in turn must confess.

Even when the Church itself began to perceive the excesses of the Inquisition, the efforts it made to correct abuses and slow its bloody progress were feeble and unavailing. By then the inquisitors saw themselves as independently powerful—independent even of the Holy See—and either ignored directions for moderation or "interpreted" such directions to the point of ineffectiveness.

As Lea has pointed out,[3] it is unfortunate that, at the time when European jurisprudence was making a fundamental change away from its ancient methods of proof and trial, the renaissance of the Roman law should hold up the tempting example of inquisitorial procedure and with it its worst abuses. The widespread adoption of those methods, to the point where they came to be a characteristic feature of the criminal law of most European countries, can be accounted for in great part by the blessings they received at the hands of the Church.

Of all the curses which the Inquisition brought in its train this, perhaps, was the greatest—that, until the

3. Lea, Henry C., *The Inquisition in the Middle Ages* (New York: Harper and Row, 1969).

closing years of the eighteenth century, throughout
the greater part of Europe, the inquisitorial process,
as developed for the destruction of heresy, became
the customary method of dealing with all who were
under accusation; that the accused was treated as one
having no rights, whose guilt was assumed in advance, and from whom confession was to be extorted
by guile or force. Even witnesses were treated in the
same fashion; and the prisoner who acknowledged
guilt under torture was tortured again to obtain information about any other evildoers of whom he per-
chance might have knowledge. . . . It would be impossible to compute the amount of misery and wrong,
inflicted on the defenceless up to the present century,
which may be directly traced to the arbitrary and
unrestricted methods introduced by the Inquisition
and adopted by the jurists who fashioned the criminal jurisprudence of the Continent. It was a system
which might well seem the invention of demons, and
was fitly characterized by Sir John Fortescue as the
Road to Hell.[4]

Toward the end of the eighteenth century, it was the judicial
abuses of the European continent which in large measure characterized that *ancien régime* against which the writers of the
Enlightenment were protesting. One of the greatest of these was
Cesare Beccaria, who, in his *Dei delitti e delle pene,* said of
torture:

No man can be judged a criminal until he be found
guilty; nor can society take from him the public protection until it have been proved that he has violated
the conditions on which it was granted. What right,

4. *ibid.,* p. 318.

then, but that of power, can authorise the punishment of a citizen so long as there remains any doubt of his guilt? This dilemma is frequent. Either he is guilty, or not guilty. If guilty, he should only suffer the punishment ordained by the laws, and torture becomes useless, as his confession is unnecessary. If he be not guilty, you torture the innocent; for, in the eye of the law, every man is innocent whose crime has not been proved. Besides, it is confounding all relations to expect that a man should be both the accuser and accused; and that pain should be the test of truth, as if truth resided in the muscles and fibres of a wretch in torture. By this method the robust will escape, and the feeble be condemned.[5]

It is against this brief account of the development of the use of torture elsewhere that we may compare Parry's subject-matter, which is the history of the use of torture in England. His principal thesis throughout is that the laws in England forbade the use of torture to produce confessions or evidence in judicial proceedings, but that such uses of torture were rather freely engaged in under the Royal prerogative, especially under the Tudors and Stuarts in cases of "religious dissention and political plots." He cites in support of the first part of his thesis the famous clause 39 of Magna Carta (p. 2), which indeed would seem to disallow torture by implication; but, does it constitute a direct prohibition? According to the *Leges Henrici,* similarly, forced confessions are not to be countenanced, but these too contain no express ban on torture. It might be more accurately stated that, while there was admittedly no consistent prohibition on torture in English law, the laws of England never, in fact, authorized it. The remainder of Parry's thesis—that it was allowed under the prerogative—seems quite supportable.

5. Beccaria, Cesare, *An Essay on Crimes and Punishments* (Philadelphia: Philip H. Nicklin, 1819), pp. 59–60.

What, then, is the nature of the Royal prerogative in England, and how did it come to be associated with those courts and procedures which have been noted historically as being the source of judicial caprice, unfairness—and torture? Stephen says of the prerogative:

> From the most remote antiquity the administration of justice was the highest or one of the highest prerogatives of the sovereigns of this country, and his council or court was the organ by which that prerogative was exercised.
>
> The original council or court was divided in course of time into the Court of King's Bench, the Court of Common Pleas, and the Court of Exchequer, each of which had originally its own peculiar province but each of which contrived to intrude to some extent upon the province of the other two, the three between them administering the known and well recognised law of the land.
>
> By the side of this comparatively well-defined jurisdiction, grew up by degrees the equitable jurisdiction (as it came to be called) of the Lord Chancellor, and the judicial authority, both civil and criminal, of the Council itself or Court of Star Chamber. The jurisdiction of the Chancellor being by experience found to be beneficial, and being wisely and justly used, was the foundation of the great Court of Chancery and of that part of our law or jurisprudence which goes by the name of equity. The judicial authority, civil and criminal, of the council or Star Chamber being used oppressively for political purposes, was destroyed.[6]

6. Stephen, James Fitzjames, *A History of the Criminal Law of England* (London: Macmillan, 1883), Vol. I, p. 182.

The traditional courts of the common law were feudal in origin and bound up in great part with the land law. Their procedures were slow and deliberate, as befits the weighty concerns of litigants in real property cases. An error in title could cause generations of strife. Pleadings set the issues, but proof relied heavily on documents; and resort to testimony usually took the form of calling a local jury to swear to the ancient knowledge of the seisin in dispute.

No more important transition exists in the history of English jurisprudence than that which took place as land slowly gave place to goods-in-commerce as the basic source of wealth and power. The rise of England as a trading nation, with all the social and economic consequences which that entailed, brought with it a need for a swifter form of legal procedure; and resort was had to what Plucknett calls the "residuum of discretion and equity," the King and Council. A litigant unable to obtain a remedy in the common-law courts petitioned the King for individual justice. Soon both King and Council became overburdened and had to seek a deputy already trained in law and involved in legal matters: they chose the Chancellor.

Petitions also came to the King alleging that individuals were being oppressed by certain of his overmighty subjects; relief in these cases was not obtainable in the local courts, where such subjects had great influence. These matters touched rather directly the interest of the Crown in maintaining and increasing the power of the Royal courts; and the parties involved might be summoned before the Council—*sub poena*—for a fairly quick, though perhaps somewhat arbitrary, disposition. When convened to hear such essentially criminal matters, the Council usually sat in the Starred Chamber of the palace and hence came to be called the Court of Star Chamber.

The jurisdiction of Star Chamber gradually expanded to include riot, perjury, conspiracy, and seditious libels—crimes more administrative in nature and tending to threaten the functioning of government rather than individual subjects or the peace of the community. It was an easy extension of this jurisdiction in the Tudor period for it to come to encompass crimes generally against the machinery of government, particularly as the bureaucratic unit of government was rapidly expanding at this time and thus the possibility of offenses against it. It is especially in these types of crimes that complaining witnesses may be lacking, and the government alone is both offended party and prosecutor. The combination of a direct threat to Royal administration (an administration weakened somewhat by its growing pains) and a lack of sufficient evidence of such wrongdoing must have sorely tempted the authorities to force the defendant to aid in his own conviction—if necessary, by torture. Moreover, Star Chamber had adopted trial procedures more consistent with Roman law than the common law, and the former had always placed greater weight on confession than on evidence.

After the Reformation, English monarchs faced the overwhelming additional task of administering the Church and enforcing religious orthodoxy within a system increasingly threatened by rival doctrines from without and schisms from within. Henry VIII and Edward VI made various attempts at such control; Elizabeth established the Court of High Commission. In the religious sphere, High Commission enforced conformity much as Star Chamber did in political matters. The court had jurisdiction over clerics in their professional roles and over both clerical and lay persons in their personal religious lives. It also punished crimes which had previously been subject to the canon law of Rome—such crimes as incest, bigamy, and slander. Finally—and most ominously—it dealt with those offenses which historically had most often been associated with the use of torture to produce confession and had led to the worst abuses of judicial process: heresy and witchcraft. In all these matters, High Commission had powers exceeding any of the lesser ecclesiastical courts, readily adopted inquisitorial procedures, and threw a net far wider than even Star Chamber.

In addition to these two most famous—or infamous—prerogative courts, the Crown itself and the Privy Council continued to be a source of judicial power; and torture was carried out by direction of the monarch and by warrant from the Council. The areas of authority of these embodiments of the Royal prerogative were, moreover, generally not clearly demarcated, resulting in a duplication and overlapping of powers which today we would judge appalling. But it was a confusing and appalling time. The Crown's sovereignty over church and state brought heresy and treason even more closely together. In Elizabeth's reign, the very question of the succession was both a religious and a political one. Witchcraft was almost universally believed in and constituted a real threat in the world-view of the Englishman of the sixteenth and seventeenth centuries.

The forms of injury inflicted simply as punishments in those days, even in ordinary criminal cases, included branding, whipping, mutilation, and other practices barbarous by modern standards. In such an atmosphere, torture was unlikely to produce the popular revulsion which it would occasion today. Moreover, the age was a hazardous one for English monarchs. The plots surrounding Elizabeth, for example, were real ones and threatened both her life and the very foundations of her government. The resort to torture to uncover and destroy such conspiracies —however much we may condemn it today—was at least consistent with the cruelties of the times. After all, the procedures in ordinary criminal cases then, even in England, though they might not have involved torture, were hardly noted for the legal niceties and the careful protection of the defendant's rights which we take for granted in modern times.

Parry notes the year 1640 as the date when torture was abolished in England, since no English monarch after Charles I caused torture to be carried out under the Royal prerogative. The reasons for its abolition are manifold and far-reaching. In referring to "abolition," however, we must, despite the detailed accounts which Parry offers of the use of torture under the prerogative, be mindful of his principal contention that at no point in English history did torture become part of the law of the land; though, as Maitland says, "The escape was narrow." This meant that the forces of abolition had less to overcome than on the Continent.

The scope of the prerogative itself diminished with the general limitation on the unfettered powers of the Crown brought about by the growing pressure of the Commons and the development and extension of relatively stable bureaucratic government. In addition, the anticlericalism of a more rational age put a stop to attempts to instill religious orthodoxy by the use of the rack and the *in pace*.

Many pervasive changes were in the air, however. Cruelties either accepted or ignored at an earlier time were beginning to be questioned by individuals, by organized groups, and by whole nations. There arose new ideas on the relationship between man and his government, ideas which were to flourish so brilliantly during the Enlightenment. And it was the brilliance of that Enlightenment, above all else, that was finally to cause the use of torture—that darkest of spots on Western jurisprudence—to shrivel and fade away.

SAWYER F. SYLVESTER, JR.

Bates College
Lewiston, Maine
September 1974

PREFACE

It may seem presumptuous to use the word "History" in connection with the title of a book, if by that word is connoted a complete record, for it is quite impossible for a work to contain all that is known of any subject. However what history of torture is contained in this book is, to the best of my belief, accurate. I have verified as far as possible every statement I have made. I have not confined myself by any means to torture in the strictly legal sense of the word, i.e. cruelty inflicted on a prisoner or a witness for the purpose of extracting information or confession. I have gone a good deal farther in describing some of the brutal sentences allowed by our judicial enactments and procedure, and passed on prisoners as part of their punishment.

In addition to referring to many cases of torture and brutality, I have recorded rather fully a few trials in which torture or some special cruelty was an important element.

I append a Bibliography of the chief works consulted in the preparation of this book. To every one of them I am indebted for some fact or opinion or quotation. I am under a debt of deep gratitude to Froude, to Lingard, and to Gardiner, for a general outlook on the legal, social, religious and political events in Tudor and Stuart times; to Mr. Pike for an enormous amount of information on many aspects of cruelty; and to Howell's State Trials for much old legal lore.

Hove, 1933.

CONTENTS

CHAPTER   PAGE

   I. THE LAW AND TORTURE 1

  II. THE COURT OF STAR CHAMBER . . . 4

 III. THE COURT OF HIGH COMMISSION . . 13

 IV. EARLY INHUMANITY 15

  V. SOCIETIES FOR PREVENTING CRUELTY . . 20

 VI. EARLY TORTURE 26

VII. ABOLITION OF TORTURE 32

VIII. TORTURE IN TUDOR TIMES 36

 IX. TORTURE IN THE STUART PERIOD . . 54

  X. TORTURE IN SCOTLAND 63

 XI. TORTURE IN IRELAND 73

XII. METHODS OF TORTURE 76

XIII. THE ORDEAL AND TRIAL BY BATTLE . . 88

XIV. PEINE FORTE ET DURE 97

 XV. BRUTAL PUNISHMENTS. HANGING, DRAWING
           AND QUARTERING 104

XVI. BEHEADING 129

XVII. THE HALIFAX GIBBET 137

XVIII. DROWNING AND BOILING 140

XIX. BURNING 146

 XX. MUTILATION AND BRANDING . . . 154

xxi

CHAPTER		PAGE
XXI.	Minor Cruelties	162
XXII.	Witchcraft and Cruelty	178
XXIII.	The Church and Cruelty	191
XXIV.	The Trial and Torture of Dr. Spreull	205
XXV.	Trial of the Suffolk Witches	216
XXVI.	Trial of Sir Thomas Picton	224
XXVII.	Trial by Battle	232
	Bibliography	241
	Index	245

THE HISTORY
OF TORTURE IN ENGLAND

THE HISTORY OF TORTURE
IN ENGLAND

CHAPTER I

THE LAW AND TORTURE

It has always been the boast of Englishmen that torture
was forbidden by the Common Law of the land. The
great charters of English liberty have not, from the time
of Magna Carta onwards, permitted the use of torture.
This Charter, rightly called the keystone of English liberty,
expressed the fundamental rights of the subject. It established the law of English freedom, including freedom from
torture in impregnable foundations. Magna Carta, wrung
from the reluctant King by his Barons, driven to desperation
by his unbearable tyranny, owes its origin to many causes,
one of the most important of which was the loss of the
Norman dominions of the Crown. As a result, the Barons
began to concentrate on the affairs of their own kingdom,
rather than on those of Normandy. The discontent which
John had roused throughout the country came to a head
and the Barons, who now consisted in great part of new
families, neither pure descendants of the Normans, nor
pure "Englishry", but derived from both sources, forced
the King to grant the Great Charter. At Runnymede,
on the Thames, between Windsor and Staines, King
John with the support of the Pope, represented by the
Papal Legate, Pandulph, the royal minister, and a few

Barons, held a conference with the remainder of the Barons, supported by the army of God and Holy Church. The result of this conference was the issue of the great charter, in 1215, which has been repeatedly confirmed in succeeding generations as the palladium of national rights, firstly by John's son, Henry III, then by Statute by Edward I (25 Ed. I), "confirmatio cartarum", and later by Edward III, Richard II, Henry IV, V and VI, altogether thirty-seven times. Later on these confirmations were followed by the Petition of Right, a declaration of the liberties of the people, agreed to by Charles I, the Habeas Corpus Act of Charles II, and finally the Bill of Rights of William III. This recognised " all and singular the rights and liberties asserted and claimed in the said declaration to be the true, ancient, and undubitable rights of the people of this kingdom". Finally the Act of Settlement (12 and 13 Wm. III, c. 2), secured the religion, law and liberties of the people of England as their birthright according to the ancient doctrine of the Common Law. These rights and liberties include the right of personal security, and from the time of the Great Charter onwards, the protection of a man from torture.

These other great charters of English liberty are merely adjuncts or reassertions of Magna Carta. Of all the articles in this document the most important is clause 39. "Nullus liber homo capiatur, vel imprisonetur, aut dissaisiatur, aut utlagetur, aut exuletur, aut aliquo modo destruatur, nec super eum ibimus, nec super eum mittimus, nisi per legale judicium parium suorum vel per legem terrae." (No freeman shall be arrested, imprisoned, dispossessed, or in any other way injured, banished, or hurt, nor will we in person or through our officers lay hands upon him save by the lawful judgment of his peers or the law of the land.)

The words *aliquo modo destruatur* include, according to the highest legal authorities an express prohibition not only of killing and maiming, but also of torture. Sir Edward Coke thus interprets the words. "No man destroyed, etc., that is forejudged of life or limb, disinherited, or put to torture or death."

Though it is clear that the common law of England forbade torture, yet torture was, from Norman times onwards, but especially in the times of the Tudors and Stuarts, very frequently used on prisoners. The rulers of the land claimed that by Royal prerogative they had the power to order torture at their discretion, and that this power overrode the common law of England. It was entirely due to the state of the country in the reigns concerned, the religious dissensions and the political plots, that this outrageous claim was allowed to pass unchallenged. Desperate diseases require, it was argued, desperate remedies, and the people realised only too late how difficult it was to dispute the claim, once it was well established. It was always employed by some tribunal of extraordinary authority not professing to be bound by the common law. The chief of these extraordinary Courts were those known as Star Chamber, and the ecclesiastical Court of High Commission. There were in addition other Courts such as the Council of the North, the Council of Wales, the Court of Racquets, and the Court of Admiralty, but these were of very much less importance than the two first named.

CHAPTER II

IT will be interesting to trace briefly the origin of some of the Prerogative Courts—the Courts without which it would not have been possible for torture to have been inflicted—the Courts which attempted to substitute the will of the sovereign for the Common Law of England.

In the reign of Edward III, the King's Continual Council was in the habit of sitting in what was called the Starred Chamber (La Chambre des Etoiles). After the establishment of the Court of Chancery, a large portion of the work of the King's Council was taken from it. The proceedings of the Council gradually fell into disrepute as its decisions were contrary to Magna Carta, and the law generally. Its jurisdiction slowly declined till the time of the Tudors. Henry VII, to restore in a legal way its power, established by law the Court of Star Chamber (3 Hen. VII, c. 1.). It was not actually called the Court of Star Chamber in the Act, though this was its popular name. It was to all effects and purposes a judicial Committee of the Privy Council.

The constitution of the Star Chamber at its inception in Tudor times, was admirably adapted for the purpose for which it was founded. It was composed of two Chief Justices, and the whole of the Privy Council, and therefore brought the highest legal and the highest political capacity to bear on cases. As a rule the causes it had to try were those in which the offenders were too powerful to be reached by the ordinary courts, or in which the evidence was too complicated for the understanding of an ordinary jury. It had become a tribunal constantly resorted to as a resource against the ignorance or prejudice of a country jury, much in the same way as a special jury is employed at the present time. In cases such as this it was an excellent court, showing ability and impartiality. It was when the trial took on a political nature that its abuses showed. Every member of the Court, except the two Chief Justices were members of the Privy Council, and as the political trials were quarrels between the defendants and some members of the Council, it was impossible that they should be in any degree impartial.

At its origin the Court was regarded with favour by the people. It was popular because it was employed in a popular cause. It protected the weak against the strong. By it the King was able to put down many prevalent evils. It was too strong for any subject to overawe, and it reached culprits too high to be made answerable to the ordinary processes of law. It brought punishment to the great at a time when it was difficult to find a jury which would not be hindered by fear from bringing in a verdict adverse to the Court even if this verdict could be sustained by the strongest evidence.

The limits of the jurisdiction of the Court as fixed by law, was gradually extended till it included such offences as contempts, misdemeanours, and libels. More important still the power of pronouncing on those found guilty of crime the judgment to which they would have been liable if they had been convicted in due course of law, grew into a power of punishing at discretion and with great severity.

The Court interfered too, with the action of juries. If a verdict were returned contrary to the wishes of the

King or the Government, the jury were brought before the Star Chamber, and its members fined or imprisoned. In the Throckmorton trial, for example, the jurors refused to find the prisoner guilty. They were called before the Star Chamber, where some made their submission, others, who refused, were fined or imprisoned.

Juries were not as they are now, men with fair and impartial minds whose verdicts must in most cases be received and acted on by the judges. It is rare at the present day for a judge to comment on the finding of the jury at all, and anything like a stricture on the verdict is very unusual. This was not so in the times under discussion.

The trial of Lady Lisle demonstrates well the way juries were influenced in giving their verdicts though this is not a case in which the Star Chamber was concerned. They were not free and independent but were terrorised by the judge, never in a more brutal manner than by the infamous Jefferies.

The night after the defeat of Monmouth at Sedgemoor, a man named Hicks who was a dissenting preacher, and another man named Nelthorp, came to Lady Lisle's house. She knew Hicks and treated him civilly, not asking where he came from but probably guessing. They told her they had been with Monmouth, so she at once sent her servant to inform the nearest Justice of the Peace, but giving the men the opportunity of escaping before they could be caught. Before anything could be done, they were all arrested. Jefferies determined to make an example of her. He even went so far as to obtain a promise from the King that he would not pardon her. This from an English judge on a prisoner who had not even been tried ! ! The account of this trial, fully set out in "State Trials," makes one blush for English Justice and bitterly ashamed of the abominable conduct of Jefferies, the judge who sat on the bench. The proceedings were conducted in a most improper and unfair way, the judge bullied the witnesses whenever an answer was given in favour of the poor wretched woman; and from beginning to end the whole trial was a farce. No legal proof was given that she knew Hicks was a rebel. The names of the two men she harboured had not been published in any proclamation, so she could not know if they were proscribed. Jefferies insisted on the jury finding her guilty. They found her not guilty, and the judge in a fury sent them out again. A second time they came back with a verdict of not guilty. Jefferies, who was a coarse minded bully, went into a transport of rage. He threatened them with all the pains and penalties possible and at last in terror of his threats and abuse, they brought her in guilty. She was sentenced to be burnt but as a concession to her position, she was beheaded.

The Court of Star Chamber gradually became more powerful and under the later Tudors and the Stuarts, was most cruel and tyrannical in its findings. It ordered the pillory, whipping, and brutal mutilations. Its decisions became so intolerable, its whole conduct so atrocious that the name of Star Chamber became synonymous with all that was tyrannical and unjust.

The Court was finally abolished by the Long Parliament in 1640. The Act which got rid of it still allowed the Privy Council to examine and commit persons charged with offences, but to prevent arbitrary use of its power, it was enacted that any person committed by it, should on application to the King's Bench or Common Pleas, have a writ of *habeas corpus* granted to him at once. The same Parliament abolished the other Prerogative Courts, including the Court of High Commission, the Council of the North, and the Council of the Welsh Marches.

Below are a few examples of the arbitrary powers exercised by the Court of Star Chamber, together with instances of the brutal punishments inflicted.

In 1628, Leighton, a Scotchman and preacher, ventured to criticise the Government in various matters, religious and political. He was charged in 1630 with "framing, publishing, and dispersing a scandalous book, against kings, peers, and prelates". The book certainly contained criticisms of the King and Government, worded in very intemperate language, but nothing more.

The Court of Star Chamber was called upon to deal with him. The two chief justices informed him that it was by the goodness of the King that he was not charged with high treason. It was the King's mercy that had left him to be tried by Star Chamber. To show this mercy and goodness of the King, Leighton was condemned to pay a fine of £10,000, to be set in the pillory in Westminster, and there whipped, and after his whipping "to have one of his ears cut off, to have his nose slit, and to be branded on the face with the letters SS (sower of sedition). At some later date he was to be taken to the pillory at Cheapside, again lashed, his other ear cut off, and then imprisoned for life". The most insistent on his inhuman sentence were the bishops.

Before the horrible sentence was carried out, Leighton was degraded from his ministerial office by the High Commission, in order that he might not appear at the pillory in his clerical dress. He went nobly to his punishment. "All the arguments brought against me," he said, "are prison, fine, brands, knife, and whip." The sharp knife of the executioner cut away his ear, and he was carried back to prison bleeding and fainting. The "great and noble heart" of Charles did not spare him the second mutilation. A week later, the sores on his back, nose, ears, and face unhealed, the rest of his sentence was carried out. He was whipped again at the pillory, his other ear was cut off, the other side of his nose slit, and the other cheek branded.

The constant passing of the death cart along the road to Tyburn raised no pity or protest from the citizens. The pillory, the brandings, the mutilations, were quite ordinary punishments and there was nothing in the sentence of Leighton which was not common in the practice of the Star Chamber.

Hudson, in his treatise on the Star Chamber, which was written in the reign of James I, gives good evidence as to what took place. "The punishment is by fine, imprisonment, loss of ears or nailing to the pillory, slitting the nose, branding the forehead, whipping; of late days, wearing of paper in public places, or any punishment but death." He adds, "Loss of ears is the punishment inflicted on perjured persons, infamous libellers, scandalers of the State, and such like. Branding in the face and slitting the nose is inflicted upon forgers of false deeds, conspirators to take away the life of innocents, false scandals upon the great judges, and justices of the realm. Whipping hath been used as the punishment in great deceits and unnatural offences, as the wife against the husband, but never constantly observed in any case, but where a clamorous person *in forma pauperis* prosecuteth another falsely, and is not able to pay him his cost."

A year or two later, in 1632, William Prynne was tried in the Star Chamber for writing and publishing a book entitled, *Histrio-mastix, or a Scourge for Stage Players*. In this book, "with very profuse collections, he exposed the liberties of the stage, and condemned the very lawfulness of acting. In this way of writing he could not refrain from over-doing any subject and from many appearances of railing. And because the Court became now more addicted to these ludicrous entertainments, and the Queen herself was so fond of the amusement that she had bore the part of a pastoral in her own royal person; therefore this Treatise against Plays was suspected to be levelled against the practice of the court, and the example of the queen; and it was supposed an Innuendo, that in the Table of the Book this reference was put, 'Women actors notorious whores'. The Attorney-General prosecuted Prynne for this libel in the Star Chamber".

The Earl of Dorset in his judgment spoke as follows. "But, Mr. Prynne, your iniquity is full, it runs over, and Judgement is come; it is not Mr. Attorney that calls for judgement against you; it is all mankind, they are the parties grieved, and they call for judgement. Mr. Prynne, I do declare you to be a Schism-Maker in the Church, a Sedition-Sower in the Commonwealth, a woolf in sheep's clothing; in a word *omnium malorum nequissimus.* I shall fine him 10,000£, which is more than he is worth, yet less than he deserveth; I will not set him at liberty no more than a plagued man or a mad dog, who though he cannot bite, he will foam; he is so far from being a sociable soul, that he is not a rational soul; he is fit to live in dens with such beasts of prey, as wolves and tigers, like himself; Therefore I do condemn him to perpetual Imprisonment, as those monsters, that are no longer fit to live among men, nor to see light. Now for Corporal Punishment, my lords, whether I should burn him in the forehead, or slit him in the nose; for I find that it is confessed of all, that Dr. Leighton's offence was less than Mr. Prynne's, then why should Mr. Prynne have a less punishment? He that was guilty of murder was marked in a place where he might be seen, as Cain was. I should be loth he should escape with his ears, for he may get a periwig, which he now so much inveighs against, and so hide them, or force his conscience to make use of his unlovely love-locks on both sides: Therefore I would have him branded in the forehead, slit in the nose, and his ears cropped too." The sentence was carried out at Westminster and Cheapside, and in addition he was expelled from Lincoln's Inn, rendered incapable of practising his profession, and degraded from his university.

In 1637 Prynne was again before the Star Chamber for the same kind of offence. He had printed secretly a book on God's Judgment on Sabbath breakers. When Prynne took his place at the bar on a charge of libel, Finch, one of the members of the Court told the usher to hold back the locks which hid the scars left by the execution of his former sentence. "I had thought Mr. Prynne had no ears, but methinks he hath ears." The executioner had dealt mercifully three years before and some portion of his ears was left. He was fined £5,000, condemned once again to lose his ears, and to be imprisoned for the rest of his life.

Those responsible for the brutalities of the Star Chamber saw that the sentence was carried out effectually. For two hours he stood in the pillory, talking with the bystanders. "The hangman burnt Prynne in both cheeks, and as I hear, because he burnt one cheek with the letter the wrong way, he burnt that again: presently a surgeon clapped on a plaster to take out the fire. The hangman hewed off Prynne's ears very scurvily, which put him to much pain: and after he stood long in the pillory, before his head could be got out." On his way back to prison Prynne composed a Latin distich in which he interpreted the letters SL (seditious libel), which he bore branded on his cheeks as Stigmata Laudis—The Scar of Laud. The conditions of his imprisonment were hard. No pens or ink, only a few religious works, and a prison—Mont Orgueil in Jersey—remote from accessible places.

In 1629 a man named Savage, who was either insane or desired some foolish notoriety, claimed that Felton had asked him to join in the assassination of Buckingham. He was sentenced by the Star Chamber to have his ears cut off. Selden, one of the leading lawyers of the day greatly concerned at the increasing use of the arbitrary powers of this Court, made a vigorous protest. "One had lately lost his ears by a decree of the Star Chamber, by an arbitrary judgement. Next they will take away our arms, and then our legs, and so our lives; let us see we are sensible of this. Customs creep on us; let us make a just representation hereof unto his Majesty."

CHAPTER III

THE High Commission was another of those Courts which attempted to over-ride the common law, and although it was not allowed to inflict death or torture, it was in its nature tyrannical and its methods were oppressive in the hands of the Crown. A short account of it naturally follows that of the Star Chamber.

A clash between Queen Elizabeth and her Commons gave rise to the establishment of the Commission. The Commons demanded a much greater range of liberty for the clergy and this the Queen strenuously opposed. She appointed Whitgift, Archbishop of Canterbury, to carry out her wishes and he took office with the determination to put an end to the inequalities which prevailed, not because they were inconsistent with sound doctrine, or with the practical usefulness of the Church, but because he considered them disorderly. He wished to raise the Church of England to great power, equalling that of Rome, and he considered this impossible unless he had obedience to authority and uniformity of worship. So the Court of High Commission was established in 1583. It based its legality on the Act of Supremacy, passed twenty-four years before. It is certain that the framers of that Act did not contemplate that the powers which they had entrusted to the Queen would be stretched to include those claimed by High Commission. The means used were in

13

absolute contradiction to the spirit of our law. A man was more or less compelled to accuse himself or his friends. His guilt was assumed on very slender grounds—grounds to which the ordinary law court would not have listened.

The Court consisted of forty-four Commissioners, twelve of whom were prelates. It had enormous powers. It was both arbitrary and inquisitorial. It was directed to enquire on all questions affecting religion, such as heretical or schismatic opinions, absence from church, seditions, slanderous words and sayings, incests, adulteries and other immoralities.

Lord Bolingbroke, in his *History of England*, says, "The prerogative certainly ran high in the days of Queen Elizabeth. Her grandfather had raised it by cunning, and her father by violence. The power of the privy council in civil affairs and the power of the Star Chamber in criminal affairs, as my Lord Bacon very properly stiles it, took too much of the pleas of the crown and the common pleas out of their proper channels, and served rather to scare men from doing wrong, than to do any man right. But the executive of these powers having continued in four preceeding reigns, the people were accustomed to it, and care being taken to give no flagrant occasion of clamour against it, we are not to wonder if it was born, without opposition or murmur, in a reign as popular as this". The Court was abolished in the reign of Charles I (16 Car. I, c. 11). James II, in his last tyrannical efforts established a new High Commission Court, a "Court of Commission of Ecclesiastical causes", in defiance of the Act of Charles I, one of his many attempts to over-ride the common law, which ended in his dethronement in 1688.

CHAPTER IV

UNCIVILISED man was by nature a cruel animal. His environment compelled him to be brutal and unscrupulous. If he wished to survive in the struggle for existence it was impossible for him to be anything else. As civilisation progressed, man became perhaps less brutal, but many centuries were to pass before even the worst of the cruel tendencies of the human race became subdued. At the end of the eighteenth century the law of England inflicted capital punishment for over 200 crimes: stealing property of the value of five shillings, picking pockets, robbing a rabbit warren and similar minor offences, all entailed the death penalty.

In 1833, just a hundred years ago, Nicolas White, a boy of nine, was charged at Maidstone with breaking a window and stealing paint of the value of twopence. At the Old Bailey Mr. Justice Bosanquet sentenced him to be hanged by the neck till he was dead. This brutal sentence, one is glad to know, was subsequently commuted.

In 1831, John Bell, a boy of thirteen, was actually hanged at Maidstone for a trifling offence. Greville narrates a trial at which he was present when several boys were sentenced to be hanged. "Never did I see boys cry so." And Rogers the poet tells how he saw "a cartload of young girls, in dresses of various colours, on their way to be hanged at Tyburn Tree". These are by no means isolated examples and they show the condition of public feeling on the question of punishment for slight breaches of the law. When early in the nineteenth century some humanitarian tried to introduce legislation to mitigate the severity of the law, the great lawyers bitterly opposed him, on the ground that he would be encouraging crime. It was not till William IV was on the throne that some semblance of humane legislation regarding punishment for crime became apparent. Gradually the death penalty for minor offences began to be abolished. First in 1832, for cattle, horse, and sheep stealing, later for· larceny, forgery, burglary and other crimes. For some time prior to the passing of these Acts, the growing feeling of humanity in the people had prevented the death penalty from being carried out so frequently, but hanging for sheep stealing took place so late as 1831, for letter stealing in 1832, for housebreaking in 1833, and for robbery in 1836.

Up to early in the nineteenth century, the conditions of child labour were so inhuman that the story of them is almost unbelievable at the present day. There was no public or organised supervision of their work. There was free and unrestricted traffic in the use of children. Little ones of four and five years of age were employed in factories all day long, they had no time for play, no education, no recreation of any kind. In coal mines the conditions were even worse. Children of seven or eight were taken down the shafts before sunrise and did not come up again till after sunset. They rarely saw the light of day. The darkness of the night was followed by the darkness of the mine.

Boys and girls as young as five were hired out to farmers, herded in barns regardless of any claims of sanitation or decency and driven in gangs to work on the farms.

At a meeting of the Social Science Association in 1870, Mr. George Smith presented a lump of clay weighing forty-three pounds. This he had taken from a boy of nine who had daily to walk twelve miles in a brick yard, half the distance carrying this weight. Here are extracts from the fourth report of the Children's Employment Commission of 1862. A boy of nine worked at hardening and tempering steel, from 7 a.m., till 9.30 p.m. Four nights a week he worked till midnight. Another boy of nine sometimes made three twelve-hour shifts running, another of thirteen worked from 6 p.m. till noon next day.

These facts did not shock contemporary opinion, as witness the following from the press of the day.

The Edinburgh Review of 1819 says: "After all, we must own that it was quite right to throw out the Bill for prohibiting the sweeping of chimneys by boys, because humanity is a modern invention; and there are many chimneys in old houses that cannot be swept in any other manner." *The Gorgon*, a Radical paper, sneers at Parliament for "its ostentatious display of humanity in dealing with trivialities like the slave trade, climbing boys, and the condition of children in factories".

Chimneys were at this time swept by sending boys to climb inside with a brush to remove the soot. If the poor child got wedged in the narrow space, his ascent was hastened by lighting straw beneath him and thus driving him up. Death often resulted. Orthodox opinion saw nothing inhuman in this.

The following is an extract from the work of Mr. Bray on Boy Labour, an eloquent and convincing picture of two views of the work of children, one that of the individualist of the Industrial Revolution, the other of the idealist, the latter of whom has fortunately gradually triumphed. "Every proposal for regulating child labour was fought on the same lines; there were the same arguments and the same replies. The individualist urged that State inter-ference was in itself an evil, that, though the consequences might be delayed and the immediate effect even beneficial, you might rest assured that in the long run your sin would find you out. The wealthy citizen declared that if boys might not climb his chimneys, his chimneys must go unswept; the manufacturer predicted certain ruin to his trade if he were forbidden to use children as seemed best to him; while all united in urging that if children were not at work they would be doing something worse, and pointed out the obvious cruelty of depriving half starved parents of the scanty earnings of their half starved children.

"To all these and similar objections the idealist, with his clearer vision of the reality of things, and firm in his faith that the prosperity of a people could never be the final outcome of allowing an obvious wrong, made response. He sympathised with the individualist for the dreary pessimism of a creed which could see the future alone coloured with hope if heralded by the sobs of suffering children. The wealthy citizen he bade roughly burn his house and build another sooner than sacrifice the lives of boys to the needs of his chimneys. While as for the manufacturer, he told him, as Mr. Justice Grose had told him earlier, that, if his engines needed children as fuel, his was a trade the country was best rid of. To those employers who pleaded the small wages of the parents he suggested the crude and obvious remedy of paying these parents more. And the idealist, with the sentiment of the British public to back him, won the day."

The first of the long series of Factory Acts, designed to abolish these almost unbelievable conditions of work by children was passed in 1802. Other Acts followed, each one doing something to remedy the abuses. But it was many years before anything approaching an endurable state was reached. Among the provisions of the earlier Acts were: (1) prohibition of the employment of children under *nine*, except in silk mills: (2) limitation of the hours

of work to *twelve* per day, exclusive of meals: (3) the forbidding of male and female apprentices sleeping in the
same room, and of more than two in the same bed. Such
was the state of public feeling in the early nineteenth century,
that it was considered right even by the humanitarians
that children of nine should work twelve hours a day.
The many other Factory Acts which have since been
passed have made the conditions under which children
and young persons are employed quite satisfactory. (No
child can now be employed in a factory.)

CHAPTER V

Young children are still subject to many cruelties from their parents. Even at the present day there is in existence a Society for the Prevention of Cruelty to Children. The necessity for such a Society is clearly shown by a reference to its Annual Reports. It deals each year with over 40,000 cases, the great majority of them fortunately examples of neglect rather than deliberate brutality, but the following extracts from recent issues of *The Child's Guardian*, describe conditions which are unfortunately by no means rare, and justify the continuance of the activities of the Society:

" *The Brute.*—'Yes, he had beaten the girl and would do it again if she did not do what he told her.' This is the statement of a father to the Windsor Inspector, who had questioned him about the ill-treatment of his eight-year-old daughter. On the child's back were five large round bruises, inflicted, in the Inspector's opinion, by a sharp instrument. Later on the man assaulted the child again, which resulted in the latter's removal to a place of safety, the prosecution of the man and a sentence of six months' hard labour. Even while the Inspector was at the house the accused, against whom there were thirty-four previous convictions for all kinds of offences, said even if he got time for it he would split the heads open of all of them.

The child's mother gave evidence, first expressing regret that she was the wife of the defendant, and relating how, on arriving home on one occasion and asking where her daughter was, the man told her he had sent her to bed. Bruises were found on the child. Two days later her husband returned home the worse for drink and threw a pile of books at her and chased the child upstairs."

"*Most Atrocious.*—Six months' imprisonment with hard labour was also the sentence on a father at the Gateshead Police Court for the brutal ill-treatment of his four-year-old son. The Chairman of the Bench said that it had never before been their painful duty to listen to such a story of ill-treatment.

"The mother's story to the Court was that the father punched the child in the face so violently that two of its front teeth were knocked out. He recently returned home drunk, having the previous day drawn £3 12s. due to him as a reservist in the Royal Artillery. The child was asleep on a mattress on the floor—the family occupied a single room—and he punched it in a brutal way, leaving large bruises on the face. Not content with this he nipped it till it screamed with pain.

"The child was brought into Court so that the Magistrate might see the marks, and the Police Surgeon told the Court that one side of the child's face was black and blue with bruises.

"'Your assaults upon this child have been most atrocious and unworthy of any man,' said the Chairman of the Court.

"No one will disagree."

"*In the Cause of Humanity.*—In convicting a father of what the prosecuting solicitor described as a 'most fiendish act of cruelty' against a baby boy, the Mayor of Stockton-on-Tees said the Magistrates were of opinion there was

hardly a sentence severe enough to impose upon him—
and sent him to prison for one month. The man was a
moulder's labourer, and the baby upon whom the assault
was committed seven weeks old. Accused returned home
the worse for drink with another man and demanded
the baby from the mother, who was nursing it. She went
downstairs, but on hearing the child scream returned to
the room, when the man who had accompanied her
husband told her to take the baby and watch her husband.
Later the child began to cry and the wife got up to attend
to it. Thereupon the father snatched the child to his
side of the bed. While absent the mother heard the child
being 'thumped,' and when she returned found the man
had half smothered it by putting it under the bed-clothes.
As the mother went to take the child he caught hold of
the baby's left ear and twisted it like a piece of paper until
blood ran down the child's neck and the woman's arm.
Medical evidence was given that the child suffered from
a lacerated left ear and injuries to the left eye and leg.
The man admitted to the Court he was drunk, and said
he did not know anything about the child's injuries. He
added that his wife saw him playing with the child's ear
and pulled it away from him, thereby making it worse!"

In Lincolnshire a boy, aged eleven years, was found in a
shed with his neck in a dog collar attached to the roof.
His ankles were fastened to a stake. He collapsed when
found by the Inspector.

An illegitimate child was allowed to be "savaged" by a
dog several times. He had to be taken to hospital for treatment. The parent calmly said he thought more of the animal
than of "that child".

In 1932 there was an increase of cases of violent brutality
to children, the figures being the highest for twenty-eight
years.

The Royal Society for the Prevention of Cruelty to Animals is an analagous Society dealing with animals. In one year they dealt with 25,000 cases. Again actual examples prove the real necessity for some method of protection of animals from horrible atrocities. The number of persons convicted for this offence in 1931 was 2,152.

These are instances from the report of the Society for 1931:—

A man put four live kittens on a fire and burnt them to death. Another cut off the toes of five sheep to prevent them from jumping over the wall into his field.

Giving evidence in a case at Builth Wells, an inspector described how he had found four pole traps, each five feet high. In some thorn bushes near the traps he found the dead bodies of three brown owls, two barn owls, three buzzards, and a sparrow hawk. The legs of the birds were broken or damaged.

A man beat a horse with a whip which had nearly a foot of steel exposed. "This is not a whip, it is an instrument of torture," said the magistrate. Examples such as these could be multiplied indefinitely, but enough have been quoted to prove the point.

" Lieutenant-Colonel Roland Gwynne, at Hailsham Petty Sessions, in sentencing John Henry Everett, a farmer, of Primrose Farm, Arlington, to the maximum penalty of three months' hard labour, said ' It is difficult for any decent-minded persons to restrain themselves or control their feelings when talking about an inhuman brute such as you are. If we had the power, we should order you to be flogged with the cat, and that would give you pain for the wretched and awful cruelty you have meted out to this poor animal.

Everett was charged with causing unnecessary suffering to a dog by failing to give it sufficient food and proper care and attention. He pleaded not guilty.

P.C. Hullock said he found a brown collie sheep dog tied to a kennel with six feet of plough trace chain. The dog was lying down, and when he tried to get it to stand up, it rolled over on its side.

It was nothing more than skin and bone, and there was no hair round its neck where the collar was.

There was no water or food except a calf skin, and the dog was in such a bad state that witness thought it would die very shortly.

Inspector Winn, of the R.S.P.C.A. shot the dog at once, and he said it was in the most terrible condition he had seen.

Inspector Holloway read a number of convictions against Everett, including: 22nd July, 1919, at Lewes Petty Sessions, £25 and £2 2s. costs for causing cruelty to a horse. 13th April, 1920, at Lewes Sessions, £2 for permitting cruelty to a horse. 14th September, 1920, £25 for moving pigs across the highway contrary to the provisions of the Foot and Mouth Disease Order. 3rd May, 1922, at Hailsham Sessions, £5 and £2 2s. costs, for causing cruelty to a horse. 4th October, 1922, at Hailsham, one month's imprisonment with hard labour, for causing a horse to be worked in an unfit state; and on the same date, at Hailsham, £5 with £2 2s. costs, for another offence in respect of a horse."

" *Three Cruelty Cases.*—Revolting as the cock-fighting cases were, there were two other cases of cruelty to animals tried last week which were infinitely worse. At Nottingham, two gamekeepers (Charles Edward Snowden and John Harry Pounds) were found guilty of gross cruelty to a dog. The two men admitted to a police officer that they beat the dog to death with staves like policemen's truncheons. A witness said that the noise they made sounded like a carpet being beaten. Lord Belper inflicted the proper punishment on these brutes by sending them to two months' hard labour. At Worksop another brute—William Stevenson —also got two months' hard labour for cruelty to a horse. This man, assisted by his son, beat the horse with a strap, after which he harnessed a pony to a chain, and flogged it to make it pull the horse, which eventually squealed, shivered and fell down dead. These two salutary sentences are a welcome sign that the bad old days—when the bench usually visited crimes of this sort with grossly inadequate fines—are gone."

CHAPTER VI

EARLY TORTURE

MAN, then being what he is, it is not to be wondered at that torture has been employed by him since the dawn of civilisation, either as a means of wringing confessions, real or false from his prisoners or of punishment to his enemies. In Greece, the Athenians admitted the principle of torture as a good method of eliciting the truth, but used it for slaves and not for citizens. Among the Romans the application of torture to witnesses and suspected persons for the purpose of eliciting information, was recognised, and the tradition was handed down to the nations which sprang from and succeeded the disruption of the Roman Empire in the fifth century. It pervaded nearly all the criminal jurisprudence of Europe until the eighteenth century.

In this country it is difficult to trace cases of torture before the reign of Edward VI, for torture warrants were not entered in the Council books before this date, but there are some scanty records. In some of the last entries made in the Anglo-Saxon Chronicle by a monk of Peterborough in the twelfth century, the brutal treatment of the oppressed is related. The upper classes "torture them with pains unspeakable, for never were any martyrs tortured as these were". There follows a passage narrating the kind of cruelty used, such as imprisonment in oubliettes, filled with adders, snakes and toads. There are also records dating back to the reign of Henry II. An instance is quoted in the Pipe Roll Henry II, Northampton Ro. 10. "Petrus Filius Ade reddit compotum de xxxv marcis, quia crepit quondam mulieremet eam tormentavit, sine licentia regis."

There can be no doubt that it was used, probably very freely under Normans and Angevins. There is plenty of proof of the employment of illegal torture during these periods by gaolers either for the purpose of extracting money or to induce prisoners to give false evidence against others. But during all this time in the greater number of cases it was not used in the name of the law or as part of the legal machinery of the country. After the departure of the Romans, it was many centuries before there were "Jurisdictions" and "Courts" for the decision of cases. A permanently settled government was scarcely thought of. It was only after the Norman conquest that the barbarous customs which preceded law developed into legal processes. Before the time of William I there was, for all practical purposes, no central authority to demand an account from its distant subordinates. At the end of the reign of Henry II the second of the Public Records was written. In this an attempt was made to give the kingdom what it had never possessed before—uniformity in its laws and in the method of administering them. It was in the reign of Henry II, that the local and private jurisdictions which had grown up after the fall of the Roman Empire yielded slowly and sullenly to the institutions which men who had studied the Roman civil law believed to be better alike for King and people.

One of the earliest cases of which there is record is that of Sir Thomas Coke, Lord Mayor of London, who was tried in 1468, and convicted of the crime of misprison of treason on the evidence of one man only, and this evidence was obtained by torture.

It was under the Tudors and the Stuarts that torture was commonly used in the name of the law and by the administrators of the law. It was during this period that it flourished. In these times we have the detailed records of an enormous number of cases of torture of all sorts and conditions of men and for all sorts and conditions of crimes. This is perhaps due to a small extent to the fact that there are such abundant records of all the events of the Tudor and Stuart reigns, far more than in those preceding them. It is only in this short period of a little over a hundred years that "the question" was employed in this country. The last instance was in the reign of Charles I, when John Archer was racked in order to get him to make revelations concerning his companions in rioting.

Lecky, speaking of the attitude of men who, on the one hand were high minded and religious, who in zeal, courage, and self-sacrifice were far above the average, yet who on the other hand had a total absence of natural affection, who were always ready to inflict suffering for the sake of the views they held, and were always ready for the most brutal and horrible persecutions, and who exhibited an amount of cold, passionless, and studied barbarity unrivalled in the history of mankind, makes these remarks.

"Nor was it only towards the heretic that this inhumanity was displayed; it was reflected more or less in the whole penal system of the time. We have a striking example of this in the history of torture. In ancient Greece, torture was never employed except in cases of treason. In the best days of ancient Rome, notwithstanding the notorious inhumanity of the people, it was exclusively confined to the slaves. In mediaeval Christendom it was made use of to an extent that was probably unexampled in any earlier period, and in cases that fell under the cognisance of the clergy it was applied to every class of the community.

And what strikes us most in considering the mediaeval tortures, is not so much their diabolical barbarity, which it is indeed impossible to exaggerate, as the extraordinary variety, and what may be termed the artistic skill, they displayed. They represent a condition of thought in which men had pondered long and carefully on all the forms of suffering, had compared and combined the different kinds of torture, till they had become the most consummate masters of their art, had expended on the subject all the resources of the utmost ingenuity, and had pursued it with the ardour of a passion. The system was matured under the mediaeval habit of thought, it was adopted by the Inquisitors, and it received its finishing touches from their ingenuity. In every prison the crucifix and the rack stood side by side, and almost in every country the abolition of torture was at last effected by a movement which the Church opposed, and by men whom she had cursed. In England, it is true, torture had always been illegal, though it had often been employed, especially in ecclesiastical cases; but almost every other country illustrates the point I have stated. In France, probably the first illustrious opponent of torture was Montaigne, the first of the French sceptics: the cause was soon afterwards taken up by Charron, and by Bayle; it was then adopted by Voltaire, Montesquieu, and the Encyclopaedists; and it finally triumphed when the Church had been shattered by the Revolution. In Spain, torture began to fall into disuse under Charles III, on one of the few occasions when the Government was in direct opposition to the Church. In Italy the great opponent of torture was Beccaria, the friend of Helvetius and Holbach, and the avowed exponent of the principles of Rousseau. Translated by Morellet, commented on by Voltaire and Diderot, and supported by the whole weight of the French philosophers, the work of Beccaria flew triumphantly over Europe, and vastly accelerated the movement that produced it. Under the same influence, Frederick of Prussia, whose adherence to the philosophical principles was notorious, took the same step, and his example was speedily followed by Duke Leopold of Tuscany. Nor is there, upon reflection, anything surprising in this. The movement that destroyed torture was much less an intellectual than an emotional movement. It represented much less a discovery of the reason than an increased intensity of sympathy. If we asked what positive arguments can be adduced on the subject, it would be difficult to cite any that was not perfectly familiar to all classes at every period of the middle ages. That brave criminals sometimes escaped, and that timid persons sometimes falsely declared themselves guilty; that the guiltless frequently underwent a horrible punishment, and that the moral influence of legal decisions was seriously weakened; these arguments and such as these, were as much truisms as in the eleventh and twelfth centuries as they are at present. Nor was it by such means that the change was effected. Torture was abolished because in the progress of civilisation the sympathies of men became more expansive, their perceptions of the sufferings of others more acute, their judgments more indulgent, their actions more gentle. To subject even a guilty man to the horrors of the rack, seemed atrocious and barbarous, and therefore the rack was destroyed. It was part of the great movement which abolished barbarous amusements, mitigated the asperities and refined the manners of all classes"

As an instance of the state of feeling on the subject of punishment, I mention the following, not, remember, the views of irresponsible and unthinking people, but the views of specially selected men, the members of the House of Commons.

An old Catholic barrister named Floyd was imprisoned in the Fleet because he had been so foolish as to rejoice at the news of the Battle of Prague. Floyd denied the charge, but the House of Commons, anxious to make an example of this man, seriously debated in the House what his punishment should be. Phelips proposed that he should ride with his face to a horse's tail, from Westminster to the Tower, with a paper inscription on his hat, " A popish wretch that hath maliciously scandalised his Majesty's children", and that he should be imprisoned in the dungeon known as Little Ease, "with as much pain as he shall be able to endure without loss of his life". Sir George More suggested that he should be whipped and then left for the Lords to deal with. Seymour moved that his beads should be hung about his neck and that he should have a lash for every bead. Darcy went further, he wanted him twice pilloried and twice whipped. Each member seemed more savage than the last. One wanted his tongue cut out, another wished him to be branded, a third suggested that his ears and nose should be cut off, and yet another that he should be made to swallow his beads. Walter would have all his lands and goods ·confiscated and then have him whipped till he shed tears. The final sentence after a long discussion by the members of one of the most important Parliaments in the world, was that this poor old man who, even if he had committed any offence, had certainly not been guilty of any particularly heinous crime, was to be pilloried three times, to ride on a bare-backed horse, facing the tail, with a paper on his hat explaining his crime, and to pay a fine of 1,000 pounds. This deplorable exhibition shows the state of feeling as regards punishments held, not by a mob of unthinking men, but by a grave deliberative assembly in the reign of James I.

CHAPTER VII

ABOLITION OF TORTURE

IT is difficult to see on what grounds the sovereign could claim to be superior to the law as established by all the Charters from Magna Carta onwards. One of the justification to this claim was founded on the Pipe Roll 34 Henry II, Northamptonshire Ro. 10, where the following words are written. "Petrus Filius Ade reddit compotum de xxxv marcis, quia capet quondam mulierem et eam tormentavit, sine licentia Regis." This seems a very slender ground for claiming such a tremendous power. Even if this Pipe Roll could supersede Magna Carta (an untenable supposition) all that is here stated is that someone was tortured without the licence of the King, a very different thing to a statement that power had been granted to the King to employ torture.

The use of torture was discontinued in England in 1640. No King, after Charles I, ever claimed that the Royal prerogative could supersede the common law at least as regards the employment of torture. In other countries the discontinuance of this inhuman practice was much later. In France it was abolished at the time of the Revolution of 1798, in Russia in 1801, and in Germany in 1831. It ceased in Scotland in 1708 by Act of Parliament.

It has never been abolished by Act of Parliament in England, for as has been repeatedly stated, it has never been the law of our country; when used it was always carried out by the order of the King as one of the rights he claimed as pertaining to his position.

In Scotland, the law of torture was very different to that of England. There were many Acts of Parliament which recognised it as lawful, and in addition many warrants were issued by Parliament for the carrying out of this procedure. The Crown and the Privy Council also granted warrants for the same purpose. In the sixteenth century there were many examples of its use. In 1567 four people were ordered by the Privy Council to be tortured for complicity in the murder of Darnley. A little later some persons accused of witchcraft were put to the torture, and rioters and others were similarly treated. In 1600, a man named Rhynd was accused of being implicated in the Gowrie House plot and was tortured. Many further cases occurred in the later part of this century. Some of these are referred to later. The last instance is that of a man accused of rape and murder in 1690.

In Ireland torture was only resorted to on rare occasions. It was not recognised either by common or statute law. In the sixteenth and seventeenth centuries a few cases are recorded. In 1627 the Lord Deputy doubted whether he had authority to put a priest named O'Cullenan to the rack. An answer was sent back by Lord Killultagh to the effect that he ought to be racked if cause was seen, and hanged if reason could be found.

Some further cases are described later.

In British colonies torture has always been regarded as unlawful. Very few instances are recorded of its use. The trial of Sir Thomas Picton for torturing a girl in Trinidad is dealt with in another chapter.

Warren Hastings had as one of the counts against him

at his trial, the accusation of the use of torture of the servants of the Begums of Oude.

It is important to consider whether the attempt to extract a confession or to obtain information from a prisoner by means of torture was of any avail. Most authorities on the subject have expressed a decided opinion against its value as a means of eliciting the truth. They contend and I think most people will be in agreement with them, that words extracted from a witness under the stress of acute agony can have little if any value, and are probably in many cases actually misleading, implicating the innocent. Montaigne, the great French essayist says, "All that exceeds a simple death appears to me absolute cruelty: neither can our justice expect that he whom the fear of being executed by being beheaded or hanged will not restrain, should be any more awed by the imagination of a languishing fire, burning pincers, or the wheel." I doubt if many will go so far as this. The terrible pain of the instruments of torture will "awe" most people into anything for the sake of immediate relief. But it is very doubtful if this "anything" obtained by such means was of any value whatever. The poor tortured wretch for the sake of obtaining ease from his agony would in most cases implicate anyone, even the innocent, and there is little doubt that many, guiltless of any crime, have suffered as the result of accusations made under torture.

The case of Squires will illustrate this point. He was a soldier who was accused before the Earl of Essex and Sir Robert Cecil, in 1598, of a design to poison the Queen. At first he loudly maintained his innocence, but after five hours of the rack, he confessed that he had been instigated by a Jesuit named Walpole to commit the crime, and had provided him with a powerful poison with instructions as to the manner of using it. He had rubbed part of the poison into the pommel of the saddle on which the Queen rode, and part into the chair in which Essex usually sat, hoping it would in both cases be successful. This utterly ridiculous tale extorted under torture of the rack brought him to the scaffold. He protested his innocence with his last breath.

CHAPTER VIII

TORTURE IN TUDOR TIMES

It was during the times of the Tudors that the use of torture reached its height. Under Henry VIII it was frequently employed, it was only used in quite a small number of cases in the reigns of Edward VI and of Mary. It was whilst Elizabeth was on the throne that it was made use of more than in any other period of history. "The Common Law of England . . . neither admits of torture to extract confession, nor of any penal infliction not warranted by a judicial sentence. But the law, though still sacred in the Courts of Justice, was set aside by the Privy Council under the Tudor line. The rack seldom stood idle in the latter part of Elizabeth's reign." (Hallam.)

The excessive severities of the prerogative Courts, i.e., the Courts which claimed to be superior to the common law, mostly under the pretext of punishment for treason, excited great indignation, not only in our own country, but also throughout the greater part of Europe, where the Queen was looked on as a usurper, heretic, and tyrant. So clamant were the protests of the people that it was considered necessary to publish a pamphlet to refute these views. This brochure, issued in 1583, was attributed to Lord Burleigh, and made an attempt to justify the prosecutions for treason. "It is affirmed for truth that the forms of torture in their severity or rigour of execution have not been used and in such manner performed, as the slanderers

36

and seditious libellers have published. And that even the principal offender, Campion himself, who was sent and came from Rome, and continued here in sundry corners of the realm, having secretly wandered in the greater part of the shires of England in a disguised suit, to the intent to make special preparations of treasons, was never so racked but that he was perfectly able to walk and to write, and did presently write and subscribe to his confessions. The Queen's servants, the warders, whose office and act it is to handle the rack, were ever by those that attended the examinations especially charged to use it in so charitable a manner as such things might be. None of those who were at any time put to the rack were asked, during their torture, any questions as to points of doctrine, but merely concerning their plots and confessions, and the persons with whom they had had dealings, and what was their own opinion as to the Pope's right to deprive the Queen of her crown. Nor was anyone so racked until it was rendered evidently probable, by former detections or confessions, that he was guilty; nor was the torture ever employed to bring out confessions at random; nor unless the party had at first refused to declare the truth at the Queen's commandment."

This is a very inadequate and unconvincing defence. The outcry against the excessive barbarities of the torture chamber, in spite of the defence of Lord Burleigh, became so great that the Government was compelled to take some steps to placate the people. They tried the expedient of keeping the sufferings of the victims more or less secret. They gave authority for private torture. "Master Topcliffe to torment priests in his own house in such manner as he shall think good." Meyer thus describes the activities of this brutal man. "No blot is more foul on the history of Elizabeth's later years than the name of Richard Topcliffe. Every inhuman quality which the most heated imagination can picture is embodied in this example of unspeakable degradation: Greed and perverse delight in inflicting suffering, rather than religious fanaticism were the motives of Topcliffe's conduct. His name became a synonym for brutality. . . . Prolonged practice had made him familiar with the amount of suffering of which man's nervous system was capable, and to invent fresh tortures became his business and his delight. The accounts handed down by eye-witnesses and the sufferers themselves surpass all power of description, and we gladly draw the veil over the last and most frightful scene when the condemned were handed over to Topcliffe without witnesses and inquisitors. Only a man like Topcliffe was capable of torturing afresh a man who had already been broken on the rack, who had confessed and admitted everything asked of him, and had even renounced his faith. Only a man like Topcliffe was capable of continuing to insult his victim so long as he drew breath and of stifling the last words of farewell and prayer. Had he not been sure of the Queen's approval, the wretch could not have plied his trade.

"When we hear of a recorder who could no longer control himself when presiding over the application of torture, but burst into tears, or of a Governor of the Tower, who was so overcome by the constancy of a man under torture that he resigned his post, we are led to the conclusion that the administration of penal justice during the persecution exceeded the horrors common at the period. We get the same impression from the treatment of prisoners during that time; they were confined in foul and stinking dungeons, and were given the worst food and water; sometimes they were tied to a manger like animals and had their scanty viands flung at them; sometimes they were yoked like beasts of burden to a sort of mill and whipped if they did not perform their tasks willingly or were unable to work from illness. Possibly we might reject these accounts as

inventions of exaggerations of catholics, were they not corro-
borated by the large number of deaths which took place
in prison. To every four or five catholics who suffered death
by execution, we must add one who died while in prison.''

Topcliffe boasted that the rack in the Tower was child's
play compared with his. Among the many atrocities
committed by him was that of hanging up Robert Southwell
till he lost consciousness over and over again, and when
he had vomited blood he wrote the Government that he
was sure to get some information from him soon.

In 1594 he brought an action against Fitzherbert, for
the sum of £5,000, which he said had been promised him
if he would torture to death three recusants, including
Fitzherbert's father and uncle. The facts of this horrible
contract were not disputed, but Fitzherbert refused to
pay on the grounds that one of the recusants was still alive
and that the other two had not actually died of torture.
As a matter of fact they had died in prison after their terrible
sufferings. The case was too abominable even for Elizabeth
and was hushed up, but Topcliffe somehow became
possessed of the Fitzherbert estates.

The light methods with which Elizabeth resorted to
the rack cannot be better illustrated than the following,
related by Lord Bacon in one of his letters. "The Queen
was mightily incensed against Haywarde, on account of
a book he dedicated to Lord Essex, being a story of the
first year of Henry IV, thinking it a seditious prelude to
put into the people's heads boldness and faction: She
said, she had an opinion that there was treason in it,
and asked me, if I could not find any places in it, that
might be drawn within the case of treason? Whereto I
answered, for treason, sure I found none; but for felony
very many: And when her majesty hastily asked me,
Wherein? I told her, the author had committed very
apparent theft: For he had taken most of the sentences

of Cornelius Tacitus, and translated them into English, and put them into his text. And another time when the Queen could not be persuaded that it was his writing whose name was to it, but that it had some more mischievous author, and said, with great indignation, that she would have him racked to produce his author; I replied, nay, madam, he is a doctor, never rack his person, but rack his style: Let him have pen, ink, and paper, and help of books, and be enjoined to continue the story where it breaketh off, and I will undertake, by collating the styles, to judge whether he were the author or no." Had it not been for Bacon, Haywarde would have been racked by Elizabeth for dedicating a book to Essex, when that nobleman happened to be out of favour with her.

Lytton Strachey in his *Elizabeth and Essex*, one of the latest studies of this Tudor Queen, shows how impossible it was to get justice in any case of treason and the reasons for this impossibility. "It was virtually impossible for anyone accused of High Treason—the gravest offence known to the law—to be acquitted. The reason for this was plain; but it was a reason not of justice but of expediency. Upon the life of Elizabeth hung the whole structure of the State. During the first thirty years of her reign, her death would have involved the accession of a Catholic sovereign, which would have inevitably been followed by a complete revolution in the system of Government, together with the death or ruin of the actual holders of power. The fact was obvious enough to the enemies of the English policy, and the danger that they might achieve their end by the Queen's assassination was a very real one. The murder of inconvenient monarchs was one of the habits of the day. William of Orange and Henry III of France had both been successfully obliterated by Philip and the Catholics. . . . In such a situation only one course of action seemed to be possible: every other consideration must be subordinated to the supreme necessity of preserving the Queen's life. It was futile to talk of justice; for justice involves, by its very nature, uncertainty; and the Government could take no risks. The old saw was reversed; it was better that ten innocent men should suffer than that one guilty man should escape. To arouse suspicion itself became a crime. The proofs of guilt must not be sifted by the slow processes of logic and fair play; they must be multiplied—by spies, by *agents provocateurs*, by torture. The prisoner brought to trial should be allowed no counsel to aid him against the severity of iron-hearted judges and the virulence of the ablest lawyers of the day. Conviction should be followed by the most frightful of punishments. In the domain of treason, under Elizabeth, the reign of law was, in effect, superseded, and its place was taken by a reign of terror.

It was in the collection of evidence that the mingled atrocity and absurdity of the system became most obvious. Not only was the fabric of a case often built up on the allegations of the hired creatures of the Government, but the existence of the rack gave a preposterous twist to the words of every witness. Torture was constantly used; but whether, in any particular instance, it was used or not, the consequences were identical. The threat of it, the hint of it, the mere knowledge in the mind of a witness that it might at any moment be applied to him—those were differences merely of degree; always, the fatal compulsion was there inextricably confusing truth with falsehood."

His description of the state of affairs in England at the end of the middle ages as regards the punishments awarded to offenders is very illuminating. "The gibbet, with a robber hanging in chains, was one of the objects most frequently presented to the eye. A petty thief in the pillory, a scold on the ducking-stool, a murderer drawn to the gallows on a hurdle, were spectacles as familiar when Henry VII ascended the throne, as a messenger from the telegraph office is to ourselves. London Bridge, which is now thronged with travellers peaceably making their way to a railway terminus, was then a narrow thorough-fare, with unglazed shops on either side, with the obstruction of a drawbridge half-way across, and perhaps chains at either end. Its chief adornments were the heads of traitors, fixed on poles, as a warning to all who might lack the skill to be on the right side in any further commotions. The fatherless and the widow, if claiming kinship with the King, might sometimes gain possession of the mutilated remains of father or husband, after a few days' exposure to the jeers of the mob. Those who were less fortunate suffered, in addition to their bereavement, the pangs of reflecting that the features which were most dear to them were to be impaled, as an exhibition, during the King's pleasure, which was, in fact, the pleasure of sunshine and storm and natural decay. Nor was London the only city to which was given this impressive caution. The head of a traitor was often sent to the neighbourhood in which the treason had been committed; and there was no town so little favoured as not to receive ever and anon the ghastly present of a quarter, wherewithal to decorate its walls or gates."

An account of some of the principal cases in which torture was used during the Tudor period shows clearly in what kind of accusations it was employed. The majority of the prisoners were charged with high treason, but murder, robbery, embezzling the Queen's plate, and failure to carry out proclamations against stage players, were among the offences charged against those who were put to "the question". It was never employed in the case of members of the aristocracy. Lords and high officials were exempt, and very rarely indeed were women put to the torture.

By some it was considered that torture should not be used on minors, and by others this privilege was extended to very old people, those who were sick, and women. But though there may have been a humane section who held this view, instances quoted later will show that it was by no means universally carried out.

Jardine, in his little brochure, *Reading on the use of Torture in the Criminal Law of England,* says, "it was never used where women were concerned". But I think he was wrong here. In the case of Anne Askew the evidence is very definite and conclusive that she was put to "the question".

In 1546 Anne Askew was arrested for her religious views which were not those which happened to be prevailing at the time. She was brought before the Lord Mayor of London, and afterwards before Bonner, the fanatical Bishop of London. He tried to persuade her to recant her views, but this she refused to do. She was released on bail but again arrested in the following summer. This time she came under Gardiner and Wriothesley, who again tried to alter her views. They questioned her for five hours, but were unable to get her to recant. She was sentenced to death, but the execution was delayed as her persecutors were anxious for her to implicate others. She was taken from Newgate to the Tower, where the Chancellor was waiting for her. She was questioned as to any others who might hold the same views but refused to implicate anyone. "Then," she says in a letter which exists in her own handwriting, "they did put me on the rack because I confessed no ladies or gentlemen to be of my opinion, and thereupon they kept me a long time: and because I lay still and did not cry, my Lord Chancellor and Master Rich (the Solicitor-General) took pains to rack me with their own hands till I was nigh dead." Sir Anthony Knyvet, the Lieutenant of the Tower, lifted her off in his arms. She fainted and was laid on the floor, and after her recovery, the Chancellor again questioned her for two hours. Her execution was carried out on July 16th, when she was carried to Smithfield with three others. She was chained to a stake, and a sermon was preached. The victims, full of courage to the last, refused to recant and said they were not come there to deny their Lord and Master. The Mayor rose and said "fiat Justicia", the fire was lighted, and the victims done to death.

Foxe's account of the torture of Anne Askew is as follows. "At length they put her on the rack, because she had confessed no ladies or gentlemen to be of her opinion, and thereon they kept her a long time, and because she lay still, and did not cry, the lord chancellor, and Mr. Rich took pains to rack her with their own hands till she was nigh dead—an instance of unusual cruelty even for that age. After that she sat two hours reasoning with the lord chancellor upon the bare floor, where he with many flattering words persuaded her to leave her opinion; but her Lord God, thanks to his everlasting goodness, gave her grace to persevere."

Although torture warrants were undoubtedly issued before the Tudor period, records were not kept, and the first warrant to be found in the books of the Privy Council is in the reign of Edward VI, when, on November 15th, 1551, one was issued against those concerned in the treason of the Lord Protector, Somerset, who ordered his own brother Thomas, Lord High Admiral, whom he suspected of aiming at the crown, to be put to the rack. Later he had him beheaded.

In the reign of Mary, the first recorded instance was in 1555, "to bring such obstinate persons as will not otherwise confess, to the tortures ". In this year Dr. Caius, Physician to the Queen, and founder of Caius College, Cambridge, was robbed, and a warrant was issued "to bring Richard Mulcaster, a servant to Dr. Caius, to the rack, and to put him in fear of the torture if he would not confess".

Another instance is that issued to the Lieutenant of the Tower, giving him authority to examine a person "vehemently suspected of robbery and if they saw cause, to bring him to the rack, and to put him to some pain if he would not confess".

Elizabeth, directly she came to the throne, commenced her long series of tortures. The first entry in the Council books is dated four months after her accession. It was to the Lieutenant of the Tower, dated March 15th, 1558/9, to examine two men, Pitt and Nicolls, accused of robbing a widow in London. If they persisted in their denial, they were to "be brought to the rack, and to feel the smart there if as the examinees by their discretion shall think good for the better boulting out of the truth of the matter".

In a letter from the Privy Council, to the Attorney-General and others, dated December 28th, 1566, was the following. "Where they were heretofore appointed to put Clement Fisher, now prisoner in the Tower, in some fear of torture whereby his leudness and such as he might detect, might the better come to light, they are requested for that the said Fisher is not minded to be plain, as thereby the faults of others might be known, to cause the said Fisher according to their discretion to feel some touch of the rack, for the better boulting out and opening of that which is required to be known."

In a letter to the Lieutenant of the Tower, January 18th, 1567, these instructions were given.—"One Rice, a buckle maker, committed there, is discovered to have been a robber of plate four years before; the lieutenant to examine the said Rice about this robbery, and if they shall perceive him not willing to confess the same then to put him in fear of the torture, and to let him feel some smart of the same whereby he may be the better brought to confess the truth." (Irish MSS. Rolls House.)

In 1570 a Papal Bull, excommunicating Queen Elizabeth, was issued a copy of which was nailed on the door of the house of the Bishop of London by a young man of good family. He was captured and under torture, confessed to the act. He was of course sentenced to death, and at the place of his crime, he was executed with the usual horrible tortures which the hangman was allowed to carry out.

At this same time, among those who were engaged in circulating seditious pamphlets was a Dr. Story, a man who was noted for his cruelties during the persecutions in the reign of Queen Mary. He was captured and when he found that he was fast in the hands of his enemies, he wrote to Cecil that "as he was old and decrepit, one iron on his sound leg would be sufficient to hold him", and praying that he might be sent to a comfortable prison, "that he perished not before his time". He was sent to the Lollard's Tower, the place where he himself had sent so many victims, and which had been empty since he had lost the power to persecute. At first he bore his fate with courage, but under the terrible pains of the rack, he, an old man of seventy, was unable to hold out and confessed the secrets of his treason, was tried and sentenced to death.

At the trial of the Duke of Norfolk in 1572, the principal evidence against him was extorted by the rack applied to witnesses. It was contended that all the confessions had been made voluntarily, but on September 15th, the Queen through Lord Burghley ordered the prisoners "to be put to the rack, and find the taste thereof": Sir Thomas Smyth in a letter of a few days later date says, "I suppose we have gotten so mych at this time as is lyke to be had; yet to-morrow we do intend to bryng a couple of them to the rack, not in any hope to get to any thyng worthy that payne or feare, but because it is earnestly commanded unto us"; and yet a few days later "of Bannister with the rack, of Barker with the extreme fear of it, we suppose we have gotten all".

In November, 1577, the Attorney-General was directed to examine Thomas Sherwood, a Catholic layman, and an educated man, for hearing mass and confessing his belief that the Queen was a heretic and had no lawful claim to the throne. The Lieutenant of the Tower was ordered to "place the prisoner in the dungeon among the rats" which was a cell below high water mark, and totally dark. The water flowed in and out according to the tides, and the rats which infested the muddy banks of the Thames poured in through holes in the wall. During his sleep the animals actually tore the flesh from his arms and legs. He made no confession under this treatment so he was put on the rack. He revealed nothing of importance under his torture, and was as usual, executed for high treason.

There are many instances of similar tortures of Catholics. In 1580 the feeling against them ran very high, especially when the Jesuits were concerned. Some seven or eight young priests were in this year arrested and taken to the Tower. They were asked to give the names of those who had taken them into their houses and the names of their leaders. This they refused to do. Under a warrant signed by six members of the Council and in the presence of the Lieutenant whose duty it was to direct the application of the torture, they were laid on the rack, the commissioners sitting by the side of them and asking them questions in the intervals of the winding of the winch to wrench their limbs. Froude in describing this case says, "A practice which by the law was always forbidden, could be palliated by a danger so great that the nation had

become like an army in the field.   It was repudiated on
the return of calmer times, and the employment of it
rests as a stain on the memory of those by whom it was
used.   It was none the less certain however that the danger
was real and terrible, and the same causes which relieve
a commander on active service from the restraints of the
common law, apply to the conduct of statesmen who
are dealing with organised treason.   The law is made
for the nation, and not the nation for the law.   Those
who transgress, do it at their own risk, but they may
plead circumstances at the bar of history, and have a
right to be heard ".   As some palliation of the Elizabethan
brutalities, the following were typical reasonings, "None
was put to the rack that was not at first by some manifest
evidence known to the Council to be guilty of treason,
so that it was well assured beforehand that there was
no innocent tormented.   Also none was tormented to
know whether he was guilty or no: but for the Queen's
safety to know the manner of the treason and the accomplices ".   (Thomas Norton to Walsingham, March 27th,
1582.   MSS. Domestic.)

Some of the horrible tortures to which the Jesuits were
subjected in the reign of Elizabeth are vividly described
by a letter written by a priest in the Tower, written in
July, 1581.   (MSS. Domestic.)   The cells were underground, lighted by tunnels sloping upwards, and closely
grated to prevent communication.   The prison diet was
bread, beer, salt fish, and stale water.   Some of the older
ones died as the result of imprisonment only.   Others
were subjected to greater tortures.   A youth of twenty-
four, named Bryant, who was known to be aware of the
hiding place of a companion, and refused to reveal it,
was threatened with the rack.   "If he would not tell the
truth for his duty to God and the Queen, he should be
made a foot longer than God had made him."   He defied

them and they kept their word. He laughed when on the rack and asked his torturers if that was the best they could do. Campion, another of the Jesuits, was racked two days in succession. Mendosa the Spanish Ambassador in a letter to the King of Spain, says, "that when this torture failed, needles were run under the nails of the fingers and toes". This barbarity is probably exaggerated, there is no record of this method having been used in England, and the Ambassador may have been thinking of the thumbscrews.

Campion was promised his freedom if he would attend the Protestant service once only. He refused and the rack was again resorted to. His trial had to be postponed on account of his condition after the last torturing. His limbs had been dislocated by the force used. When at the bar at Westminster Hall, Campion was unable to raise his hand to plead, so it was lifted by two of his companions.

At the execution of this group of Jesuits, Campion as the oldest, was allowed the privilege of dying first. He ascended the cart, and spoke a few words. Criers for the Government proclaimed that he was being executed for treason and not for religion. "We are come here to die," cried Campion, "but we are not traitors. I am a Catholic man and a priest. In that faith I have lived and in that faith I mean to die. If you consider my religion treason, then I am guilty. Other treason I never committed, as God is my judge."

Froude's comments on these proceedings are of the utmost interest. "The modern reader will find it hard to judge fairly the men who ordered these things. Abhorrence of deliberate cruelty provokes abhorrence also of those who were guilty of it, and the long impotence of the Catholic clergy in England renders us incredulous of the dangers that were to be feared from them. For

the rack, the thumbscrew, the Tower dungeons, and the
savage details of the execution, no detestation can be too
strong, no gratitude too vehement that we have left them,
with stake and wheel, and red-hot pincers, and the ferocious
refinements of another age, long and for ever behind us.
But there is a common level of humanity among contemporary civilised nations, from which there is seldom
any very large deviation for good or evil; and Protestant
England, notwithstanding the cruelties to the Jesuits,
was not below but above the average continental level.
The torture chambers of the Inquisition were yet more
horrible than the cells of the Tower, and the use of torture
in England, though forbidden by the law, was inherited
by the council, through a long series of precedents.
Protestant prisoners had been racked by Mary, as Catholics
were racked by Elizabeth. We condemn Burghley and
Walsingham, not because they were worse than Pole
and Gardiner, but because they were not better, while
the atrocious sentence for treason was repeated for two
more centuries from the bench whenever rebel or conspirator was brought up for justice. The guilt of judicious
cruelty to criminals must be distributed equally over the
whole contemporary world. The mere execution of these
Jesuits, if political executions can be defended at all, was as
justifiable as the execution of the meanest villain or wildest
enthusiast who ever died on the scaffold. Treason is a
crime for which personal virtue is neither protection nor
excuse. To plead in condemnation of severity, either
the general innocence or the saintly intentions of the
sufferers, is besides the issue; and if it be lawful in defence
of national independence to kill open enemies in war,
it is more lawful to execute the secret conspirator who
is teaching doctrines, in the name of God, which are
certain to be fatal to it. The Catholics throughout Europe
had made war upon Protestants. They had taught as

part of their creed the duty of putting heretics to death. England had shaken off their yoke, but it had not retaliated, and although the professors of such an accursed doctrine might have been treated without injustice as public enemies, Elizabeth had left her Catholic subjects to think as they pleased as long as they would remain quiet under the law. They refused to accept her forebearance. They availed themselves of her lenity as a shelter. They conspired against her throne and life, and they brought down upon themselves at last with overwhelming force the heavy hand of justice."

Throgmorton, accused of treason in 1583, was known to have important information in respect of the plot in which he had been engaged. His friends hoped that he would refuse to betray them, but his courage was not equal to the cruel treatment of the rack. "Interrogated in the gloomy cell which had rung with the screams of the Jesuits, the horrid instrument at his side, with the mute executioners standing ready to strain his limbs out of their sockets, his imagination was appalled, his senses refused to do their work. He equivocated, varied in his story, contradicted himself in every succeeding sentence. Pardon was promised him if he would make a free confession. He still held out, but he could not conceal that he had much to tell, and the times did not permit humanity to traitors to imperil the safety of the realm. The Queen gave the necessary authority to proceed with 'the pains'. Her Majesty thought it agreeable with good policy and the safety of her person and seat, to commit him to the hands of her learned council, to assay by torture to draw the truth from him. Again he was proffered pardon: again he refused, and he was handed over 'to such as were usually appointed in the Tower to handle the rack'. His honour struggled with his agony. On the first racking he confessed nothing; but he could not encounter a second trial. When he was laid again upon the frame, before he was strained to any purpose, he yielded to confess everything that he knew. Sitting in wretchedness beside the horrid engine, the November light faintly streaming down the tunnelled windows into the dungeon beneath the armoury, he broke his pledged word, and broke his heart along with it." (Froude, quoting from Throgmorton's treason. Official narrative.)

Throgmorton was of course hanged. A confession under torture carried with it no mercy.

In 1591, Eustace White and Brian Lassy were ordered manacles and such other tortures as are used in Bridewell. This is the first occasion in which any reference to this instrument occurs. After this date it appears to have been in common use. It was kept in Bridewell till about 1598. Exactly what this instrument was, is obscure. The ordinary meaning is simply that of handcuffs or some such appliance, but it is probable that the old "manacles" was an instrument which compressed the whole body, similar to one which existed in the Tower of London as late as 1837.

The type of prison used in these Tudor times is well illustrated by the following description from a letter from a Charles Bailey, one of the many young men who devoted their services and their lives to Mary, Queen of Scots, during her imprisonment in England. He was captured and sent to the Tower, the most dreaded prison in Europe, where he was confined in a cave, which he describes as rheumatic and unsavoury, foul with the uncleansed memorials of generations of wretches who had preceded him there, without a bed, with only a little straw on the moist earth-floor to lie upon, the wardens answering to his complaints that they provided prisoners only with place and room, beds and other necessities they must obtain from their friends.

Burghley ordered Sir William Hopton, Lieutenant of the Tower, to examine Bailey concerning certain letters written by him in cipher to the Bishop of Ross. "You will ask him for the alphabet of the cipher, and if he shall refuse to show the said alphabet, or to declare truly the contents of the said letters in cipher, you shall put him upon the rack; and by discretion with putting him in fear, and as cause shall be given afterwards, you shall procure him to confess the truth with some pain of the said torture." Soon afterwards, Bailey was so severely racked that he was hardly able to stagger back to his dungeon. He was "discoloured and pale as ashes". He confessed nothing, but further torture was to be applied and he was sent to his filthy prison to reflect in the darkness on this further punishment. This second racking was unnecessary as the information desired was obtained from Bailey by a trick.

CHAPTER IX

TORTURE IN THE STUART PERIOD

In the reign of James I, torture was frequently resorted to, but mainly in cases of high treason, and only rarely for other crimes such as murder and robbery, as in Tudor times. The first case occurred in April, 1603, before the King reached London on his journey from Scotland. The Attorney-General himself personally conducted an examination under torture of an accused individual.

Perhaps one of the best known instances of torture in Stuart times, is that of those concerned in the gunpowder plot. The proceedings against the conspirators in this plot, in 1605, is an excellent illustration of a trial for treason in early Stuart times. Guy Fawkes was sent to the Tower, and when examined concerning the plot refused to answer any questions which would incriminate anybody else. A list of queries which he was required to answer was sent to him by the King, who ordered that in the event of his refusal to comply he should be put to the torture, though recourse was not to be had to the rack unless he proved obdurate. The directions to the Lords Commissioners for the torture of Guy Fawkes, given by James I exist in the King's own handwriting. "If he will not otherways confess, the gentlest tortures are to be first used unto him; *et sic per gradus ad ima tenditur*, and so God speed your good work."

Nothing of importance was ascertained by his answers, and he was therefore, examined again the same day, probably after "gentle torture"; and he then gave further particulars.   He was in a few days subject once more to torture, this time of a severe nature, for his signature to his examination was in a trembling and broken hand. He and all his fellow conspirators were found guilty and condemned to death.   Early in 1606, the sentence on Guy Fawkes, Thomas Winter, Rokewood, and Keyes, was carried out.   As they passed down the streets, each dragged on his separate hurdle, they moved through long lines of hostile faces.   The only word of sympathy they received was in the Strand, when they came to the house in which Rokewood's wife was staying.   Her husband on seeing her begged her to pray for him.   "I will, I will, and do you offer yourself with a good heart to God and your creator."

Digby, Robert Winter, Grant, and Bates had been executed the day before in St. Paul's Churchyard.   Tresham who had died had his head cut off after death and exhibited at Northampton.   The brutal nature of the times is shown by the action of a member of Parliament who moved a petition to the King to stay judgment till some extraordinary method of punishment could be found which might surpass in horror even the ghastly executions usually carried out on traitors.   The proposal was fortunately negatived at once.   The execution of those concerned in the plot did not end the action of the Government in the matter.   They were fully convinced and anxious to prove to the people that the Jesuits in England were largely responsible for the plot.   Bates, one of those concerned, had acknowledged that he had revealed the plan to a priest, Greenway, in confession, and had also been in communication with others, Gerard and Garnet. The first two escaped from the country, Garnet was arrested.   Incidents in connection with this arrest are strange reading to-day.   Garnet had gone in hiding to the house of a priest named Oldcorne, in Hindlip.   This house was amply provided with secret chambers.   Nearly every room had its hiding place in the thickness of the walls; even the chimneys led to rooms, the doors of which were lined with smoke covered bricks.   The house was searched.   Several hiding places were discovered but not that of Garnet.   It was not till ten days later that the priest stepped out of his secret chamber, unable any longer to endure the close confinement.   He had been in no danger of starvation for there was a communication between the place of hiding and one of the rooms through which broth was passed by means of a quill.   It is very difficult to understand how a thorough search of the house did not reveal the secret chamber.   A Scotland Yard man would not take many minutes to discover such a hiding place.   No information could be got from Garnet. He was threatened with torture but the King had expressly forbidden its actual use in the case of the priest.   Garnet's servant, Owen, however was put to the torture.   He was fastened by his hands to a beam above his head, and fear of the repetition of the agony caused him to commit suicide the next day.   He used a blunt knife supplied for feeding purposes to rip up his abdomen after getting rid of his keeper on some subterfuge.   He covered himself with straw and his condition was only discovered by the oozing through of blood and the ghastly appearance of the man.

The first torture warrant (but not by any means the first case of torture) of which there is trace in the reign of Charles I was in 1626.   William Monke was falsely accused of treason, and was put to the rack.   So severely was he tortured that he was totally disabled and quite unable to maintain himself or his wife and nine children.

Later he was granted some compensation from the property of those who had falsely accused him.

In 1614, Edward Peacham, Rector of Hinton St. George, in Somersetshire was one of those who protested strongly against the ecclesiastical abuses of the time. His chief objection was to the Ecclesiastical Court of the Bishop of Bath and Wells. He made charges against the Consistory Court for which he was sent up to Lambeth for trial before the High Commission. He was adjudged to be guilty of libel, and was deprived of his orders in December, 1614. Ten days before this he had by order of the Privy Council been transferred to the Tower of London. In searching his house, some papers were discovered, part of which was a composition in the form of a sermon. The papers were examined by the Council and were declared to contain treasonable matter. The sermon was undoubtedly of an aggressive nature. It abused the Government, it referred to the misconduct of officials, and the extravagance of the King. It was suggested that when the Prince came to the throne he might attempt to seize the Crown lands which had been given away and this would cause the owners to rise in rebellion and slay him. Peacham acknowledged that he had intentionally aimed at the King and he justified his action. It was supposed that in the composition of these notes which were evidently intended to be preached, as a sermon or issued in the press, Peacham had been helped and instigated by the gentry of the County of Somerset, where there was so much discontent at the levy of the Benevolence, which the King, always in want of money, was trying to raise. So convinced was the Court that he had the help of others in his work that directions were given if he would not confess he was to be tortured. Winwood, Secretary of State, and the Chancellor of the Exchequer, together with Bacon, Yelverton, Montague, and Crew, the four law advisers of the Crown, were ordered by the Council to renew the examination, and if they saw fit to put Peacham in "the manacles". He, although an old man, was actually put to the torture.

Gardiner in his *History of England*, commenting on procedures such as these says: "There is no reason to suppose that any of those who were entrusted with this odious work imagined, for a moment, that they were doing anything wrong. Though the common law expressly rejected the use of torture, it was generally understood that the Council had the right of obtaining information by its means whenever they might come to the conclusion that the evidence of which they were in search was of sufficient importance to render it necessary to appeal to such a mode of extracting a secret from an obstinate person. The distinction, then so familiar, between the law which ruled in ordinary cases, and the prerogative by which it was overruled in matters of political importance, has happily passed away even from the memory of men. It is, therefore, not without difficulty that we are able to realise to ourselves a state of feeling which would regard proceedings of this kind as contrary to the law, and yet it is indubitable that such feeling existed and there can be little doubt that it was shared by all those who witnessed the scene. Bacon's part as Attorney-General was entirely subordinate and, though he may have possibly regarded the use of torture as inopportune in this particular case, there is no reason to suppose that in the general question he felt in any way different to those who were associated with him."

Secretary Wenwood makes these remarks regarding Peacham's torture. "Peacham was this day examined before torture, in torture, between torture, and after torture: notwithstanding nothing could be drawn from him, he stood persisting in his obstinate and insensible denials and firm answers."

One of the most important, perhaps the most important declaration ever made on the subject of torture was that of the judges in 1628.

In 1628 John Felton was put on trial for the assassination of the Duke of Buckingham. The King wished him to be tortured, in order to obtain information as to any accomplices he may have had. Before doing so, he put the following question to the judges. "Felton, now a prisoner in the Tower, having confessed that he killed the Duke of Buckingham, and said that he was induced to this partly by private displeasure, and partly by reason of a Remonstrance in Parliament, having also read some books which he said defended that it was lawful to kill an enemy to the republic: the question is whether by the law he might not be racked, and whether there were any law against it, for, said the King, if it might be done by law, he would not use his prerogative on this point."

All twelve judges, assembled at Sergeant's Inn, on November 14th, declared unanimously "he ought not by the law to be tortured by the rack, for no such punishment is known or allowed by the law".

This answer given by the judges has often been misquoted or misinterpreted. The decision was not definitely that torture was never to be allowed but that it was not allowed *by law*. They made no statement as to the use of torture by the Royal prerogative, a prerogative which preceding sovereigns had used freely and almost as a matter of course in grave cases, uncontrolled by any law, but a prerogative which was to cease for ever a few years later.

On November 27th, Felton was removed from the Tower to the Gatehouse and brought to trial, when he pleaded guilty. He was sentenced to death. "Whereupon

he offered the hand to be cut off that did the fact;
but the court could not, upon his own offer, inflict that
further punishment upon him; nevertheless the king sent
to the judges to intimate his desire, that his hand might
be cut off before execution.   But the court answered
that it could not be; for in all murders, the judgement
was the same."

Felton was hanged and afterwards hung up in chains.

The last case of torture in England took place in 1640.
Riots had occurred at Southwark in connection with the
grievances of the people against Laud.   Most of those
engaged in the rioting were journeymen and apprentices.
Several of them were arrested and tried before a special
commission.   The judges laid it down that the disturbances
amounted to high treason.   One prisoner a man of very
humble origin, was sentenced to be hanged and quartered,
and this was carried out at Southwark, though the
authorities, in their mercy, allowed him to hang till he
was dead, instead of cutting him up when he was only
half strangled.   Another poor victim, John Archer, who
had beaten the drum in advance of the crowd, was
believed to possess information as to the instigators of
the riots.   He was put to the torture in an attempt to
get him to confess anything he knew, but he made no
revelations.   He was hanged, after being racked.   This
was the last attempt in this country to enforce confession
by torture.   The reign of this abominable cruelty was
over for ever.

In 1680, in the reign of Charles II, Elizabeth Cellier
was charged with writing and publishing a libel, and
Baron Weston who was trying the case made the following
remarks, after the accused had asserted that the principal
witness against her had been tortured and that therefore
the evidence so obtained was of no value.   "For knowing
Praunce to be a principal witness, she undertakes to let

the world know, that Praunce was tortured in prison, to insinuate, that the evidence he gave against these persons that were executed for this murder, was extorted from him by ill and cruel usage (this was a reference to part of the alleged libel). But you must first know the laws of the land do not admit a torture, and since Queen Elizabeth's time there hath been nothing of that kind ever done. The truth is, indeed, in the twentieth year of her reign, Campion was just stretched upon the rack, but yet not so but that he could walk; but when she was told that it was against the law of the land to have any of her subjects racked (though that was an extraordinary case, a world of seminaries being sent over to contrive her death, and she lived in continual danger), yet it was never done after to anyone neither in her reign, who reigned twenty-five years after, nor in King James' reign, who reigned twenty-two years after: nor in King Charles the first's reign, who reigned twenty-four years after; and God in heaven knows that there hath been no such thing offered in this King's reign, for I think we may say, we have lived under as lawful and merciful a government as any people whatsoever, and have had as little blood shed, and sanguinary executions as in any nation under heaven. Well, but (contrary to the law in this case), she does suppose extraordinary ways were used to make Praunce give this evidence. She says, she thought what she first heard was the noise of a woman with child, and that Harris, the turnkey, did tell her it was a woman in labour; but when she desired to be let in to help her, he turned her away rudely; but listening, she perceived it was the groans of a strong man that must be in torture: She asked some of the gaolers what was the matter? They told her, they durst not tell her, but it was something they could not endure; and they heard him cry, What would you have me confess? Would you have me belie myself? I know nothing of it; and such words as these.

"Whereupon we have called Praunce, and here, upon oath, he tells you there was no such matter. That he was used very kindly, had all things fitting, and under no compulsion, so that this is an high libel against the government."

It is remarkable that Baron Weston should have made a statement so entirely opposed to fact as this. The torture warrants issued by Elizabeth and her Privy Council were more frequent than in any other reign, the rack was seldom idle with her, and many and many a time after Campion's case was some poor wretch put to "the question ". In the time of the first two Stuarts case after case is recorded, Guy Fawkes and his companions, Wm. Monke, Paecham, John Archer and a host of others. Yet we have a judge of the High Court, some forty years after torture had ceased, stating during the course of a trial, that no instance had occurred since that of Campion in 1581. Torture was in actual fact in common use till 1640.

CHAPTER X

In Scotland, torture had a much surer legal status than it had in this country. It was acknowledged by many Acts and warrants of the Scottish Parliament, and warrants both of the Crown and Privy Council. Sometimes a special Act was passed to deal with one particular offender. .

In 1542, Lord Glammis was condemned to "forfeiture", but this was later altered by the Parliament on the grounds that the evidence had been obtained from a confession extorted by threat of the "pynebankis". In the register of the Scottish Council is a warrant ordering the torture of four people in 1567 for complicity in the murder of Darnley, another in 1591 to torture certain people accused of witchcraft, and another in 1600 to torture a man, Rhynd, for participating in the Gowrie House plot. There are numerous other instances in the records of the Privy Council and Parliament.

A report of some of the well known Scotch cases of torture are appended.

On June 14th, 1596, John Stewart, Master of Orkney, was indicted for consulting with Alison Balfour, a witch, for the destruction of Patrick, Earl of Orkney, brother of the master, by poison. The confession of Alison was put in and read. The Master of Orkney, in his defence said, "No regard can be had to it (the confession) in respect the said confession was extorted by force of torment; she having been kept forty eight hours in the Caspie laws; her old husband, a man about ninety years of age, put in heavy irons; and her little daughter, about seven years old, put in the pilniewinks; all in the poor woman's presence to make her confess".

This torture of a child of seven is the youngest case of which I have found any record, though there are other instances in which children were put to the "question".

The Torture of William Spence

"July 26th, 1684. Mr. William Spence, late servant to the earl of Argyle, by order of the Privy Council, is put and tortured in the boots, to force him to reveal what he knows of the earl's and other persons accession to the late English fanatic plot, and the association and design of rising; and in regard he refused to depone upon oath, if he had the key whereby he could read some letters of the earl's, produced by Major Holmes, written in cyphers; and seeing that he would not say upon oath that he could not read them, and that they offered to secure him by a pardon for his life, it rendered him very obnoxious and suspect of prevarication; so that after the torture, he was put in general Dalzell's hands; and it was reported that by a hair shirt and pricking (as the witches are used) he was five nights kept from sleep, till he was turned half distracted. He ate very little, of purpose that he might require the less sleep, yet all this while he discovered nothing, and though he had done it, yet little credit was to be given to what he should say at such a time.

"August 7th, 1684. At Privy Council, Spence is again tortured and his thumbs crushed with thumbikins: It is a new invention used among the colliers when transgressors; they having seen them used in Muscovy. After this, when they were about to put him again in the boots, he being frightened, desired time, and he would declare what he knew; whereon they gave him some time, and sequestrated him in the castle of Edinburgh, as a place where he would be free from any bad advice or impression, to be obstinate in not revealing.

"August 22nd. Mr. William Spence, to avoid any further torture, reads these hieroglyphic letters; and agrees with Mr. Holme's declaration, that Argyle, Loudon Campbell, the late President Stair, Sir John Cochran and others, had formed a design to raise an army in Scotland, and to land at such convenient places as they hoped the people would join with them, and hoped, if they once gave the King's forces a foil, they would get many to flock into them; and had advanced money to this purpose; and that there were three keys, whereof he had one, and Mr. Carstairs another (which caused him to be tortured) and Holmes a third. . . . They resolved not to admit of his madness for an excuse, which they esteemed simulate: as the late Chancellor had done."

The case of William Carstairs

"September 5th and 6th, 1684. Mr. William Carstairs, son to Mr. John Carstairs, once minister at Glasgow, is brought before the secret committee of council and is tortured with the thumbikins. (According to Carstairs himself The King's smith was called in to bring in a new instrument to torture by the Thumbikins, that had never been used before and under this torture I continued an hour and a half.) He confessed there had been a current plot in Scotland these ten years past. . . . He named many that were upon the knowledge of it. . . . Such of them as could be got are presently apprehended, and put in close prison; and then Major Monro and Philiphaugh

are first examined; and standing on their denial, they
are threatened with the boots; which makes them
ingenuous, and confess their accession. This did so dis-
compose and confound Alexander Monro, to discover
others, that he desperately offered money to the keeper
of the tolbooth's man to run him through with his sword,
and roared, that he knew he behoved to do some base
thing before he died. . . . Duke Hamilton opposed this
torturing much, and alledged that, at this rate, they
might, without accusers or witnesses, take any person
off the street and torture him; 'et nemo in aliorum caput
est torquendus'; and he retired and refused to be present,
on this ground, that if the party should die in the torture,
the judges were liable for murder, at least were severely
censurable.

"It was doubted how far these testimonies extorted
per torturam can be probative against third parties, seeing
witnesses should be so far voluntary and spontaneous as
to be under no impressions, or terrors of fear of life and
limb; others judge them best to be credited then. Some
thought our privy council would have been at some loss,
and contracted some tash by this cruel torture, had they
suffered it as they did the boots (which they regarded
not, their legs being small) without discovering or revealing
this conspiracy; but their confessing tends to justify the
privy council's procedure.

"The Privy Council of Scotland passed this Act to
deal with the case of Carstairs. 'An Act anent Mr.
William Carstairs' Torture. Edinburgh, September, 5,
1684.'

"It appearing that Mr. William Carstairs is concerned
in the late conspiracy, and there being pregnant presumptions of his knowledge of this atrocious villany, to the
effect that the whole plot may be known, and the truth
expiscated; and having called the said Mr. William

Carstairs, he would not answer and depone thereanent, albeit it was allowed by the advocate, that what he declared or deponed should not militate against him. The lords of his majesty's privy council, considering that thereby he renders himself most suspect, do ordain that Mr. William Carstairs be questioned in torture this afternoon, upon the questions agreed upon in the council, and appoint one of the bailies of Edinburgh to be present, and the executioner.

"In the afternoon of the same day, September 5, the council called and interrogated Mr. Carstairs, 'If he would now answer the queries upon oath ingenuously'. He still shunned so to do, albeit the advocate declared what the said Mr. Carstairs deponed should not militate or operate against him in any manner of way, whereunto the council assented. The council called for one of the Bailies of Edinburgh, and the executioner with the engines of torture being present, the lord chancellor commanded the bailie to cause the executioner to put him in the torture, by applying the thumb-screw to him, which being done, and he having for the space of an hour continued in the agony of torture, the screw being by space and space stretched until he appeared near to faint; and being still obstinate and refractory to depone, the lords thought fit to ease him from the torture for that time, but certified him that to-morrow by nine of the clock, he would be tortured by the boots if he remained obstinate."

Extracts from the Privy Council records:—

November 13th, 1684. Three fellows . . . who were suspected and apprehended as owners of the late apolegitical of war against the King, and threatening to murder all their persecutors . . . were brought in and examined, and they owned the contents of that scandalous paper, and did obstinately abide the torture of the thumbikins without shrinking, till they were taken out of them, and then they fell down.

August, 1687. James Muir, . . . pursues Sir John Ramsay of Whitehall, sheriff-depute of East Lothian, for oppression, in holding a pretended court at Cockney without a clerk or fiscal, and fining him in 100 dollars far above his jurisdiction, and for detaining him *in privato carcere* in Seton, and putting him in the irons and thumbikins, though torture belongs only to the privy council. Answered, that Sir John Ramsay had also a reconvention against him, for tearing papers and discharges he had given, and for beating, blooding and deforcing the sheriff's officers which were heinous crimes, and proven to him, not only as justice of peace, but also as sheriff . . . and that he was so furious, he behoved to be kept in irons like a madman, and having brike them, the thumbikins were put upon him, not to torture, but to secure him from flying. Yet a guard of men could have done that. The privy council admitted both libels (documents) to probation; and at advising, were clear, that a sheriff-depute nor no inferior judge could use torture; and that Sir John Ramsay had exceeded his power: Yet not to discourage the Government, both were called in, and Muir was rebuked for his violence, and Sir John was desired to exercise his power with greater moderation, and to restore the fine.

The records of the Scotch Privy Council mention two cases of torture which occurred in the reign of William III, probably the last cases before the Act abolishing torture in Scotland which was passed in the reign of Queen Anne.

"Forasmuch as ther has been a treasonable and hellish plot contrived and carried on against their maties persons their government and their good subjects and the neighbouring nations; and that ther is evident presumptions and documents that Henry Nevill Pain prisoner within their castle of Edinburgh . . . therefore, and for detecting and discovering thereof, ther maties high commissioner and the lords of privy council do ordaine the Tortur to be put to the saids Henry Nevil Pain. . . ."

At Edinburgh, December 10th, 1690, the following letter direct from the King, William III, to the Privy Council was read and ordered to be recorded. . . . "Whereas we have full assurance upon undeniable evidence of a horrid plott and conspiracy against our government, and the whole settlement of that our ancient kingdom, for introducing the authoritie of the late king James and Popery in these kingdoms, and setting up an intire new forme of government, whereof there has been several contrivers and managers, and Nevil Pain, now prisoner in our castle of Edinburgh, hath lykways been an instrument in that conspiracie, who having neither relation nor business in Scotland, went thither on purpose to maintain a correspondence, and to negotiat and promott the plott: And it being necessary for the security of our government, and the peace and satisfaction of our good subjects, that these foul designs be discovered: Therefore we doe require you to make all legal inquirie into the matter; and we have transmitted several papers and documents for your information, some whereof have been read amongst you; and particularly wee doe require you to examine Nevil Pain strictly; and in case he prove obstinate or disengenious do you procees against him to torture, with all the rigour that the law allows in such cases; and not doubting your ready and vigorous applications for the furder discovery of what so much concerns the public safety, we bid you heartily fareweell. . . . By his majesty's command (Sic Sub.). Melville.

"The brave prisoner being brought to the bar, and being several times removed and called in again, and being asked several questions anent a conspiracie against the government, and for restoring the late king James, whereof the council had strong and evident presumption of his knowledge; . . . and therfor required him to be ingenious and frank in his confessione, oyrwayes they would . . . put him to the torture; and the prisoner having still refused to make any acknowledgement, and in a boasting manner bid them doe with his body what they pleased the councill resolved to proceed to torture; but first called for and read at the board (the prisoner being removed) ane former warrant of councill for putting this prisoner and others to torture, in respect of the evident presumptions against them, signed by their majesties' commissioner and fifteen lords of the council of the 4th of August last.

"It being moved att the bar, Whether Nevill Pain the prisoner in case of his disingenuity or refusall to answer notwithstanding of the torture he is to be put to this night, may be put to new torture the morrow; the same went to the vote, and carried in the affirmative, that he might be putt to the torture again upon interrogators not coincident with these, which he shall be this night interrogate upon.

"December 16, 1690. Anent the Petition given into the lords of their majesties' privy council be Francis Pain, nevoy to Henry Nevill Pain, shewing that the petitioner being informed that his said uncle was committed close prisoner after torture; and that his own physicians and chirurgeons have not liberty to attend him, and seeing these circumstances may endanger his life; and therefore humbly craving their (lordships) to allow him the benefite of open prisone, and to allow his ordinary phisitians and chirurgeons to attend him, since they only could know his constitutione, as the said petition bears: The lords of their majesties privy councill having considered the above petitione, they grant the desyre thereof, and allows the above Henry Nevill Pain the benefit of open prisone, and allows his ordinary physitians and chirurgeons to attend him. . . ."

"1683. Gordon of Earlstone is brought to the bar of the criminal court, and the sentence of forfeiture and death formerly pronounced, is read to him, and the time of execution prefixed, viz. 28th September next: But there came a letter from the king proroguing the time, and appointing him to be put to the boots anent his accomplices, he having been hitherto very disingenuous. The council wrote back to the king, that it was not very regular or usual to torture malefactors after they were condemned to die, but only before conviction. He attempted to escape but was hindered. Earlston (conform to his majesty's command) being brought to the council chamber to be tortured, he through fear or distraction roared out like a bull, and cried and struck about him, so that the hangman and his man durst scarce lay hands on him; at last he fell in a swoon, and then reviving, he was told that general Dalziel and Drummond were to head that fanatic party, and duke Hamilton was on their side; which improbable things made some call it revery, and others, a politic design to invalidate all he should say; and the physicians were ordained upon soul and conscience to report his condition, if they judged him really mad, or only feigned, as David at Gath with Achish, as also to prescribe him a diet for curing him; and for more quietness, they sent him to the Castle."

Burnet (*History of Our Own Times*) after mentioning that the unrelenting severity of the Duke of York had appeared very indecently in Scotland, says: "When any are to be struck in the boots it is done in the presence of the council: And upon that occasion almost all offer to run away. The sight is so dreadful, that without an order restraining such a number to stay, the board would be forsaken. But the Duke, while he had been in Scotland, was so far from withdrawing, that he looked on, all the while, with an unmoved indifference and with an attention, as if he had been to look on some curious experiment. This gave a terrible idea of him to all that observed it, as if a man that had no bowels nor humanity in him. Lord Perth observing this, resolved to let him see how well qualified he was to be an Inquisitor General. The rule about the Boots in Scotland was, that upon one witness and presumption together, the question might be given: but it was never known to be twice given; or that any other species of torture besides the boot might be used at pleasure. In the Court of Inquisition they do upon suspicion, or if a man refuses to answer upon oath as he is required, give him the torture; and repeat it, or vary it, as often as they think fit; and do not give over, till they have got out of their mangled prisoners all that they have had a mind to know from them."

CHAPTER XI

IRELAND was comparatively unaffected by the torturers. This custom was recognised neither by common nor statute law and only a few cases are recorded in this country.

On February 1st, 1506, an order was issued by the Presidency of Munster. "Also it shall be lawful for the President and Council or any three of them, the President being one, in cases necessary, after vehement suspicion and presumption of any great offence in any party committed against the Queen's Majesty, to put the same party to torture as they shall think convenient."

In 1583, when Elizabeth was Queen, an Irish priest named Hurley was discovered in Drogheda with secret letters addressed to Catholic noblemen of the Pale, who were under suspicion. He had brought with him introductions from Pope Gregory XIII who had appointed him Archbishop of Casel, and he had arrived to take possession of his see. He was taken before the Lords Justices, Archbishop Loftus and Sir H. Wallop. Hurley refused to give any information about himself, maintaining an obstinate silence. The Irish Council wrote to London for instructions and were told to torture him unless he answered the questions put to him. There was no rack in Dublin, so the Justices suggested he should be sent to London. This was refused, and Hurley was then threatened with torture unless he spoke. He still refused to speak. Walsingham, Secretary of State to Queen Elizabeth, suggested to Archbishop Loftus that Hurley's feet should be "toasted against the fire with hot boots". This was done (Irish tradition says that melted rosin was poured into his boots). Yielding to the agony he confessed something, but probably less than the truth. He insisted that his mission to Ireland was religious and not treasonable. Archbishop Loftus consulted the Dublin lawyers. They were Catholics and "found scruple to arraign him for that his treason was committed in foreign parts". It was thought that his vigorous denials in open Court would have a bad effect on the people. To allow him to escape could not be entertained. The Lords Justices therefore suggested that with the approval of the Queen it would be best to execute Hurley "by martial law, against which he could make no just challenge, for that he had neither lands nor goods". Forfeiture of property could only be enforced after a legal trial and conviction. Martial law was therefore confined to the poor. The Queen sent a reply that the man being so notorious and ill a subject, as he appeared to be, the Lords Justices should proceed to his execution by ordinary trial first: if they found the effect of that course doubtful, through the affection of such as should be of the jury, on the interpretations of the lawyers on the Statute of Treasons, they might then take the shorter way which they had proposed. No further confession being expected, there was to be no more torture, but the Queen generally commended the Lords Justices for what they had already done. The Irish Judges could find no ground for a trial, so Loftus and Wallop, determined that their victim should not escape them, had him executed by martial law.

There are not many other instances of torture in Ireland recorded. A few years before the case of Hurley, a man named Myagh had actually been sent over from Ireland to the Tower to be put to the torture. Later on, in the reign of Charles I, Dublin possessed its own rack, and men were tortured on it.

In 1628, the Byrnes of Wicklow were indicted for conspiracy against the King in Ireland. They immediately replied that they had been ill treated and petitioned the King to this effect. The King directed that a Committee of the Irish Privy Council should make an impartial investigation. The witnesses upon whose testimony the Byrnes had been indicted were mostly condemned felons, who had saved their lives by offering to give evidence for the Government. Other evidence had been obtained by threats of, or, actual torture. One witness against the Byrnes had been placed on the rack, another had been put naked on a burning gridiron. Those who had got up the case against the Byrnes by such means included Lord Esmond, Sir Henry Bellings, and other influential persons. One witness, Hugh Macgarrald, deposed "that he was apprehended by William Graham, the Provost Marshal, who had kept him seven days in his custody tied with a hand lock, and two several times the said Graham threatened to hang the examinate if he would not do service against Phelim MacPheag (Byrne) one time sending for a ladder, and another time showing him a tree whereon he would hang him with, and the ropes and withs".

CHAPTER XII

METHODS OF TORTURE

A LARGE number of methods and many instruments have been used at various times for torturing prisoners, and much ingenuity displayed, especially in Scotland. Of some of them we have the name only left, their construction and use having been lost in the mists of time. In England, the rack was by far the most frequent implement of torture of which use was made. There is, I believe, no example of it in existence, at the present time, though a model of it is shown in the Tower of London.

It was first used in this country in the reign of Henry VI. The instrument consisted of a large oak frame raised some three feet from the ground. The prisoner was placed under it on his back, with wrists and ankles fixed by cords to two rollers at the end of the frame. By means of levers worked in opposite directions, the body of the prisoner was pulled up level with the frame and left thus suspended by ankles and wrists. If the prisoner did not then give the required information, the levers were moved. The cords pulled on the joints until the bones started from their sockets. There was the danger of the fingers being pulled from the hands, the toes from the feet, the hands from the arms, the feet from the legs, the forearms from the upper arms, the legs from the thighs, and the thighs and upper arms from the trunk. Every ligament was strained, and every joint loosened in its socket, and sometimes even dislocated.

The Scavenger's Daughter, called after its inventor Skevington, was an instrument working on just the opposite principle to the rack. Instead of pulling the body asunder, it compressed it in all its parts. It came into use in the reign of Henry VIII. It consisted of a broad iron hoop, divided into two, and working on a hinge. The prisoner was made to kneel on the floor, the hoop was put over him, and the executioner compressed his victim till the hoop could be fastened round him. The legs were forced back on the thighs, the thighs on to the abdomen, and the miserable victim was pressed almost into the shape of a ball. He was kept thus for some considerable time, generally well over an hour. So great was the crushing of the body that blood usually started from the mouth and nostrils, even from the toes and fingers and often the ribs and breast bone were broken.

Iron Gauntlets. These were gloves of iron which could be compressed by a screw. They were fixed on the wrists and tightened up. The prisoner was then hung in the air by his hands fixed to points wide apart on a beam. Three pieces of wood were placed under each foot, and these were withdrawn, one after the other, leaving the prisoner hanging by his wrists from the beam.

Bartoli narrates the case of Gerard, one of the Jesuit Priests who was thus tortured in Queen Elizabeth's time. "I felt," says Gerard, "the chief pain in my breasts, belly, arms and hands. I thought that all the blood in my body had run into my arms and began to burst out at my finger ends. This was a mistake, but the arms swelled till the gauntlets were buried within the flesh. After being thus suspended an hour I fainted, and when I came to myself I found the executioners supporting me in their arms; they replaced the pieces of wood under my feet: but as soon as I was recovered, removed them again. Thus I continued hanging for the space of five hours, during which I fainted eight or nine times."

The Boots was an instrument made either of iron or of iron and wood combined, fastened on the leg, between which and the boot, wedges were introduced and driven in by repeated blows with a mallet, with such violence as to crush both muscles and bones. A much milder variety consisted of a boot or buskin made wet and drawn upon the legs and then dried by heat so as to contract and squeeze the tissues of the leg.

Burnet in his *History of Our Own Times*, says of the boots: "They put a pair of iron boots close to the leg, and drive wedges between these and the leg. The Common Torture was only to drive these in the calf of the leg: but I have been told they were sometimes driven upon the shin bone." The boots and thummikins were imported into this country from Russia by a Scotsman who had been long an officer in the service of that power.

The common instruments employed in Scotland were the boots and the thummikins. On the matter of torture, Lord Roystoun observes: "The instruments in use amongst us in later times were, the boots and a screw for squeezing the thumbs, hence called the thummikins. The boot was put upon the leg, and wedges driven in; by which the leg was squeezed sometimes so severely, that the patient was not able to walk for a long time after (note the word 'patient'), and even the thummikins did not only squeeze the thumbs, but frequently the whole arm was swelled by them. Sometimes they kept them from sleep for many days, as was done to one Spence, A.D. 1685. And frequently poor women accused of witchcraft were so used. Anciently I find other torturing instruments were used, as pinniewinks or pilliwinks, and caspitaws or caspicaws, in the master of Orkney's case, June 24, 1596; and tosots,

August, 1632. But what these instruments were I know not, unless they are other names for the boots and thummikins."

The thumbscrew consisted of a frame with three uprights or bars, between which the thumbs were passed: a piece sliding on the bars was forced down upon the thumbs by turning a screw. This instrument inflicted great agony without danger to life and was a great favourite in use for inflicting torture. One of the earliest references to this instrument is contained in the register of the Privy Council of Scotland, July 23rd, 1684. "Whereas . . . there is now a new inventione and Ingyne called thumbekins . . . (the Lords) ordaine that when any persone shall be (by their order) put to torture that the said thumbekins or bootes or both shall be applyed to them."

According to the Oxford English Dictionary, the pilliwinks was a special form of thumbscrew to crush all the fingers. "Johan Skypwyth . . . adonques esteant viscont de Nicole per colour de son office aresta le dit Johan . . . et lui mist en ceppes . . . et sur sez smaynes one paire de pyrowykes. 1397." This is the earliest reference to the use of this instrument.

Another early reference is the following: "Quendam Robertum Smyth de Bury . . . Ceperunt . . . et ipsum . . . in ferro posuerunt, et cum cordis ligaverunt, et super pollicis ipsius Roberti quoddam instrumentum volatum *Pyrewinkes* ita stricte et dure posuerunt, quod sanguis exivit, de digitis illius." (Carturla Abbatiæ S. Edmundi. About 1401.)

The cashilaws or casicaws is said to have been invented by the Master of Orkney in 1596. It appears to have been an instrument to draw forcibly together the body and limbs of the victim and hold him in this cramped position much in the same way as the Scavenger's Daughter.

By others it is said to have been an iron frame to hold the limb of the victim which was then roasted in it.

The construction of some of the other instruments such as the tosots, the long irnis, and the narrow bone is unknown. They have left no record behind but the name.

Other methods which were occasionally used were the following: The victim was hung up by the wrists till he became senseless. Sometimes under his foot as he hung was placed a sharp piece of wood, on which the whole weight of his body rested. This was named the piquet, and was at one time a well-known military form of punishment. (See case of Picton, described in a later chapter.)

The exquisite sensitiveness of the fingers was sometimes utilised by the torturers to produce pain. The nails were pulled off, or sharp spikes driven between the nails and the quick.

Little Ease. This method of torture was as follows. The prisoner was confined in a very small cell, so that he could neither walk, stand, sit, nor lie at full length. He was obliged to sit in a squatting position and was kept confined there for many days. Another method of this nature was to put the victim in an underground, damp cell, overrun with rats.

There are old torture chambers in existence in many places, e.g. Nuremberg, in Germany, Andorra, the little Pyrennean Republic, and Gruyère in Switzerland, and many other places, where, more or less, the old instruments are preserved in their original form.

In the Tower of London are the bilboes, the iron collar, the thumbscrew, the scavenger's daughter, and a model of the rack.

A few instances of methods of torture in foreign countries during this period are quoted, not as showing treatment more savage and uncivilised than our own, but as describing rather different methods. There was in France

an instrument of torture called the brodequin which cor-
responded to the boots. It is thus described in the trial
of Ravaillac for the assassination of Henry IV of France
in 1610.

"The brodequin is a strong wooden box, made in the
form of a boot, just big enough to contain both the legs
of the criminal, which being put therein, a wooden wedge
is then driven with a mallet between his knees, and after
that is forced quite through; a second wedge, of a larger
size, is applied in the same manner." The barbarous
sentence and execution of Ravaillac is thus recorded.
"We the presidents, and several of the councillors being
present, the prisoner, Francis Ravaillac, was brought into
Court, who having been accused and convicted of parricide
(this term included the murder of a royal personage)
committed on the person of the late King, he was ordered
to kneel, and the clerk of the court pronounced the sentence
of death given against him; as likewise that he should
be put to the torture to force him to declare his accomplices. His path being taken, he was exhorted to redeem
himself from the tortures preparing for him, by acknowl-
edging the truth, and declaring who those persons were
that had persuaded, prompted, and abetted him, in that
most wicked action, and to whom he had disclosed his
intention of committing it. He said, by the salvation I
hope for, no one but myself was concerned in this action.
He was then ordered to be put to the torture of the brodequin, and the first wedge being driven, he cried out,
'God have mercy upon my soul, and pardon the crime
I have committed; I never disclosed my intention to anyone.' This he repeated as he had done in his interrogation.

"When the second wedge was driven, he said with loud
cries and shrieks, 'I am a sinner, I know no more than
I have declared, by the oath I have taken, and by the
truth which I owe to God and the Court; all I have said

was to the little Franciscan, which I have already declared;
I never mentioned my design in confession, or in any other
way; I never spoke of it to the visitor of Angouleme, nor
revealed it in confession in this city. I beseech the court
not to drive my soul to despair.'

"The executioner continuing to drive the second wedge,
he cried out, 'My God, receive this penance as an expiation
for the great crimes I have committed in this world; Oh
God! accept these torments in satisfaction for my sins.
By the faith I owe to God, I know no more than what
I have declared. Oh! do not drive my soul to despair'.

"The third wedge was then driven lower near his feet,
at which a universal sweat covered his body, and he fainted
away. The executioner forced some wine into his mouth,
but he could not swallow it; and, being quite speechless,
he was released from the torture, and water thrown upon
his face and hands. Some wine being forced down his
throat, his speech returned, and he was laid upon a mattress
in the same place, where he continued till noon. When
he had recovered his strength he was conducted to chapel
by the executioner; and two doctors of the Sorbonne
being sent for, his dinner was given him; but before the
divines entered into a conference with him, the clerk
admonished him to think of his salvation, and confess
by whom he had been prompted, persuaded, and abetted
in the wicked action he had committed, and so long designed
to commit; it not being probable, that he should of himself
have conceived and executed it without communicating
it to any other. He said, that if he had known more than
what he had declared to the court, he would not have
concealed it, well knowing, that in this case he could
not have mercy of God, which he hoped for and expected;
and that he would not have endured the torments he
had done, if he had any further confession to make. He
said, he acknowledged he had committed a great crime,

to which he had been incited by the temptation of the devil; that he entreated the King, the Queen, the court, and the whole kingdom to pardon him, and to cause prayers to be put up to God for him, that his body might bear the punishment for his soul. And being many times admonished to reveal the truth, he only repeated what he had said before. He was then left with the doctors, that they might perform the duties of their office with him.

"A little after two o'clock the clerk of the court was sent for by the divines, who told him, that the condemned man had charged them to send for him, that he might hear and sign his confession, which he desired might be revealed and even printed, to the end, that it might be known to the whole world; which confession the said doctors declared to have been, That no one had been concerned with him in the act he had committed; that he had not been solicited, prompted, or abetted, by any other person whatever, nor had he discovered his design to any one; That he acknowledged he had committed a great crime, for which he hoped to have the mercy of God, which was still greater than his sins, but which he could not hope to obtain if he concealed any thing. Hereupon the clerk asked the condemned, if he was willing that his confession should be known and revealed? and, as above, admonished him to acknowledge the truth for the salvation of his soul. He then declared upon his oath, that he had said all he knew, and that no one had incited him to commit the murder. At three o'clock he came from the chapel; and as he was carried out of the Conciergerie, the prisoners, in great numbers, thronged about him, with loud cries and exclamations, calling him traitor, wicked wretch, detestable monster, damned villain, and the like; they would have struck him, had they not been hindered by the bailiffs, and the other officers of justice, who kept them off by force. When he was put into the tumbril, the crowd was so great, that it was with the utmost difficulty that the bailiffs and officers of justice could force themselves a passage; and as soon as the prisoner appeared, that vast multitude began to cry out as above, wicked wretch, traitor, and the enraged populace continued their cries and exclamations till he arrived at the Greve, where, before he was taken out of the tumbril to mount the scaffold, he was again exhorted to reveal his accomplices; but he persisted in his former declaration, that he had none; again imploring pardon of the young King, the Queen, and the whole kingdom for the crime he had committed.

"When he had ascended the scaffold, the two doctors comforted him, and exhorted him to acknowledge the truth; and after performing the duties of their function, the clerk approached him and urged him to think of his salvation now at the close of his life, and to confess all he knew; to which he only answered as he had done before. The fire being put to his right hand, holding the knife with which he had stabbed the King; he cries out, Oh God! and often repeated Jesu Marie! While his breast, etc., were tearing with red-hot pincers, he renewed his cries and prayers; during which, being often admonished to acknowledge the truth, he persisted in denying that he had any accomplices. The furious crowd continued to load him with execrations, crying, that he ought not to have a moment's respite. Afterwards by intervals, melted lead and scalding oil, were poured upon his wounds; during which he shrieked aloud, and continued his cries and exclamations. The doctors again admonished him, as likewise the clerk, to confess, and were preparing to offer up publicly the usual prayers for the condemned; but immediately the people, with great tumult and disorder, cried out against it, saying that no prayers ought to be made for that wicked wretch, that damned monster. So that the doctors were obliged to give over. Then the clerk remonstrating to him, that the indignation of the people was a judgment upon him, which ought to induce him to declare the truth, he persisted to answer as formerly, saying, I only was concerned in the murder. He was then drawn by four horses, for half an hour by intervals. Being again questioned and admonished, he persisted in denying that he had any accomplices; while the people of all ranks and degrees, both near and at a distance, continued their exclamations, in token of their great grief for the loss of their King. Several persons set themselves to pull the ropes with the utmost eagerness, and one of the noblesse, who was near the criminal, lighted off his horse, that it might be put in the place of one which was tired of drawing him. At length, when he had been drawn for a full hour by the horses, without being dismembered, the people, rushing on in crowds, threw themselves upon him, and with swords, knives, sticks, and other weapons they struck, tore, and mangled his limbs; and violently forcing them from the executioner, they dragged them through the streets with the utmost eagerness and rage, and burnt them in different parts of the city."

I have been able to find very few instances of the use of the wheel in Great Britain. Cawdor, a trooper who was responsible for the assassination of the Regent of Scotland, Lennox, in 1571, was punished in this way. He met his death by being broken on the wheel.

A horrible variation of the torture of being drawn asunder by having the limbs tied to horses and making them gallop in different directions is illustrated by the punishment of a prisoner, captured by the Spaniards in 1582. They treated him as a pirate and arranged to kill him by tying his limbs and attaching them to four boats, and then rowing them in different directions.

A very horrible and vindictive punishment was meted out to the murderer of the Prince of Orange, in 1584. After firing three poisoned balls at the Prince, the assassin, Balthazar, made an attempt to escape but was caught at once. The people, maddened at the murder of their ruler, seized Balthazar and resolved that he should suffer as much pain as it was possible to inflict. They flogged him with knotted cords, they cut his flesh with split quills and dipped him in salt water. They then wrapped him in a garment soaked in vinegar and brandy. He was left all night in this condition, and in the morning placed on the rack. Finally his flesh was torn from him by red-hot pincers.

The following example of brutality to English sailors by the Spaniards is from the Commons Journal of 1607. "The purser of the *Trial* was summoned on board the Spanish Admiral's ship and told that his vessel was to be searched for the goods of Turks and Jews (which were not allowed by the Spaniards). They were told that if none were found there would be no trouble. None were found, but allegations were made that the ship was a ship of war and that various things found on board had been taken from a French vessel. These accusations were denied but the Spaniards commanded the purser to be put to the torture and hanged him up by the arms on the deck of the ship, and the more to increase his torture they hung heavy weights to his heels. Nevertheless he endured the torture the full time and confessed no more than the truth. So they put him the second time to torture again and hanged him up as aforesaid; and to add more torment they did tie a live goat to the rope, which with her struggling did, in most grievous manner, increase his torment, all which the full time he endured. The third time, with greater fury, they brought him to the same torment again, at which time by violence, they broke his arms, so as they could torment him no longer, nevertheless, he confessed no otherwise but the truth of their merchant's voyage.

"Another sailor, Ralph Boord, was twice tormented and had given him a hundred bastinados to enforce him to confess, and for not saying as they would have him, was committed to a wet vault, where he saw no light, and lay upon the moist earth, feasted with bread and water for eight days, and being then demanded if he would not confess otherwise than before, he replied he had already told them the truth, and would not say otherwise; whereupon they took from him his allowance of bread, and for seven days gave him no sustenance at all, so that he was constrained to eat orange peels which other prisoners had left there, which stunk, and were like dirt, and at seven days' end could have eaten his own flesh; and the fifteenth day the gaoler came unto him and not finding him dead, said he would fetch him wine and bread to comfort him, and so gave him some wine and two loaves of bread, which he did eat and within a little while after, all his hair did fall off his head; and the day after a malefactor, for clipping of money, was put into the same vault, who, seeing what case his fellow prisoner was in, gave him some of his oil he had for his candle to drink, by which means his life was preserved."

CHAPTER XIII

THE ORDEAL AND TRIAL BY BATTLE

FOR the first few hundred years after the conquest, the method of trial of accused persons was very unfair and inadequate. There was no central judicial body in the country which had control of criminal matters. Local potentates had the power, if not the right, of trying, condemning, and punishing offenders and it was only very gradually that our present system of police courts, juries and just judges enabled an accused person to obtain a fair and impartial hearing.

The ordeal by water or fire, trial by battle, and compurgation were the principal methods by which an offender was found innocent or guilty.

The ordeal was legalised in England by William I, and was regarded as a direct appeal to God, who would by His divine power intervene to punish the guilty and save the innocent. When the ordeal by water was employed, the person accused was taken to a Church, and the spectators divided into two equal lines, one representing the accuser the other the accused. Between them, in the middle of the Church was the fire which was to free or condemn the prisoner. Those who were present were expected to be fasting. The priest first sprinkled all the assembly with Holy Water. The vessel of ordeal, filled with water, was then put on the fire. Two chosen from each side were appointed judges; they gave the signal when the water boiled. The congregation joined in prayer for a just issue. The accused was taken to the boiling vessel, his arms wrapped in numerous linen bandages. At the bottom of the vessel was a stone and if he could snatch this away from the vessel, in the cloud of smoke and steam arising from it, without injury to himself, the first act of the ordeal was over. Three days were allowed to elapse, when the bandages were taken off and the arm exposed. If it were unsinged he was declared innocent, if there were any trace of scalding, he was guilty and suffered such punishment as was awarded.

The ordeal by fire was of much the same nature. The accused, his arm protected as before by bandages, had to lift a piece of hot metal, weighing from one to three pounds. If, after three days there was no burn, he was innocent: if there were signs of burning, he was guilty. The Lateran Council, in 1215, forbade the priests any longer to take part in this mummery and it was abolished by law in 1219.

The question which was asked of prisoners put on their trial was, "Prisoner how wilt thou be tried?" although generally answered "By God and my country", should really have been "By God or my country", that is either by ordeal or by jury. The question supposes an option to the prisoner who could choose either the judgment of God, the ordeal, or the judgment of his country, the jury.

As late as 1679 the question of the "ordeal" was raised in a trial. John Gavan, a Jesuit priest, was indicted at the Old Bailey for high treason, and in the course of his defence made the following statement. "And now, my lord, I humbly cast myself upon the honour and justice of this honourable and just court; to which I submit myself, with all my heart and soul, having used all the remedies I can. I have cleared myself, as to the main day, the 24th of April, whereon all the pretended plot lies; And I will bring witnesses that shall swear, I was not in London in August; and if my eternal salvation lay upon it, I could aver, I was not in London; And I wish I may be made an example of justice before all the world (in the sight of God I speak it) if I be not the most innocent person in the world. And, my lord, seeing there is only his oath for it and my denial, I have only one demand: I do not know whether it be an extravagant one or no; if it be, I do not desire to have it granted."

Sir William Scroggs, the Lord Chief Justice: "What is that demand?"

Gavan: "You know, that in the beginning of the church (this learned and just court must needs know that) that for 1,000 years together, it was a custom, and grew to a constant law, for the trial of persons accused of any capital offence, where there was only the accuser's oath, and the accused's denial, for the prisoner to put himself upon the trial of Ordeal, to evidence his own innocency."

The Lord Chief Justice: "We have no such law now. You are very fanciful, Mr. Gavan; you believe that your cunning in asking such a thing, will take much with the auditory; but this is only an artificial varnish; You may do this with hopes of having it take with those that are Roman Catholics, who are so superstitious as to believe innocency upon such desires; but we have a plain way of understanding here in England, and that helped very much by the protestant religion; So that there is scarce any artifice big enough to impose upon us. You ask a thing that sounds much of a pretence to innocency, and that it would be mighty suffering, if you should mis-carry, because you ask that you know you cannot have. Our eyes and our understandings are left us, though you do not leave their understandings to your proselytes, but you are mistaken if you think to impose that upon us that you do upon them."

Gavan: "But is it any harm, my lord, to ask whether I might be so tried?"

It is remarkable that an educated man should have suggested at the end of the seventeenth century that he should be allowed to prove his innocence in such a way. This is the last occasion in which the question of the "ordeal" was raised in a Court of Law.

The Wager of Battle or duel was practically unknown in England before the conquest. It was introduced here by the Normans. By a law of William I, Trial by Battle was made compulsory, but only when both the parties were Normans. Otherwise it was optional, and as the two nations merged into one it greatly spread so that by the time of Henry II it was quite common. The following is a description of this form of trial from the Hale MSS. Outside the walls of Northampton a plot of ground was marked out and kept by soldiers. The Justices in Eyre sat as they would have sat for an ordinary case. The parties to the suit appeared, as was the law in civil cases, not in person, but each by champion. A great crowd surrounded the field of battle, or court of law, but the parties on one side were far greater in number than those on the other. After the signal had been given, the combatants began to struggle, each bound to conquer or die, or to bear for ever afterwards the most disgraceful of all names—recreant. At length both fell at the same moment. The friends of the deforciants, fearing that the issue might be adverse to them, drew their swords, broke through the line of soldiers, and surrounded the two fallen men. Some were mounted, others on foot, and the force at the disposal of the judges was wholly unable to cope with them. They held the ground and kept off both the soldiers and the justices. The champion of the plaintiffs was unable to raise himself, the horses were made to trample on him, and when he was quite helpless, he was proclaimed a recreant. The sheriff raised the hue and cry, and the judges left the ground without any attempt to bring the proceedings to a legal termination. A complaint was afterwards laid before the King in council, when it was held that the attack upon the justices and the champion tended to the subversion of the royal dignity, peace, and crown, and that the champion should not incur the infamy and the disability of recreancy, but should enjoy his free law as fully as before the duel.

The following, also from the Hale MSS, is from the account of one John Hill, Armourer and Sergeant in the Office of Armoury, with King Henry IV and King Henry V, and describes a Wager of Battle in a case of treason. "The first honour in arms is that a gentleman fight and win the field, either as appellant or defendant, in his Sovereign Lord's quarrel, in a battle of treason sworn within lists, before the Sovereign Lord Himself." As in a court of law, the appellant had a counsel who was assigned to him before the Constable and the Marshal, and who was bound to teach him all the various tricks and devices which belong to the Wager of Battle. Not the least responsible duty of this counsel was to take care that the appellant was properly clad and armed. The details of this armour are not important but the object for which they were employed is of interest and value. The perfection of the armour and the arms was a subject of anxious forethought, but it was considered even of less importance to protect the champion, and give him the best weapon of offence, than to conceal the wounds he might receive from his adversary. To this intent he was provided with shoes made of red leather and with red hose to draw over his leg harness, so that his opponent might not see any blood which flowed. Similar devices were adopted by the old crusaders. Such courage as is evidenced by these precautions deserves to be admired: and it was because knights were so brave in battle that those who wrote of them summed up their virtues in the one word, chivalry.

It was also part of the duty of the counsel to engage three priests, each of whom was to sing a mass on the day of battle. Throughout the night before the fight, a light was kept burning in the room of the champion and his counsel watched him and observed how he slept. In the morning he went to church. His harness was laid out at the North end of the latter and covered with a cloth: the Gospel was read over it, three masses were sung and at the end, a priest gave a blessing. He then went to the enclosure fully armed and ready for the conflict: he sent his counsel to the King with a request that he might have free entry when he came to the barriers, and that a chair or tent might be set up for his use. These requests were always granted, and he approached with his confessor, counsel, armourer, and servants. His counsel bore before him a long sword, a short sword, and a dagger. At the barrier he was met by the Constable and Marshall who said, "What art thou?" He told his name and the cause of his coming, and was then admitted with his followers. As he entered, he blest himself, and then approached the King. After making obeisance twice to him, he went back to the tent. When the defendant appeared on the field, the appellant again left his tent and stood fully armed, and viewed his adversary. The weapons of both parties were then brought before the King and examined in his presence by the Constable and Marshall. If there was no fault in the arms the appellant was at once summoned to take the first oath.

When the appellant had sworn to the truth of his accusation before the King, he returned to his tent. His counsel who had carefully noted the terms of his oath, remained in the presence of the King to hear what was sworn by the defendant. Unless the defendant swore that every word and every syllable of every word sworn by the appellant was false, the appellant's counsel might ask judgment without further ceremony. But if the defendant swore as required, the counsel returned again to the appellant's chair to await the summons for taking the second oath. The second oath was followed by the third oath, and if the appellant persisted in making his accusation in the same terms and the defendant denied it every time without equivocation, evasion, or cavil, the tents were removed and the lists prepared for the actual battle. Upon this the applicant's counsel asked for a place within the bar on the right hand of the King. The reason of this was that an appeal might be made to the mercy of the King if it seemed likely that either of the combatants might die. The counsel remained in the place assigned till the King had given his judgment. But should the King not see fit to stay the trial, the order was given to cry, " Laissez Aller ", and the champions fought to the death.

Some interesting points are revealed in the story of the trial of Spencer Cowper, a barrister, for the murder of Miss Sarah Stout, at Hertford, in 1699. The facts of this trial are remarkable, but do not bear on the point under discussion. Cowper was acquitted. This acquitta led to "an appeal of murder". Upon an acquittal on an indictment for murder, the prosecutor (who in these days was usually a relative, for the Crown did not as a rule undertake prosecutions even for such a serious crime as murder) had the right to challenge the accused to the ordeal of battle. Mrs. Short, the mother of the dead woman, sued for a writ of appeal in the Chancery Court against Cowper, in the name of an infant who was her daughter's heir. She was misled as to what she was suing for, believing that it was to obtain the property of her dead daughter for this heir. When she discovered what her action actually meant, she discontinued her proceedings on this matter. Lord Justice Holt in dealing with the point said, "he wondered it should be said that an appeal is an odious persecution. He said he esteemed it a noble remedy and a badge of the rights and liberties of an Englishman".

The last instance in which this method of trial was invoked occurred in 1818, in the case of Abraham Thornton who had been tried for the murder of a young girl, Mary Ashford. He was indicted for first ravishing and then murdering her, and although acquitted, the general belief was that he was guilty.

The circumstances of the case having been investigated by the secretary of state, he granted his warrant to the sheriff of Warwick to take Thornton into custody again on an appeal of murder to be prosecuted by William Ashford, the brother and heir-at-law of the dead girl. The proceedings on the appeal were held at the Court of King's Bench at Westminster Hall. On November 6th, the appellant, attended by four counsel, appeared in Court when the proceedings were adjourned till the 17th. On that day the prisoner demanded trial by wager of battle. The revival of the obsolete law gave rise to much legal argument on both sides and it was not till April next year that the decision of the Court was given on the matter. The learned judges gave their opinion one after the other, Lord Ellenborough expressing the general view that the law of the land was that there shall be a trial by battle unless the party brings himself within some of the exceptions. The judges granted the prisoner his right. Later, on a technical point, the prisoner was released and no trial by battle took place. The law allowing this ancient right was repealed in 1819 (59 Geo. III, c. 46).

There is a record in the *Lord's Journal*, March 19th, 1629, of a bill to abolish this ancient custom having been introduced—but it did not pass into law.

An account of the proceedings in the Court of Chivalry on an appeal of high treason, in 1631, is given in a later chapter.

The last method of trial to which I wish to refer is that by compurgation. Here all that was necessary was that the accused should produce a certain number, generally twelve, of good men and true to testify that they believed him innocent. They were called compurgators and if they gave the necessary assurance, the innocence of the accused was regarded as proved. This method of trial, although it had fallen into disuse long before, was not abolished in our legal system till 1833 (2 and 3 Will. IV, c. 42).

CHAPTER XIV

PEINE FORTE ET DURE

In the thirteenth century, after the ordeal was abolished, the system of trial by jury was gradually and slowly evolved. In the period before the abolition of the ordeal and the development of the jury system, judges were confronted with the task of deciding what to do in cases in which an accused person refused to submit to any form of trial. Prisoners had begun the experiment of standing mute or refusing to plead. Under these circumstances no trial took place, but convictions automatically followed as if there had been a trial. It was recognised that this was a very unsatisfactory proceeding, and shortly afterwards, in the reign of Edward I a Statute was passed (3 Ed. I, c. 12) to remedy this.

The Act is entitled, "The punishment of Felons refusing Lawful Trial," and is as follows. "It is provided also, That notorious Felons which openly be of evil Name, and will not put themselves in Enquests of Felonies (so that they may be charged) before the Justices at the King's Suit, shall have la prisone forte et dure, as they which refuse to stand to the Common Law of the Land. But this is not to be understood of such Prisoners as be taken of light Suspicion."

A pardon granted by Edward III (quoted by Pike in his *History of Crime in England*) shows clearly the intention of this law. "The King to all his bailiffs and faithful men

to whom these presents shall come, Greeting. Whereas
Cecilia, widow of John Rygeway, lately indicted concerning
the death of her husband, was adjudged to the penance
because she held herself mute before our Justices of Gaol
delivery at Nottingham; and whereas she afterwards
sustained life without food or drink, in close prison, during
forty days after the manner of a miracle, and contrary to
human nature, as we have been informed on trustworthy
testimony: We, moved by piety, to the praise of God,
and the glorious Virgin his mother, from whom, as is
believed, this miracle has proceeded, have of especial
grace pardoned unto the said Cecilia the execution of
the judgement aforesaid, and do desire that she be delivered
from prison and be no further impeached of her body."
(Patent Roll, 31 Ed. III.)

This punishment of prison forte et dure was about the
reign of Henry IV transformed into that of "peine forte
et dure", or the torture of the press. This was a form
of torture used, not to extract evidence from a prisoner,
but to compel him to plead when he stood mute at his
trial or to punish him if he would not plead. If a prisoner
stood mute he was warned three times of what would
happen to him if he persisted in his refusal, and he was
allowed a few hours for consideration. If he then would
not plead, Judgment of Penance was pronounced as
follows: "That you go back to the prison whence you
came, to a low dungeon into which no light can enter:
that you be laid on your back on the bare floor, with a
cloth round your loins, but elsewhere naked; that there
be set upon your body a weight of iron as great as you
can bear and greater; that you have no sustenance save
on the first day three morsels of the coarsest bread, on
the second day three draughts of stagnant water from
the pool nearest to the prison door, on the third day
again three morsels of bread as before, and such bread

and such water alternately from day to day till you die."

The procedure ordered by this sentence was sometimes varied in that the arms and feet were to be tied to the four quarters of the prison.

"At the trial of Richard Weston, at the Guildhall of London, for the murder of Sir Thomas Overbury, in 1615, the prisoner was asked, after the indictment had been read to him, if he were guilty of poisoning Sir Thomas. He answered, 'Lord have mercy upon me! Lord have mercy upon me!' But being again demanded he answered 'Not guilty'. And being again demanded how he would be tried, he answered, he referred himself to God, and would be tried by God; refusing to put himself or his cause upon the jury or country, according to the law or custom. (This was considered as equivalent to refusing to plead.) Hereupon the Lord Chief Justice, and all other in their order, spent the space of an hour in persuading him to put himself upon the trial of law; declaring unto him the danger and mischief he ran into by resisting his ordinary course of trial, being the means ordained by God for his deliverance, if he were innocent; and how by this means he would make himself the author of his own death, even as if he should with a knife or dagger kill or stab himself; exhorting him very earnestly either with repentance to confess his fault, or else with humility and duty to submit himself to his ordinary trial. Whereupon he suddenly answered, welcome by the grace of God; and he referred himself to God. And so when no persuasion could prevail, the Lord Chief Justice plainly delivered his opinion, that he was persuaded that Weston had been dealt with by some great ones, guilty of the same fact, as accessory, to stand mute, whereby they might escape their punishment; and therefore he commanded (for satisfaction of the world) that the Queen's attorney there present should declare, and set forth the whole evidence, without any fear or partiality; and yet notwithstanding he used once more much persuasion to the prisoner to consider what destruction he brought upon himself by his contempt; and declaring unto him how his offence of contempt was, in refusing his trial, and how the laws of the land had provided a sharper and more severe punishment to such offenders than to those that were guilty of high treason; and so he repeated the form of judgment given against such, the extremity and rigour of which was expressed in these words, *onere, frigore, et fame.* For the first he was to receive his punishment by the law, to be extended, and then to have weights laid upon him, no more than he was able to bear, which were by little and little to be increased. For the second, that he was to be exposed in an open place, near to the prison, in the open air, being naked. And lastly, that he was to be preserved with the coarsest bread that could be got, and water out of the next sink or puddle to the place of execution, and that day he had water he should have no bread, and that day he had bread he should have no water; and in this torment he was to linger as long as nature could linger out, so that oftentimes men lived in that extremity eight or nine days; adding further that as life left him, so judgment should find him. And therefore he required him, upon consideration of these reasons, to advise himself to plead to the country, who notwithstanding absolutely refused."

It does not appear from the account of the trial that he was ever "pressed". The Lord Chief Justice directed that Weston was by his own confession guilty, and sentenced him to be hanged, which sentence was carried out at Tyburn.

One of the most remarkable instances of torture by pressing is that of Major Strangeways in 1658. He was charged with having caused the death of his brother-in-law, and when the body was viewed by the Coroner's jury, he was required to take it by the hand and to touch the wounds. It was commonly believed that if the corpse were touched by the murderer, it would bleed. But the contrary was not accepted, if the body did not bleed, it was no evidence of innocence. At the Old Bailey he would not plead, and stated, as his reason, if he stood mute he could not be convicted, and so would not forfeit his lands. He was anxious to save his property for his heir. He was warned in the usual way, and being obdurate, the sentence of peine forte et dure was passed on him.

In order to hasten death there had grown up a custom, out of pity for the sufferer, of placing a piece of sharp wood under the back, which was driven into the spine by the weight of iron above, and thus hastened death. In Strangeway's case, the gaolers placed some of the iron over the heart of their prisoner, and when they found that this was not sufficient to cause death, they added the weight of their own bodies. Even under these circumstances, it took nearly ten minutes before the sufferings of this unhappy man were ended.

A few other examples of this terrible punishment follow.

A man named Burnworth was arraigned at Kingston, in 1726, for murder. He refused to plead and stood mute after the usual warning. He was pressed with weights of about 400 lbs. for two hours. He was then taken back to the Court where he pleaded not guilty. He was however convicted and hanged.

The head of an ancient family in the north of England, in a fit of jealousy killed his wife and all his children who were at home, by throwing them from the battlements of his castle. He went to find his only remaining child who was at a farm house near by, but on his way was overtaken by a severe thunder and lightning storm. He regarded this as the vengeance of heaven threatening him. He repented and confessed, and in order to save his property for the child he had been on his way to kill, stood mute. (Unless a man stood his trial, his property could not be confiscated—this could only be done after conviction.) He was pressed to death.

One of the last instances, if not the last, in which this brutal punishment was employed was at the end of the eighteenth century when Thomas Spiggot, a highwayman, refused to plead. Whilst being tied up he broke the cords, but was eventually secured and pressed with weights amounting to 350 lbs. He sometimes lay silent, as if insensible to the pain, at other times showed by his catchy breathing, that he was enduring the pain. He complained several times that they were putting weights on his face. This was probably due to the pressure of blood in his head. After enduring the pressure of 500 lbs. for half an hour, he said he had had enough, and agreed to plead.

The peine forte et dure gradually became less and less used, and before its actual abolition by Statute a more merciful, or perhaps one should say a less brutal form of punishment was employed to compel prisoners to plead. This consisted of tying the thumbs together and twisting the cord. Some instances of this method are given below:

In 1721, a woman, Mary Andrews, refused to plead, and whipcords were applied to her thumbs with such force that they broke. She still remained mute, but after three more attempts were made, she agreed to make her plea.

At the Old Bailey, in 1734, a man, John Durant, who said he was deaf and unable to read, stood mute. The following conversation took place.

Court: If he remains obstinate, he must be pressed.

Gaoler (shouting to prisoner): The Court says you must be pressed to death if you won't hear.

Durant : Ha.

Court : Read the law, but let the executioner first tie his thumbs. (This was done and the knot pulled very tight.)

Prisoner : My dear lord, I am deaf as the ground.

Executioner : Guilty or Not Guilty?

Prisoner : My sweet sugar, precious lord, I am deaf indeed, and have been so these ten years.

Executioner : Guilty or Not Guilty?

Court : Hold him there a little . . . Now loose the cord, and give him a little time to consider of it, but let him know what he must expect if he continues obstinate, for the court will not be trifled with.

The prisoner was then taken away and shortly after he pleaded not guilty.

The peine forte et dure was abolished in the time of George III (12 Geo. III, c. 20), and by a later Act (7 and 8 Geo. IV, c. 28) it was enacted that any prisoner standing mute should be considered as pleading "Not Guilty".

CHAPTER XV

THE torture so far dealt with has been torture in its narrow sense, that is torture used as a means of extracting evidence or confession from witnesses or prisoners. In the present chapter, torture in its broader sense, that is cruel and brutal methods of punishment inflicted on those found guilty by the Courts is discussed. Starting as far back as Roman times, we find the punishments of this period very terrible: the stake and burning, crucifixion, stoning, throwing from a height, the rack, flogging with leaden balls, mutilation, the use of barbed hooks to tear the flesh, and of cords to compress the limbs are punishments which took place in England during the whole period of the Roman occupation. A very horrible vengeance was devised for parricides, which was regarded as one of the worst of crimes. The convicted person was sewn up in a sack with venomous serpents and then thrown into the river or sea to drown, so that the sight of the sky might be denied him when alive, and the earth refuse him a grave when dead.

They not only burned Christians and slaves, but made exhibition of criminals battling with wild beasts in the arena a prominent institution. The amphitheatre was the club of both sexes. That this actually took place in Britain is proved by numerous references in the Theodosian Codex, *De Criminibus deque Processu Criminale*, and by the discovery of the remains of amphitheatres in our country. The Romans also inflicted torture on their prisoners for the purpose of extracting confession.

Cruel punishment in post-Roman days was common in England, and during the times of the Norman and Angevin Kings continued without interruption. The fact that there was really no centrally controlled judicature, and that justice was dealt out by local potentates is responsible for some of the brutalities, but even after the reign of Henry II, when the germs of our present legal system had come into being, the long catalogue of horrible atrocities carried out in the name of punishment, is appalling. The following examples bear out this statement. William the Conqueror ordered as an ordinary procedure the maiming of criminals as a perpetual warning to the ill disposed. In the reign of Henry I, coiners of base money were very common. The King commanded that all the known ones should be collected and brought to Winchester. Here in one day the whole body of them had their right hands cut off, and they were afterwards castrated. Richard I, at the time of the crusades, wars carried on in the name of religion, issued an edict that any crusader who killed a man on board ship was to be tied to the dead body of his victim and drowned, if he killed a man on shore he was to be tied to the corpse and buried alive. If blood was drawn by a knife, the right hand which drew the blood was to be cut off, and the punishment for theft consisted in shaving the head of the thief, pouring boiling pitch on the shaven scalp, and then covering it with feathers. In the reign of Henry II, if the "ordeal" failed, such crimes as murder (which was not regarded by any means as one of the most serious offences), arson, robbery and coining were punished by the loss of a foot, sometimes of a hand in addition.

As time passed on and the Tudor period arrived,

punishment, irrespective of the so called legal torture, already described, continued to be very barbarous. Of all the cruelties inflicted, those on traitors were probably the worst.

Treason, which was originally defined as a breach of fealty to the sovereign or an infringement of the Royal prerogative, became a very different matter in Tudor times. To speak a word disrespectfully of the King, to differ from him in religion, to criticise him or his actions, was treason, equally with leading a rebellion, or making an attempt on his life. Even opinions became treasonable. As defined by Tudor custom, treason was a crime very easy to commit. It required very little difference with King or Government to lead one to the scaffold. In 1684, Thomas Rosewell was tried for High Treason for speaking disparagingly of the power of the King to cure tuberculous glands by touching with the Royal hand. This was not by any means an isolated instance of the kind of action which led to a trial for treason.

Treason and heresy became in the sixteenth century very much confused. In the reign of Henry VIII this confusion was due to the claim of the King to the head-ship of the Church of England; in Elizabeth's reign it was due to the close association of religious disputes with the question of the heirship of the throne. The political plotting of these times made the distinction between the two crimes, definitely separate as they actually were, very difficult. Religious feeling, too, was high and bitter. The Catholics burnt the Protestants, and the Protestants hanged the Catholics, and only too often this religious animosity was disguised under the name of treason. The prisoner accused of treason was handicapped in his trial in many ways. He was not confronted with the witnesses for the prosecution, their evidence could be given in writing, and there was therefore no possibility of cross-examination.

His own witnesses were not sworn and therefore their evidence was regarded as of less value than that of the sworn witnesses. A prisoner could not be represented by counsel, except to argue points of law. He had to prepare his own case and put it before the Court, to pit his wits and knowledge against that of the picked lawyers of the Crown. These inequalities were gradually removed as public feeling revolted against the terrible prosecutions of the so called traitors. It was not till 1696 that the prisoner was allowed the full service of counsel, and some generations later before his witnesses could be sworn. The juries were not free, they acted under pressure—if their verdict was not what the Crown required, they could be, and were fined and imprisoned.

The punishment inflicted on a traitor was one of cold and calculated ferocity. The sentence was worded as follows. "That the traitor is to be taken from the prison and laid upon a sledge or hurdle (in earlier days he was to be dragged along the ground tied to the tail of a horse) and drawn to the gallows or place of execution, and then to be hanged by the neck until he be half dead, and then cut down, and his entrails to be cut out of his body, and burnt by the executioner; then his head is to be cut off, his body to be divided into quarters, and afterwards his head and quarters to be set up in some open place directed."

In carrying out this sentence the prisoner was hanged until he was half strangled and then cut down. The executioner slit his chest open, plucked out the heart and held it up to the view of the assembled crowd, crying, "Behold the heart of a traitor", or after taking the half dead prisoner down, he cut open the abdomen, pulled out the bowels, and burnt them on a fire in face of his victim.

"*Suspendantur et viventes ad terram posternantur, et interiora sua extra ventes suos capiantur ipsiusque viventibus comburantur.*"

The head was then cut off, the body quartered, and the pieces coated with tar and fixed in public places as a warning to others.

This sentence was first carried out on a pirate named Marise, who was condemned to death in 1241.

In 1817 a few half starved labourers were induced to take part in a rising to overthrow Parliament. They were soon captured and the Government, in order to make an example, prosecuted the ringleaders and three of them were condemned to death, as traitors. The Prince Regent as an act of mercy remitted the quartering but the rest of the sentence, hanging, drawing, and beheading, was confirmed. The High Sheriff, after consultation with the prison doctor, proposed to have the head cut off with a knife by a skilled person. The authorities in London refused to allow this, and ordered the beheading to be carried out by an axe. Two, therefore were made similar to those used in the Tower. The wretched men were drawn on a hurdle by horses to the gallows. On a platform in front of this, a block was placed with sawdust, axes, knives and a basket. The body of the first man was taken down, and placed with the head on a block. It was struck with the axe and the final act was to finish the decapitation with a knife. The headsman then held up the severed head and called, "Behold the head of a traitor, Jerimiah Brandreth".

Pictures of Old London Bridge of the sixteenth and seventeenth centuries show large numbers of the heads of traitors stuck on poles. Horace Walpole in his *Letters* says, "I have been this morning at the Tower, and passed under the new heads at Temple Bar, where people make a trade of letting spying-glasses at a halfpenny a look".

The Cato St. conspirators who were executed in May, 1820, were the last on whom this degrading custom of beheading after hanging, was carried out, though it continued in force nominally till 1870.

The exhibition of vindictive cruelty and petty revenge shown by Charles II on his restoration would be difficult to beat. He determined that whatever affront he could offer to the dead Protector, should be carried out. In the Journals of the Commons for December 8th, 1660, appears this Resolution of the Lords and Commons in Parliament assembled. "That the carcasses of Oliver Cromwell, Ireton, Bradshaw, and Pride, should be taken up, drawn on a hurdle to Tyburn, and there hanged up in their coffins for some time, and after that buried under the gallows."

In the case of the Earl of Carlisle, which was heard in the reign of Edward II, the judges carefully gave reasons for some of the added atrocities of their sentence. He was found guilty of treason and was sentenced as follows. "The award of the Court is that for your treason you be drawn, hanged and beheaded, and that your heart, and bowels, and entrails, whence came your traitrous thoughts be torn out and burnt to ashes, and that the ashes be scattered to the winds; and that your body be cut into four quarters and that one of them be hanged upon the tower of Carlisle, another upon the tower of Newcastle, another upon the bridge of York, and the fourth at Shrewsbury; and that your head be set upon London Bridge, for an example to others that they may never presume to be guilty of such treasons as yours against their liege lord."

Hanging in chains was another method of insulting the dead man. When the execution had been carried out, the whole body was tarred and placed in a kind of iron cage, known as chains, and suspended on a gibbet, generally near the scene of the crime, as a warning to passers by. There are several examples of "the chains" in existence. A very perfect one is to be found at Rye, in Sussex in the Town Hall Museum. In this cage was placed and gibbetted the body of John Breed, a butcher, who murdered the Mayor of Rye. The gibbet was set up on a marsh at the west end of the town, now known as "Gibbet Marsh". Here it stood for many years, but when all the remains had dropped away except a part of the skull, the Corporation took possession of it and it is now among their treasured exhibits.

Hanging in chains was not at all uncommon from an early time in England, but according to Blackstone, was not part of the judgment though it could be ordered by the judge who tried the case. Holinshed in his *Chronicles of England*, (seventeenth century) says, "In wilful murder done upon premeditated malice or in any notable robbery, the criminal is either hanged alive in chains near the place where the act was committed, or else upon compassion taken, first strangled with a rope and so continueth till his bones come to nothing. Where wilful manslaughter is perpetrated besides hanging, the offender commonly hath the right hand struck off."

It was not till 1752 that gibbetting was legally recognised.

The Statute made in the twenty-fifth year of the reign of George II, for preventing the crime of murder enacts: "That the body of every person convicted of murder shall, if such conviction and execution shall be in the county of Middlesex, or within the city of London, or the liberties thereof, be immediately conveyed by the sheriff or sheriffs, his or their deputy or deputies, and his or other officer or officers, to the hall of the Surgeons' Company, or such other place as the said company shall appoint for this purpose, and be delivered to such person as the said company shall depute or appoint, who shall give to the sheriff or sheriffs, his or their deputy or deputies, a receipt for the same; and the body so delivered to the said company of surgeons, shall be dissected or anatomised by the said surgeons, or such persons as they shall appoint for that purpose; and that in no case the body shall be suffered to be buried, unless after such body shall have been dissected or anatomised."

John Swan and Elizabeth Jefferys were convicted in 1752, at Chelmsford, of the murder of Joseph Jefferys, uncle of the woman charged. They were both found guilty and were hanged at Epping Forest, near the Bald Faced Stag, close to the place where the murder was committed. The male prisoner was hanged in chains. At a meeting of the judges at the chambers of the Lord Chief Justice Lee, in June, 1752, to consider this case, and to see if anything could be done to prevent "the horrid crime of murder", it was agreed by the great majority of the judges that the judgment for dissecting and anatomising, and the time of execution, ought to be pronounced in cases of petty treason, though murder only is mentioned, except in the case of women. (Petty treason is aggravated murder, such as the murder of a master by his servant or of a husband by his wife.) There was some doubt whether hanging in chains might ever be made part of the judgment, but after discussion it was agreed by nine judges that in all cases within the act, the judgment for dissecting and anatomising only should be part of the sentence. If it were thought desirable, the judge might afterwards direct the hanging in chains by special order to the sheriff.

As has been pointed out before the passing of the "Murder Act of George II", there was some difficulty about hanging in chains. In 1741, James Hall pleaded guilty to the murder of his master, John Penny. The Rev. Dr. Penny, dean of Lichfield applied to the court at the Old Bailey asking that an order might be made to hang Hall in chains. The Lord Mayor, Sir Daniel Lambert, asked the advice of the recorder of London on this matter. He said that the court never made any order in such cases: they must apply to the King, the body being at the disposal of His Majesty. The King was then in Hanover, and an application was made by the relatives to the Regency. They were told that the Regency or the Council never made an order in such cases, and that it should have been done by the Court which tried the case. The relatives persisted and finally secured an order from the Regency to hang Hall in chains. This was carried out at Shepperd's Bush, just beyond Kensington gravel pits.

The last man gibbetted was James Cook, a bookbinder, of Leicester, found guilty of murder in 1832. The custom was abolished by Act of Parliament in July, 1834.

The old method of execution by hanging differed in many ways, irrespective of the accompanying brutalities, from the procedure as carried out at the present day. The execution was a long drawn out affair. The prisoner was drawn on a hurdle or driven in a cart to the scaffold, often a considerable distance: the route was lined by crowds, always ready to jeer or cheer, and to watch a gruesome sight. The whole procedure was public. The prisoner was expected to and usually did, make a dying speech to the assembled mob. He was received with approval or disapproval, according to his popularity. He stood in the cart in which he had been driven, or mounted a ladder. The rope was placed round his neck, the cart or ladder was then drawn away and the suspended victim died slowly of strangulation. Sometimes a merciful gaoler or one of the friends of the victim would hang on to his legs and so shorten the suffering. The time of execution was in the hands of the judge. He frequently had prisoners hanged on the day of conviction. It was not till the reign of George II that any time was fixed by law. By 25 Geo. II, c. 27, it was enacted that a prisoner should be executed two days after sentence. This has now been altered and a period of about three weeks is the average time of hanging after conviction.

From the method of slow strangulation there was gradually evolved the present rapid and expeditious manner of death. First there was added to the scaffold a short drop. This occasionally had the effect of breaking the neck but more generally strangulation was still the cause of death, although it was considerably quicker than formerly. Later still, about 1870, the present method of the long drop was evolved, mainly due to the hangman Marwood. This causes a fracture dislocation of the vertebrae of the neck, pressure on, or severing of the spinal cord and medulla, and instant death. There are some excellent specimens of fracture dislocation of the vertebrae as the result of executions in the Museum of the Royal College of Surgeons at Lincoln's Inn Fields.

A present day execution is soon over. From the entry of the hangman into the cell till death occurs, is usually a matter of from sixty seconds to two minutes. The hanging is and has been private since 1866, when the last public execution took place. Michael Barret, a Fenian guilty of complicity in the Clerkenwell explosions was hanged outside Newgate.

Executions which were at one time so terribly common (Stow says 72,000 in the reign of Henry VIII) are now comparatively uncommon in England, about twenty or thirty every year. By the Criminal Law Amendment Act of 1861 the death penalty is now only inflicted for murder or treason, and a few crimes against the Government.

Even with the perfected modern arrangements serious mishaps will sometimes occur. In the Babbacombe murder case three attempts were made to release the trap, and all failed. The Governor then stopped the execution, and the man was subsequently reprieved. There are recorded instances of the force of the drop being so great that the head of the victim has been pulled off. But any hitch in the procedure is most unusual under modern conditions. The execution is carried out almost invariably in as merciful a way as such a dreadful punishment can be.

The following account of the execution of Earl Ferrers will show what was the usual happening when a well-known man was hanged. The Earl was tried and sentenced to death in 1760 for the very brutal murder of one of his servants. The sentence of the Court was in these words. "That you, Lawrence, Earl Ferrers, return to the prison of the Tower from whence you came; from thence you must be led to the place of execution, on Monday next, being the 21st day of this instant April; and when you come there you must be hanged by the neck till you are dead, and your body be dissected and anatomised. And God Almighty have mercy on your soul." On the fateful day of execution Earl Ferrers left the Tower in his own landau, drawn by six horses, preceded and followed by a regular procession of constables, soldiers and officials. The crowd was so dense all along the route from the Tower to Tyburn that nearly three hours was occupied by the journey. The Earl asked the Sheriff if he had ever seen so great a concourse of people before and on receiving the answer that he had not, said that he supposed they had never seen a Lord hanged.

When the procession reached Holborn, near Drury Lane, the prisoner said he would like a glass of wine and water, and again later, seeing a friend seated in a coach, intimated that he wished to get out to say good-bye to her; but on both occasions was dissuaded by the Sheriff.

The scaffold, covered with black baize, was at last reached, the condemned man ascended, and after talking with the chaplain handed to the assistant of the executioner instead of, as he intended to the executioner himself, five guineas. This caused an unseemly wrangle on the scaffold. The hangman then proceeded with his gruesome task. The earl submitted to this with the greatest resignation. His neckcloth was removed, a white cap which he himself had brought with him was put on his head, his arms secured with a black sash and the cord placed round his neck. He then advanced to a stand raised eighteen inches above the platform (this was a new arrangement in place of the cart or ladder), and placing himself under the crossbeam asked the executioner, "Am I right?" Then the cap was drawn over his face and the signal given by the Sheriff.

For a short time there was some struggling but life was soon ended by the hangman clinging to the body of the Earl. The corpse hung for about one hour and was then cut down and taken to Surgeon's Hall to undergo the remainder of the sentence. A large incision was made from the neck to the bottom of the breast, and another across the lower part of the throat. The abdomen was opened and the intestines removed, and the body afterwards exposed to view in the Hall.

As a type of dying speech I quote one made by Mary Blandy who was hanged at Oxford, in 1752, for the poisoning of her father. She begged the prayers of all the spectators and declared herself guilty of administering the powders to her father, but without knowing that it had the least poisonous quality in it or intending to do him any injury, as she hoped to meet with mercy at that great tribunal before whom she should very shortly appear. And as it had likewise been rumoured that she had been instrumental in the death of her mother in like manner as her father and also of Mrs. Pocock, she declared herself not even the innocent cause of their deaths as she hoped for salvation in a future state.

The utter callousness of those who so arbitrarily exercised power is well illustrated by the death of the Mayor of Bodmin. He was one of those who took part in the rising of 1549, but he was not a very important personage and fully expected to be pardoned. Sir Anthony Kingston, who was appointed provost marshal visited Bodmin and sent word to the Mayor that he would dine with him. He had to hang a man and so a stout gallows must be ready. The dinner was consumed, and the gallows prepared. "Think you," said Kingston, as they stood looking at it, "think you it is strong enough?" "Yes sir," said the Mayor, "it is." "Well then get you up, it is for you." And without any delay the Mayor was hanged.

In this same rising a miller named Kingsmill was taken by the rebels and an attempt was made to persuade him to join them. He refused and was promptly hanged by the vicar, who was one of the rebels. He was captured and the body of Kingsmill found hanging outside his door. A court-martial found him guilty of murder and ordered him to be hanged. He accepted his fate without protest. A beam was thrust out from the church tower of St. Thomas, and there he was hanged in chains, with the insignia of his office round his body. There he remained till his clothes rotted away, and the crows had picked all the flesh from his body, and nothing but his skeleton was left.

The account of the hanging of Sir Robert Tresilian, Lord Chief Justice of England, is one of the earliest of which we have record. In 1388, Sir Robert Alexander Nevil,

Archbishop of York, Sir Nicholas Brambre, sometime
Lord Mayor of London and others were tried for high
treason. "Sir Nicholas Brambre was brought by the
constable of the Tower into Parliament: and being charged
with the aforesaid Articles of Treason, he desired longer
time, that he might advise with counsel learned in the law,
and might make a more full Answer to his Accusation:
but he was refused, in that he required a thing not usual,
nor allowable by law in a case of this nature, whereupon
the Judge required him then to answer severally and
distinctly in every point in the Articles of Treason contained. Whereupon Brambre answered, 'Whosoever hath
branded me with this ignominious mark, with him I am
ready to fight in the lists to maintain my innocency, whenever the King shall appoint'. And this he spoke with such
a fury, that his eyes sparkled with rage, and he breathed
as if an Aetna lay hid in his breast, chusing rather to die
gloriously in the field, than disgracefully on a gibbet. The
Appellants hearing the courageous challenge, with resolute
countenance answered. That they would readily accept
of the combat, and thereupon flung down their gages
before the King; and on a sudden the whole company
of lords, knights, esquires, and commons flung down their
gages so thick, that they seemed like snow in a winter's
day, crying out, 'We also will accept of the combat, and
will prove these Articles to be true to thy head, most
damnable Traitor'. But the lords resolved that battle
did not lie in that case, and that they would examine the
Articles touching the said Nicholas, and take due Information by all true, necessary, and convenient ways, that
their consciences might be truly directed what Judgement
to give in this case, to the honour of God, the advantage
and profit of the king and his kingdom, and as they would
answer it before God, according to the course and law
of parliament."

Tresilian, the Lord Chief Justice of England was also found guilty and when asked what he had to say why execution should not be done according to judgment passed upon him for his treasons so often committed; "but he became as one struck dumb, he had nothing to say, and his heart was hardened to the very last, so that he would not confess himself guilty of anything. Whereupon he was without delay led to the Tower, that he might suffer the Sentence passed against him: his wife and his children did with many tears accompany him to the Tower, but his wife was so overcome with grief, that she fell down in a swoon as if she had been dead. —Immediately Tresilian is put upon an hurdle, and drawn through the streets of the city, with a wonderful concourse of people following him. At every furlong's end he was suffered to stop, that he might rest himself, and to see if he would confess or acknowledge any thing; but what he said to the friar his confessor, is not known. When he came to the place of execution, he would not climb the ladder, until such time as being soundly beaten with hats and staves, he was forced to go up; and when he was up, he said, 'So long as I do wear any thing upon me I shall not die'; wherefore the executioner stript him, and found certain images painted like the signs of the heavens, and the head of a devil painted, and the names of many of the devils wrote in parchment; these being taken away he was hanged up naked, and after he had hanged some time, that the spectators should be sure he was dead, they cut his throat, and because the night approached, they let him hang till the morning, and then his wife having obtained a licence of the king, took down his body, and carried it to the Gray Friars, where it was buried."

A typical execution for treason in the time of the Tudors, that of the Nortons, uncle and nephew, is thus described by a spectator. These men were two who had taken part in a rebellion in the North in 1570. "On Saturday, May 27th, Thomas Norton, and Christopher Norton, of Yorkshire, being both condemned of High Treason, were delivered by the Lieutenant of the Tower to the sheriffs of London, and were both laid on a hurdle and so drawn from the Tower through the City of London to Tyburn, having besides many officers and a multitude of others, a godly preacher riding besides them. And being come to the place of execution proclamation was made of the cause of their death. Thomas Norton the elder man was first executed, who took his death in this wise. He being come up and standing upon the cart with rope about his neck, the cart was drawn away and there he hung a certain space and then was taken down and quartered in the presence of his nephew Christopher Norton, who then presently must drink the same cup. Then the executioner proceeded to carry out the sentence on the younger man. After he had hanged a while, he was cut down, the butcher opened him and as he took out his bowels he cried, and said, ' Oh, Lord, Lord have mercy upon me!' and so yielded up the ghost. Then being likewise quartered as the other was, and their bowels burned as the manner is, their quarters were put into a basket provided for the purpose and so carried to Newgate, where they were parboiled, and afterwards their heads set on London Bridge, and their quarters set up upon sundry gates of the City of London for an example to all traitors and rebels, for committing High Treason against God and their prince. God grant it may be a special warning for all men; and God turn the hearts of all those who are maliciously bent against Elizabeth, our Queen and sovereign of this realm, and send her a triumphant victory over all her enemies. Amen. God save the Queen."

A later instance in the time of Oliver Cromwell shows the same cruel tendencies. The state of public feeling allowed vindictive atrocities to be carried out on the human body for the offence of High Treason. The writ for the execution of Miles Sundercombe is preserved in a Roll of the King's Bench, and is, unlike previous records, written in English. Latin had been the language used up till this time. "Oliver, Lord Protector, etc., to the Sheriff of Middlesex, greeting. Whereas we, in our Court before us in the Upper Bench, have considered that Miles Sundercombe, late of the parish of St. Martin in the Fields, in the County of Middlesex, yeoman, otherwise called Miles Fish, . . . for High Treason, touching our person, whereof he is indicted and attainted, is committed by our said Court of Upper Bench aforesaid to the Lieutenant of the Tower of London and from thence through the middle of the City of London unto the gallows at Tyburn shall be directly drawn, and upon the gallows there shall be hanged and shall be (then living) laid upon the ground, and his entrails out of his body shall be taken, and shall be burned (he being then living) and his head shall be cut off," etc., etc.

It is remarkable, but yet it is a fact, that men could live and see their intestines burnt before their eyes.

The trial of Dr. William Parry at Westminster for High Treason in 1584. "In the beginning of the year, queen Elizabeth discovered a Conspiracy of which William Parry was the author. He was a gentleman of Wales, member of the House of Commons, and had signalised his zeal. for the Catholic religion in opposing alone a Bill which was preferred in the lower house against the Jesuits. He spoke upon that occasion with so much passion and vehemence, that he was committed to custody: but his submission being made he was in a few days admitted to his place in the house again. Hardly was he at liberty when Edmund Nevil, who laid claim to the inheritance of the Earl of Westmorland, lately deceased in the low countries, accused him of conspiring against the queen: whereupon he was sent to the Tower. He owned that he had a design to kill the queen, and was persuaded thereto by Morgan, an English Catholic refugee in France: that he held intelligence with Jesuits, the pope's nuntios, and cardinals; that the better to deceive the queen and get free access to her person, he returned from France into England, and discovered the whole Conspiracy to her that afterwards repenting of his wicked intention, he left off his dagger every time he went to her, lest he should be tempted to commit the murder: but that at length cardinal Allen's book, wherein he maintains it to be not only lawful, but honourable to kill princes excommunicated, falling into his hands, he read it, and felt strongly encouraged to pursue his first design: that Nevil his accuser coming to dine with him, proposed the attempting something for the deliverance of the queen of Scots, to which he answered, that he had a greater design in his head: that a few days after Nevil coming to see him, they resolved to kill the queen, as she rode abroad to take the air, and swore upon the Bible to keep the secret: but that in the meanwhile, Nevil hearing the news of the earl of Westmorland's death, accused him, in hopes of procuring thereby the earl's inheritance to which he laid claim."

William Parry who was a doctor of laws, made a voluntary confession. He had a few years before been convicted of a gross assault on Mr. Hugh Hare, of the Inner Temple, nearly killing him. He was tried and convicted for this, but escaped overseas, where he got mixed up with the Jesuits, and engaged in the plot to kill Elizabeth.

His sentence was as follows. "The court doth award, that thou shalt be had from hence to the place from whence thou didst come, and so drawn through the open city of London upon an hurdle, to the place of execution, and there to be hanged and let down alive, and thy privy parts cut off, and thy entrails taken out and burnt in thy sight; then thy head to be cut off, and thy body to be divided into four parts, and to be disposed of at her majesty's pleasure: And God have mercy on thy soul."

Dr. Parry livid with passion, called on the queen to answer for his blood. "Whereupon the lieutenant of the Tower was commanded to take him from the bar, and so he did: and as he was going away the people cried out, 'Away with the Traitor, away with him'; whereupon he was conveyed in a barge to the Tower again by water. Upon the 2d of March ensuing he was delivered by the lieutenant of the Tower, early in the morning, to the sheriffs of London and Middlesex, who received him at Tower-Hill; and according to the Judgement caused him to be forthwith set on an hurdle, on the which he was drawn through the midst of the city of London unto the place for his execution in Palace-yard, Westminster, where having long time of stay permitted him before his execution, he impudently denied that he was ever guilty of any intention to kill queen Elizabeth, and so (without any request to the people to pray for him, or using any outward prayer himself) he was turned off, and executed according to sentence."

As the cart was drawn, the executioner caught the rope at the first swing and butchered him alive, "When his heart was taken out, he gave a great groan".

Trial of Queen Elizabeth's Physician.

Ruy Lopez, a Portuguese Jew, was driven out of his own country by the Inquisition, and settled in England, at the beginning of the reign of Elizabeth. He started as

a doctor in London, where he met with great success,
being appointed to a post at St. Bartholomew's Hospital.
He had a large connection among celebrated people,
numbering among his patients Leicester and Walsingham.
After he had been in practice some seventeen years he
was appointed physician-in-chief to the Queen. In
January, 1594, he was arrested, being accused of complicity
in a plot originating in Spain for the destruction of Elizabeth.
Among the others accused were Ferreira, a Portuguese
gentleman living with Lopez, and Tinoco, also a Portuguese
in the pay of the Spanish government. They were all
three, as was inevitable in charges of treason, convicted
and sentenced to the usual barbarities. In June of 1594,
the three of them fastened on hurdles were drawn past
the doctor's house, in Holborn, to the place of execution
at Tyburn. A great crowd had assembled. The doctor
who wished to make a speech to the assembly, was refused
a hearing, and strung up. He was cut down alive, castrated,
disembowelled and quartered. Ferreira was then executed
and lastly Tinoco. He had witnessed the other two suffer
their atrocious punishment, he had seen their struggles and
their blood shed, when he himself was hanged. He was
cut down, recovered his sense, and struggled with his
executioner. The crowd cheered and sided at first with
him, making a ring to watch the fight. He nearly succeeded
in overcoming the hangman, when some of the onlookers
seized him, and held him down whilst he was like the
others, castrated, disembowelled and quartered.

The trial of Babington and his fellow conspirators for
participating in a plot to murder Queen Elizabeth, in
1586, was followed by the usual barbarities. Ballard was
the first executed. He was cut down, and bowelled with
great cruelty while he was alive. Babington beheld Ballard's
execution without being in the least daunted: whilst the
rest turned away their faces, and fell to prayers upon their

knees. Babington being taken down from the gallows, alive too, and ready to be cut up, he cried aloud several times in Latin, *"Parce mihi, Domine Jesu!* Spare me, O Lord Jesus!"* Savage broke the rope, fell down from the gallows, and was presently seized by the executioner, his privities cut off, and his bowels taken out while he was alive. Many others were similarly treated. The next day, another batch of those convicted were executed, but the Queen, "being informed of the severity of the Executions the day before, and detesting such cruelty, gave express orders that these should be used more favourable: and accordingly they were permitted to hang till they were quite dead, before they were cut down and bowelled". This is one of the few instances of the "mercy" of Queen Elizabeth during her long, cruel and brutal reign.

Dr. Bryan, in his book, *Roundabout Harley Street*, tells us some interesting facts about Tyburn, now known as Marylebone. Oxford Street was originally Tyburn Road, and the celebrated Tyburn Tree, the scene of so many terrible tragedies, was just by the Marble Arch. A triangle in the road marks its place. If the numbers of those to be hanged was excessive, the overflow were executed in that Mecca of the doctors, Harley Street. Imagine a gibbet in this exclusive thoroughfare! For 600 years, then, from Henry the Second to George the Third, there was an endless procession of unhappy wretches to Tyburn, many to die for offences which nowadays would not call for more than a caution or a reprimand. But whether it was for premeditated murder or for monkeying about with hayricks, it was all the same; they were dragged on a hurdle along Tyburn Road—which we know as Oxford Street—with their coffins in front of them (unless indeed the law decreed that they be flogged at the cart tail from gaol to gibbet) and hanged, or hanged-and-burnt, or half-hanged, and then disembowelled ere the

breath was out of their bodies. It is sufficient to say that
the gallows stood at Marble Arch. At first it appears to
have been a temporary affair, erected and re-erected as
required. At a later date it developed into a permanent
structure, and stood for many a year across the Edgware
Road. Again it reverted to a temporary erection some
time before the abolition of public executions at this spot.
Its abolition was not due to any high-minded motive
on the part of the Government of the day, nor of the
well-to-do and titled people who had built their new
mansions in Mayfair and Marylebone. For the victims, no
one seemed to have any pity; for the sight they had no
particular objection, rather the opposite. It was the
periodic incursion of the rabble into a neighbourhood
that had grown select that at long last led the residents
to protest and to shift the scene of execution to Newgate,
where it was still a public affair for almost another
century.

It was the pleasant custom of the authorities of the day
to farm out the space surrounding the scaffold to various
enterprising specimens of the human race, who thereupon erected grand stands and sold the seats at different
prices on the festive occasion of an execution. Mammy
Douglas was one of the most notorious of these "Tyburn
pew-openers", as a decadent age called them. We have
a glimpse of her in 1758 when Dr. Henesey, adjudged
guilty of treason, was bumped on a hurdle in the usual
way to Tyburn, there to be swung off into eternity. The
hanging of a doctor was not quite an everyday affair
and there was a rush for seats on the part of the crowd.
Mammy Douglas with the same discernment (but with
more moderation) than the modern commercial man
would employ, observed that the demand was greater
than the supply and promptly raised the tickets from
2s. to 2s. 6d. There was much grumbling about this sordid

piece of profiteering, but that grumbling was nothing compared with the uproar when, having paid their half-crowns and taken their seats, the Doctor was at the last moment "most provokingly reprieved"! In the ensuing riot the "pews" were reduced to matchwood and abortive efforts were made to hang Mammy Douglas in place of the reprieved Doctor; but their praiseworthy efforts appear to have failed.

Dr. Bryan, in the work already referred to, also narrates several instances of survival after hanging by the old method. "One was in his coffin, and created a sensation by pushing off the lid and asking for a drink. With ill-judged kindness they gave him a jug of wine which he swallowed, and dropped back dead. Another lived for many a year, but all he could tell the excited crowd was that he had at first experienced a fleeting second of agonising pain, followed by a dull sensation and accompanied by much flashing of lights before his eyes—and then nothing. Another did not recover until he had been taken back to the Surgeons' Hall at Newgate, and was about to be dissected. The Law demanded that he be handed over to them to be hanged again, as the sentence was *that he be hanged until dead;* but a threatening crowd cowed the officers of the Law and he was transported instead."

The strangest story of all, however, concerns a young surgeon, Abraham Chovet, who exactly two hundred years ago (April, 1733) deliberately and ingeniously endeavoured to prevent the full execution of the law by pitting science against the hangman's rope. A butcher-cum-highwayman, named Gordon, having been condemned to death for a series of "hold-ups", set London by the ears in his efforts to secure a reprieve. Having failed in that, and in subsequent efforts to bribe his gaolers, he offered a reward to whomsoever would help him to escape the fate that awaited him. Chovet conceived the bold idea of earning the reward. After carrying out certain experiments on dogs, "hanging" them for varying periods and then restoring them to life, he managed to get admission to Newgate, and to interview Gordon in his cell. He informed him of his plan but first demanded the reward, which the desperate man perforce handed over. Chovet then performed what amounted to a tracheotomy, and inserted a tube down the condemned man's throat with the instruction that the moment he was "swung off" he was to close his mouth, nose, *and ears*.

Mr. Gordon, for reasons readily understood, endeavoured to carry out these difficult instructions to the best of his ability, and it must be admitted with no little success; for when he was cut down *at the end of three-quarters of an hour* he was still breathing, or rather his heart was still beating. . . . He was conveyed without loss of time to a public-house where Chovet was anxiously awaiting him. Instantly opening a vein he was rewarded by seeing the "dead" man open his eyes and heave a deep sigh. But that was all. The eyes closed as quickly again, and this time, despite feverish efforts, Gordon was really dead.

Two other cases are quoted of attempts to revive a hanged man, one successful, one the reverse.

Patrick Ledmond was hanged for a street robbery, in February, 1767. He had been suspended for twenty-eight minutes, when he was rescued by the mob and carried to an appointed place, where a surgeon was in attendance who performed tracheotomy. The criminal was restored to life.

George Foster was executed for murder in 1803. After his body had hung the usual time, it was cut down and moved to a house close by where Professor Aldin subjected the corpse to galvanism, which had been recently discovered. This caused violent muscular contractions but nothing else. The Beadle of the Surgeons' Company was so terrified that he died of fright.

A case is recorded in which a medical man, Sir William Petty, was about to dissect the body of a woman who had been hanged when he noticed signs of life and thereupon he restored her. She later on had several children.

CHAPTER XVI

Of the many methods of execution in the times under discussion, that of beheading was perhaps on the whole the least cruel. It was merciful and quick, but a very great deal depended on the skill of the headsman. Some of them removed the head with one stroke of the axe, others had to make several attempts before they succeeded in severing the head from the body. The whole procedure had its conventional aspect, just as in other methods of carrying out the death sentence. The prisoner usually addressed the assembled crowd (the executions were always public), made a present to the headsman, placed his head on the block and then gave the signal for the descent of the axe.

Sometimes instead of the axe, a sword was used. The method of death by beheading was reserved for those of high rank only. It was considered a great favour to have one's head cut off, rather than to be hanged: James II, as a concession to the pressure brought to bear on him, allowed Dame Alice Lisle to be beheaded instead of being strung up by the hangman. This punishment was introduced into England by the Conqueror. The first victim was the Earl of Huntingdon, in 1076, the last, Lord Lovat, in 1747. "Decollat. April, 1747." Between these two, a long, long list of celebrated names appear, names which have made English history, Kings, Queens, statesmen, lawyers, bishops, Lords and Ladies of all kinds and descriptions, Charles I, Mary, Queen of Scots, Lady Jane Grey, the Lord Protector, Somerset, Anne Boleyn, Catherine Howard, Archbishop Laud, Dame Alice Lisle, Fisher, Bishop of Rochester, the Duke of Norfolk, Sir Thomas More, Sir Walter Raleigh, and countless hosts of other celebrities, some of them justly, some of them unjustly suffering their death.

The execution of Sir Walter Raleigh illustrates the usual procedure of the time. After many delays he was told that he must prepare to die on the following morning. As he was to suffer at Palace Yard, he was taken to the Gatehouse at Westminster to pass the night. In the evening his wife paid him her last visit and informed him that she had obtained permission to dispose of his body. At midnight she left him and he went to sleep for a few hours. In the morning he had a long conference with the Dean, who was surprised at the courageous manner in which Sir Walter faced the prospect before him. The Dean administered the Communion, after which Raleigh took his breakfast and smoked his pipe as usual. His spirits seemed even excited at the scene which was before him. Being asked how he liked the wine which was given to him he replied, "it was good drink, if a man might tarry by it". At eight o'clock he was summoned to execution, and as he passed the scaffold he noticed that one of his friends had difficulty in getting near it. "I know not what shift you will make, but I am sure to have a place," he called to him. Directly he mounted the scaffold, he asked leave to address the throng. His speech had been carefully prepared. Every word he spoke was a protest against the accusations which had been made against him. He denied any disloyalty to his King or country. "And now," he concluded, "I entreat that you all will join with me in prayer to that Great God of Heaven

whom I have so grievously offended, being a man full
of all vanity, who has lived a sinful life in such callings
as have been most inducing to it; for I have been a soldier,
a sailor, a courtier, which are causes of wickedness and
vice: that His Almighty goodness will forgive me; that
he will cast away my sins from me, and that he will
receive me into everlasting life: so I take leave of you
all, making my peace with God."

When all was ready, Raleigh turned to the executioner
and said he would like to see the axe. He ran his finger
down the edge, saying to himself, "This is sharp medicine,
but it is a sound cure for all diseases". He then knelt down
and placed his head on the block. After a short prayer he
gave the signal, and with two blows the head was severed
from the body. He was buried at St. Margaret's, Westminster.

The death of Lady Jane Grey is surely one of the most
pathetic tragedies in the history of England. This young
girl, only seventeen years of age, forced by political
circumstances, against her will, into claiming the queen-
ship of her country, suffered the terrible fate awaiting
her with a calmness and courage which must earn her
the admiration of everyone. Her husband was also
condemned to the same death, and on the morning of
the execution he begged for a last interview and a last
embrace. She refused, believing it would only make it
harder for them both. He died without meeting her,
but Lady Jane saw him led to the scaffold and his headless
body as it was brought back, passed her. When the time
came for her to die, she was taken by Sir John Bridges
down the Tower Green, her attendants prostrate with
grief. The eyes of Lady Jane were dry. She prayed quietly
till she reached the scaffold when she sprang up the steps,
let down her hair, and uncovered her neck. "The hangman kneeled down and asked her forgiveness, whom she

forgave most willingly. Then he willed her to stand upon the straw, which doing, she saw the block. Then she said, I pray you despatch me quickly. Then she knelt down, saying, Will you take it off before I lay me down? and the hangman answered, No, madam. She tied a kerchief about her eyes; then, feeling for the block, she said, What shall I do; where is it? One of the bystanders guiding her thereunto, she laid her head down upon the block, and stretched forth her body, and said, Lord, into thy hands I commend my spirit. And so ended." (Chronicle· of Queen Mary.)

Anne Boleyn was in 1536 tried for adultery, and after a hearing of considerable length and care was found guilty. The judgment was that the Queen be taken by the Constable to the King's prison within the Tower, and then as the King shall command, be brought to the green within the said Tower, and there burned or beheaded, as shall please the King. A short interval between the sentence was allowed. Of the five gentlemen who were found guilty of offences with Anne Boleyn, four were beheaded and one hanged. On May 19th, at nine in the morning, Anne, Queen of England, was taken to Tower Green, which was open to those of the public who wished to see their Queen die. On the scaffold were present Cromwell, the Lord Chancellor, the Duke of Suffolk, and the Duke of Richmond. The Queen was led to execution by the Lieutenant of the Tower. She seemed dazed, but on reaching the platform asked if she might say a few words. "Christian people, I am come to die. And according to law, and by law, I am judged to death; and therefore I will speak nothing against it. I am come hither to accuse no man, nor to speak anything of that whereof I am accused and condemned to die. But I pray God save the King, and send him long to reign over you; for gentler and more merciful prince was there never; and to me he was ever a good, a gentle, and sovereign lord. If any person will meddle of my cause I require him to judge the best. And thus I take my leave of the world and of you: and I heartily desire you all to pray for me. Oh, Lord have mercy on me! To God I commend my soul." She removed her head-dress and one of her attendants gave her a cap into which she fitted her hair. She then knelt and as she prayed, the executioner with one blow of the sword severed her head from her body. A handkerchief was placed over it and it was carried away by one of her ladies in attendance. The others carried her body to the Tower where it was buried. This was the first Queen of England to perish in this way.

Whether Anne Boleyn were guilty or innocent (and the evidence is very conflicting) these words are remarkable in their expressions of love and admiration for the man who, by a word could have pardoned the wife whom he had professed to love so much, and thus have saved from such a terrible fate.

The execution of Mary, Queen of Scots, whatever view one may take of her life and conduct, was attended with much sadness. She had been kept in prison by Elizabeth for nearly twenty years and believed that the warrant for her death would never be executed. When the time came she bore her fate with quiet resignation. On the scaffold after praying for a short time she placed her head on the block. The hard wood seemed to hurt her for she put her hands under her neck. The executioners gently removed them lest they should interfere with the blow of the axe. One of them held her slightly, and the other struck the blow. He, although a practised headsman, was unnerved, and his aim was erratic and struck the knot of the handkerchief binding her eyes. The blow scarcely cut the skin. Mary neither spoke nor moved and at the second stroke the aim was accurate, her head fell from her shoulders, and all was over.

The Earl of Essex, who was beheaded at the end of the reign of Queen Elizabeth, is another of the celebrated figures of history who ended his life on the scaffold. For his execution, he was dressed in a black cloak with a black doublet, and a scarlet waistcoat with long scarlet sleeves. After he had prayed long and earnestly, including in his words the welfare of the Queen, he removed his outer clothing and placed his head on the block. Telling the executioner that he would be ready when he stretched out his arms, he lay flat on the scaffold. Crying out, "Lord, into thy hands I commend my spirit", he put out his hands as arranged, and the axe fell, but it required three strokes to sever the head. The headsman then lifted this up by the hair and called, "God save the Queen".

Hakluyt describes a death by the axe which took place during the voyage of Sir Francis Drake, in 1578. Doughty, one of the crew, was tried and condemned for desertion. "Which our general saw, although his private affection to Mr. Doughty, as he when in the presence of us all sacredly protested, was great, yet the care he had of the state of the voyage, of the expectation of her Majesty, and of the honour of his country, did more touch him, as indeed it ought, than the private respect of one man; so that the cause being thoroughly heard and all things being done in good order, as near as might be to the course of our laws in England, it was concluded that Mr. Doughty should receive punishment according to the quality of the offence. He, seeing no remedy but patience for himself, desired before his death to receive the communion, which he did at the hands of Mr. Fletcher our minister, and our general accompanied him in the holy action. Which being done, and the place of execution being made ready, he, having embraced our general and taken leave of all his company with prayers for the Queen's Majesty and our realm, in quiet sort laid his head to the block: here he ended his life."

The Duke of Monmouth who was beheaded on Tower Hill, had the misfortune to have a very clumsy headsman. He went to the place of execution with calmness and courage. When he saw the axe he touched it and said it was not sharp enough. He gave the executioner half of the present he intended, telling him the other half would be given him if he did his work expeditiously. He was thinking of the manner in which Lord Russell had been beheaded by this same man. The headsman seemed in a state of great perturbation, trembling all over. He struck at Monmouth's neck two or three times, but did not succeed in severing the head from the body. He threw down his axe but the sheriff compelled him to take it up. He took another three or four strokes before he was able to cut off the head.

Strafford, whose execution was witnessed by a crowd estimated at 200,000 people, thus addressed those who could hear him. He told them he had always regarded Parliaments in England to be the happy constitution of the kingdom and nation, and the best means under God to make the King and his people happy. He wished that all who were present would consider whether the beginning of the people's happiness should be written in letters of blood. Having professed his attachment to the Church of England, he knelt for a while in prayer, remaining on his knees for a quarter of an hour. He then rose, took leave of his brother, and sent messages to his wife and family. Having done this he took off his upper garment and said, "I thank God I am not afraid of death, nor daunted with any discouragement rising from my fears, but do as cheerfully put off my doublet as ever I did when

I went to bed". The executioner then drew out a hand-kerchief to blindfold him. "Thou shalt not bind my eyes for I will see it done." He placed his neck upon the block, spread his hands as a sign that he was ready, and the axe fell.

Often more than one victim was executed at the same time, and this added to the awful ordeal through which the condemned had to pass, for the later ones saw the scaffold drenched with blood from those who had been executed before.

After the execution the heads were placed on poles and exhibited in prominent places such as the Tower of London, and Temple Bar, as a warning to others. The Tower has been described as "the grim fortress from whose battlements as from the towers of the bridge which faced it hung the bodies of scores of traitors drying in the sun. The heads of many another grinned at the passers by, from the pikes upright along the tops of the walls, food for the carrion birds that fought for their possession till only a whitened glistening skull remained".

CHAPTER XVII

THE HALIFAX GIBBET

THE guillotine, or rather its early prototype, was used in England long before it was introduced into France. Holinshed's Chronicle published in 1587 refers to this instrument known as the Halifax Gibbet. "There is, and has been of ancient time, a law or custom at Halifax, that whosoever doth commit any felony and is taken with the same, or confesses the fact upon examination, if it be valued by four constables to amount to the sum of thirteen pence halfpenny, he is forthwith beheaded upon one of the next market days (which fall usually upon Tuesdays, Thursdays, and Saturdays), or else upon the same day that he is convicted, if market be holden. The engine wherewith the execution is done is a square block of wood, of the length of four feet and a half, which doth ride up and down in a slot, rabet, or regall, between two pieces of timber that are framed and set upright. In the nether end of a sliding block is an axe, keyed or fastened with an iron into the wood, which being drawn up to the top of the frame, is there fastened by a wooden pin (with a notch made in the same, after the manner of a Samson's post) into the middest of which pin also there is a long rope fastened that cometh down among the people; so that when the offender hath made his confession, and hath laid his neck over the nethermost block, every man there present doth either take hold of the rope (or

putteth forth his arm so near the same as he can get in token
that he is willing to see justice executed), and pulling
out the pin in this manner, the head block wherein the axe
is fastened doth fall down with such a violence, that if
the neck of the transgressor were so big as that of a bull,
it should be cut in sunder at a stroke, and roll from the body
by a high distance. If it be so that the offender be apprehended for an ox, sheep or kine, or any such cattle, the
self beast or other of its kind shall have the end of the rope
tied somewhere unto them, so that they, being driven,
do draw out the pin, whereby the offender is executed."

There are records in the Parish Register of Halifax
of forty-nine people who suffered in this way between
1541 and 1650, since when no executions in this manner
have taken place.

This account of the last execution by the "Halifax
Gibbet" is from a work entitled, *Halifax and its Gibbet Law
placed in a true light*, by Dr. Samuel Midgley, published in
1708. "About the latter end of April, A.D. 1650, Abraham
Wilkinson, John Wilkinson, and Antony Mitchell were
apprehended within the Manor of Wakefield in the liberties
of Halifax, for divers felonious practices, and brought
or caused to be brought into the custody of the chief baliff
of Halifax, in order to have their trials for acquittal or
condemnation according to the custom of the forest of
Hardwick, at the complaint of Samuel Colbeck, of Wardley,
within the liberty of Halifax; John Fielden at Stansfield,
within the said liberty, and John Cushforth of Dunker,
in the parish of Sandall, in the Manor of Wakefield."

A summons was issued to the constables in the district,
ordering them to appear accompanied by men of the best
ability in their constabulary, to try the cases. They viewed
the stolen goods, and after hearing the evidence, they
found the prisoners guilty, and adjudged them to suffer
death by having their heads severed and cut off from

their bodies at the Halifax Gibbet. They were executed on the same day.

A similar instrument for beheading criminals was introduced into Scotland, in 1565, by the Earl of Morton, Regent of Scotland, where it was known as the Scottish Maiden. He himself met his death by this instrument sixteen years after. The first to be executed by this instrument in Scotland were some of those implicated in the murder of Rizzio, in Holyrood Palace in 1566. Large numbers afterwards fell victims to this instrument including Sir John Gordon of Haddo, and the Earl of Argyle. The last occasion on which the Scottish Maiden was used was in 1710. It is now in the Museum of the Society of Antiquaries, at Edinburgh, and the remains of the Halifax Gibbet are still preserved in the town.

CHAPTER XVIII

DROWNING AND BOILING

DROWNING was never a common method of punishment in this country, though it was occasionally used up to the commencement of the seventeenth century. It seems to have been more or less reserved for women rather than men. In Anglo-Saxon times women guilty of theft were drowned, and in the early middle ages, the Barons had their gallows for men and their drowning pits for women.

Richard I ordained that any soldier who killed a fellow crusader on board ship should be tied to the dead man's body, and cast into the sea. In Boy's *History of Sandwich* is the following. "In 1313 a presentment was made before the itinerant justices at Canterbury that the prior at Christ Church had for nine years obstructed the high road leading from Dover Castle to Sandwich by the seashore by a water mill, and the diversion of a stream called the Gestlyng, where felons condemned to death within the hundred should be drowned, but could not be executed that way for want of water. Further that he raised a certain gutter four feet and the water that passed that way to the gutter ran to the place where the convicts were drowned and from whence their bodies were floated to the river and that after the gutter was raised the drowned bodies could not be carried into the river by the stream as they used to be for want of water."

In Scotland execution of the death sentence by drowning was more common and there are many recorded examples. This method of execution existed here till 1685.

In 1544, a friar, preaching in one of the churches at Perth, was interrupted by one of the congregation, Robert Lamb, who disagreed with his views. He committed the additional sin of holding a feast at his home on All Hallows Eve, when he should have fasted. As a result of complaints a nest of heretics was rooted out and arrested. A court was held at Gray Friars' place. Indictments were found against the party where a woman, the wife of one of accused was included. They were all found guilty. Lest their friends should attempt a rescue at the execution, Cardinal Beaton had a large guard present. The three men were brought to the scaffold, the woman, Helen Stirk, with her baby in her arms was taken to see her husband suffer before she received her punishment. She asked to die with the rest but this was refused. She embraced her husband under the gallows. "Husband", she said, "we have lived together many joyful days; but this day in which we must die ought to be most joyful for us both, because we must have joy for ever. Therefore I will not bid you good night. Suddenly we shall meet again in the kingdom of heaven."

The men were hanged and then she was taken away to be drowned, the punishment in Scotland for witches. "Ah!" she said, as they led her past where Cardinal Beaton was sitting, "they sit in that place quietly who are the cause of our death this day; but He who seeth this execution upon us shall shortly see their nest shaken." They reached the water, she gave her baby to a bystander and was flung in to drown. Surely even Beaton must have been satisfied with this brutality.

In Ireland in 1570 large numbers of prisoners captured

by the government troops were stripped naked and put in the bog to drown in the mud. Two years later the Irish captured a number of Scottish prisoners and drowned four hundred of them.

Early in the eighteenth century, eleven gipsy women were condemned to be drowned at Edinburgh in the Nor' Lock. In May, 1685, Margaret Mc'Lachlan, aged 63, and Margaret Wilson, aged 18, were drowned in the Blednock for denying that James VII of Scotland was entitled to rule the church as he wished. In 1697, Janet Grant was tried for theft in the Baronial Court of Sir Robert Gordon, and for this offence was drowned in the loch of Spynie.

In 1567 the Regent of Scotland determined to make an attempt to restore order on the border, where anarchy was reigning. He made an unexpected raid at Hawick on market day, and seized thirty-six of the Border thieves, catching them red-handed. Thirteen were at once hanged and nine were drowned in the nearest pool with stones round their necks.

Boiling to death.

In the reign of Henry VIII, in 1531, an Act was passed which made boiling alive the punishment for the then rare crime of poisoning. Of course at this time there was no such science in existence as that of toxicology, and instances of poisoning may have escaped detection simply because there were so few means of proving the crime.

Fisher, Bishop of Rochester, who lived in Lambeth, was very hospitable and fed many of the poor of the neighbourhood. In the year 1531, a number of those whom he had entertained were taken alarmingly ill, as were also several members of his household. One of these and one

of the poor whom he entertained, died. It was discovered
that the yeast which had been used in the preparation
of several dishes had been poisoned. The guilty person
was found to be a cook named Richard Rouse. The
motive of this crime is obscure. It may have been political
or it may have been religious, or more likely it may have
been both. But it aroused a great feeling of horror in
England. Poisoning was looked upon as a peculiarly
continental method of murder, and not one which the
English could possibly tolerate. The result was that a special
Act of Parliament was passed to deal with this crime.
The wording is very remarkable. The Act (22 Henry
VIII, c. 9) is as follows: "The King's royal Majesty calling
to his most blessed remembrance that the making of good
and wholesome laws, and due execution of the same
against the offenders thereof, is the only cause that good
obedience and order hath been preserved in this realm:
and his Highness having the most tender zeal for the
same, considering that man's life above all things is chiefly
to be favoured, and voluntary murders most highly to be
detected and abhorred; and specially all kinds of murder
by poisoning, which in this realm hitherto, our Lord be
thanked, hath been most rare and seldom committed
or practised; and now, in the time of this present Parliament, that is to say, on the eighteenth day of February,
in the twenty-second year of his most victorious reign,
one Richard Rouse, late of Rochester, in the county of
Kent, cook, otherwise called Richard Cook, of his most
wicked and damnable disposition, did cast a certain venom
or poison into a vessel replenished with yeast or barm,
standing in the kitchen of the reverend father in God,
John, Bishop of Rochester, at his place in Lambeth Marsh;
with which yeast or barm, and other things convenient,
porridge or gruel was forthwith made for his family,
there being; whereby not only the number of seventeen

persons of his said family, which did eat of that porridge, were mortally infected or poisoned, and one of them, that is to say, Bennet Curwan, gentleman, is thereof deceased; but also certain poor people which resorted to the said bishop's palace, and were there charitably fed with remains of the said porridge, and other victuals, were in likewise infected; and one poor woman of them, that is to say, Alice Trypitt, widow, is also thereof now deceased. Our said sovereign lord the King, of his blessed disposition inwardly abhorring all such abominable offences, because that in manner no person can live in surety out of danger of death by that means, if practices thereof should not be eschewed, hath ordained and enacted by authority of this present Parliament, that the said poisoning be adjudged and deemed as high treason; and that the said Richard, for the said murder and poisoning of the said two persons shall stand and be attainted of high treason.

"And because that detestable offence, now newly practised and committed, requireth condign punishment for the same, it is ordained and enacted by authority of the present Parliament, that the said Richard Rouse shall be therefore boiled to death, without having any advantage of his clergy; and that from henceforth every wilful murder of any person or persons hereafter to be committed or done by means or way of poisoning, shall be reputed, deemed, and judged in the law to be high treason; and that all and every person or persons which shall hereafter be indicted and condemned by order of the law of such treason, shall not be admitted to the benefit of his or their clergy, but shall be immediately after such attainder or condemnation, committed to execution of death by boiling for the same."

He was boiled to death at Smithfield a few days later.

The Act was repealed in 1547, in the reign of Edward VI. There were very few cases in which the punishment was carried out. The only records which I can trace are that of Rouse and that of a maid servant, who in 1531 was boiled to death at Kings Lynn for the murder of her husband by poison.

CHAPTER XIX

BURNING

BURNING as a method of punishment, dates back to very early times. The ancient Britons sacrificed their prisoners to the Gods in this way. The offenders were placed in wicker cages made in the form of some well-known idol, and big enough to hold several persons. The cage was surrounded by wood and was then set on fire and the wretched victims destroyed. This was 1,500 years before the fires of Smithfield.

As a punishment for heresy, it was inflicted long before the conquest. St. Alban was the first to suffer at the stake. It was probably employed on occasion for heretics in the period before Henry IV, but there was not much heresy before the fourteenth century. In the reign of this King when the ecclesiastical party triumphed, the burnings commenced in full force.

The first Act of Parliament which allowed heretics to be burnt was passed in the reign of Henry IV (2 Hen. IV, c. 15. De Heretico Comburendo). The Bishops by this Act received power to arrest and imprison on suspicion without any check or restraint, at their will and pleasure. Prisoners who refused to acknowledge their errors, who persisted in heresy, or who relapsed after abjuration, were sentenced to be burnt alive.

In the long list of those who suffered death from burning for the sake of their religion, Protestant burnt by Catholic

146

or Catholic burnt by Protestant, were Archbishop Cranmer, Sir Thomas More, Bishops Hooper, Ridley, Latimer, Fisher, and countless others, both clerical and lay; many of whom had, when their religion was supreme, taken part in the burning of those opposed to them in religious beliefs.

The first to suffer under the 'De Heretico Comburendo' Act was William Sautre, "sometime chaplain", accused of "most damnable heresy". The sentence passed on him by the Convocation of the province of Canterbury was that he should be degraded from all ecclesiastical rank, and that afterwards he should be left to the secular power, Holy Mother Church having no further concern in him. The King informed the Mayor and Sheriffs of London that such heretics should be burnt. William Sautre was to be taken to some public place and there burnt alive. This sentence was duly carried out. No outcry was raised by the public to such proceedings.

In Tudor times, the burning of heretics was quite a common spectacle. The case of an Observant Friar, named Forest who was condemned to death as a heretic in 1539, is a typical instance. "For him was prepared at Smithfield, in London, a gallows on which he was hanged in chains, by the middle and arm-holes, all quick; and under the gallows was made a fire, and he so consumed and burnt to death. At his coming to the place of execution, there was prepared a great scaffold on which sat the nobles of the realm, and the King's majesty's honourable council —only to have granted pardon to that wretched creature, if any spark of repentance would have happened to him. There was also prepared a pulpit where a Right Reverend in God, and a renowned and famous clerk, the Bishop of Worcester, called Hugh Latimer, declared to him his errors; but such was his forwardness that he neither would hear nor speak. And a little before his execution, a huge and great image was brought to the gallows, which image was brought out of Wales, and of the Welshmen much sought and worshipped, and was burnt under Forest. This frear (friar) when he saw the fire come, and that present death was at hand, caught hold upon the ladder, which he would not let go, but so impatiently took his death that no man that ever put his trust in God never so unquietly nor so ungodly ended his life."

Some other instances are here quoted. Information was given to Bonner, Bishop of London, that a boy named Richard Makins, had spoken some idle words which it was said affected the sacrament of the altar. He probably did not know even what they meant. The boy, scarcely fifteen years old, was burnt alive by the Church, at Smithfield.

James Bainham, a barrister of the Middle Temple, was in 1532 guilty of daring to express his religious convictions which did not happen to be in agreement with those held by the Government at that particular moment. No mercy was possible. He looked for none. The authorities decided they could not give him a pardon in this world on any terms; but they would not kill him till they had tried to save his soul. He was removed to the coal cellar of the Bishop of London, at Fulham. Here he was ironed and put in the stocks, in the cold of March, and left for many days. He would not recant, so was taken to the house of Sir Thomas More, at Chelsea, where for two nights he was chained to a post and whipped; then he was taken back to Fulham for another week of torture, and finally to the Tower for another fortnight and more whippings. Mercy could no longer be shown to this obstinate man. The authorities had done everything possible. But he remained firm in his belief. He was burnt alive at Smithfield.

The light-hearted way in which the burning of a heretic was regarded is illustrated by the following quotation from a letter of Cranmer's.

"Other news we have none notable, but that one Frith, which was in the Tower in prison, was appointed by the King's Grace to be examined before me, my Lord of London, my Lord of Winchester, my Lord of Suffolk, my Lord Chancellor, my Lord of Wiltshire, whose opinion was so notably erroneous that we could not dispatch him but were fain to leave him to the determination of his ordinary, which is the Bishop of London. His said opinion is of such nature that he thought it not necessary to be believed as an article of our faith that there is the very corporeal presence of Christ within the host and sacrament of the altar; and holdeth on this point much after the opinion of Oecolampoedius. And surely I myself sent for him three or four times to persuade him to leave that imagination. But for all that we could do therein, he would not apply to any counsel. Notwithstanding he is now at a final end with all examinations; for my Lord of London hath given sentence, and delivered him to the secular power, when he looketh every day to go unto the fire. And there is also condemned with him one Andrew, a tailor, for the self-same opinion; and thus fare you well."

The victims perished by fire at Smithfield. Twenty years later, the author of this callous letter, was burnt to death at Oxford, for holding the very opinions for which these two men had been burnt.

After Monmouth's rebellion, as is well known, the inhuman brutality and atrocity of the most infamous Judge this country has ever known, Jeffreys, accounted for many hundreds of deaths by his method of so-called justice.

There was in London a woman named Gaunt who was accused of harbouring a rebel. She was a good woman who had spent her life in acts of charity, visiting jails, and looking after the poor. One of the rebels went to her one

night and she gave him shelter, and attempted to get him
out of the kingdom. He heard that the King had expressed
the view that he would rather catch those who sheltered
the rebels than the actual rebels themselves. So utterly
lost was this man to common decency and gratitude that
he actually betrayed his benefactress. She was arrested
and tried. It was necessary that her act of treason should
be proved by two witnesses. The only witness was the
degraded betrayer. But the judge, in order to secure a
conviction, accepted the evidence of a maid who knew
nothing of the alleged treason. Such was English justice
in the time of James II and Jeffreys! She was condemned
to be burnt. She died as such a noble woman would.
Penn the Quaker, who witnessed her death, said she laid
the straw about her for burning, and behaved herself so
magnificently that all the spectators were in tears.

The powers at the head of the nation not content with
burning men alive, went so far as to burn the dead bodies
of those who differed from them in religious matters. A
man named William Tracey left a will in which some
words were written which might be construed into some
heretical meaning. His body was exhumed by order of
Cranmer, Archbishop of Canterbury, and burnt.

The last heretic burnt in England was Edward Wightman,
in 1612. He was convicted by Bishop Neile of holding
several distinct heresies. About the same time the question
arose as to what was to be done with a man, Bartholomew
Legate, who professed to be an Arian. James I was
very anxious to burn him, but there was some doubt
as to whether he could do this legally so the judges
were consulted. Coke, the Lord Chief Justice believed it
was illegal, and therefore James asked that when the
Judges were consulted Coke should not be included
among them, another example of Stuart justice. Conviction followed as a matter of course, and Legate was

burnt at Smithfield and Wightman a few days later at Lichfield.

Neile, Archbishop of York thus describes the fate of this poor victim of the Church. After he had been bound to the stake, and the wood lighted, "the fire scorched him a little. He cried out that he would recant. The people thereupon ran into the fire and suffered themselves to be scorched to save him. There was then prepared a form of recantation, which he there read and professed before he was unchained from the stake." He was carried back to prison but he refused to renounce his heresies and was once again bound to the stake and burnt alive.

Although these were the last to be executed in this way for heresy, it was not till 1648 that burning for this crime was abolished by law. Burning still remained the method of putting to death of female traitors.

In 1721, Barbara Spencer was convicted of coining, an offence which was at this time high treason. She was sentenced to be burnt alive. She was taken to Tyburn, and bound to the stake. She wished to say a last prayer in peace, but the mob, ever ready for a day's pleasure at a sight like this, would not leave her alone and amused themselves by stoning her before she died.

In 1726, Catherine Hayes was convicted of aiding and abetting in the murder of her husband. This was petty treason and the punishment was the same as for high treason, namely, burning alive. This sentence was duly carried out.

In the reign of William III the law of treason was considerably modified, but the punishment for women remained the same, and many cases are recorded of women being burnt for various offences in this reign. In 1784 a man named John Quin, and a woman, Mary Bayler were accused of murdering the husband of the latter at Portsmouth. The two were charged that they did feloniously and traitorously kill Cornelius Bayler and each with both their hands and both their feet in and upon the head, belly, breast, sides and stomach of him the said Cornelius Bayler, did beat, strike and kick so that he died. The woman was convicted and was ordered to be drawn on a hurdle to the place of execution, on Monday the eighth of March, and burned with fire until she died. This sentence was carried out.

In 1777, a girl of fourteen concealed whitewashed farthings made to look like shillings at the command of her master. She was ordered to be burnt alive and was actually tied to the stake and the fire about to be lighted when a reprieve arrived.

The last instance of this punishment being carried out was in 1789, when Christian Murphy was burnt for coining. By an Act of George III (30 Geo. III, c. 48) the punishment for women for capital offences was for the future to be that of hanging.

The authorities burnt women instead of hanging them as a concession to the sex. Blackstone expresses the prevailing view. "For as the decency due to the sex forbids the exposing and publicly mangling their bodies, their sentence (which is to the full as terrible to sensation as the other is) is to be drawn to the gallows and there to be burnt alive", and he adds, "the humanity of the English nation has authorised, by a tacit consent, an almost general mitigation of such part of these judgements as savours of torture and cruelty, a sledge or hurdle being usually allowed to such traitors as are condemned to be drawn, and there being very few instances (and these accidental and by negligence) of any person being disembowelled or burnt till previously deprived of sensation by strangling."

The merciful executioner often tied a rope round the neck of the prisoner, and strangled her. Sometimes bags of gunpowder were provided and placed in the armpits of the victims. As a result they were killed by the explosion of the powder before much of the fire had touched them.

A refinement of the punishment of burning alive was the estrapade, a machine introduced into France in the sixteenth century by Francis for the better correction of heresy. The offender was slung by a chain over a fire, and by means of a crane was dipped up and down into the flame, the torture being thus prolonged for an indefinite time. Francis was occasionally present in person at these exhibitions, the executioner awaiting his arrival before commencing the spectacle.

The burning to death of heretics is discussed more fully in the chapter on the Church and cruelty.

CHAPTER XX

MUTILATION AND BRANDING

MUTILATION of the body as a method of punishment and warning to others dates back to pre-Conquest days and is referred to in the Codes of Alfred, Athelstan, and Canute. Eyes and tongues were plucked out, the nose, ears, lips, hands and feet cut off, the scalp torn away, and even the whole body flayed alive. Men without hands, without feet, with the tongue cut out and branded on the forehead, all this for some petty crime, could frequently be seen walking about, and were regarded as warnings to others.

A law of Henry VIII made an act of bloodshed within the King's Court punishable with the loss of the right hand (13 Henry VIII, c. 12). There was a carefully arranged ceremony to be carried out on those convicted. The trial was before the Lord Great Master or Lord High Steward of the household. If found guilty, the prisoner was brought before the Marshall. The Sergeant of the Woodyard brought blocks and cords and bound the hand in a convenient position. The master cook was present with his knife which he handed to the Sergeant of the Larder who adjusted it and held it till the execution was done. The Sergeant of the Poultry was close by with a cock which was to have its head cut off on the block with the same knife, and the body of which was afterwards used to wrap about the stump. The Yeoman of the Scullery stood

near watching a coal fire, with the Sergeant Farrier ready
to hand the searing irons to the Surgeon. The Chief
Surgeon seared the stump and the Groom of the Salcery
held vinegar and water in case of fainting. The Sergeant
of the Ewry and the Yeoman Chandry attended with
basons and towels for the Surgeon. After the hand had
been struck off, and the stump seared, the Sergeant of
the Pantry offered bread, and the Sergeant of the Cellar
a pot of red wine to the sufferer.

A case of mutilation, not of a legal character, occurred
in a church brawl in the reign of Henry II, and is quoted
only as showing the nature of public feeling at that time.
Guy Mortimer, who was rector of the church of Kingston-
on-Hull, bore a grudge against one of his parishoners,
William Joye. He hired men to attack him and as he
lay helpless on the ground, Mortimer came up, drew
his knife, and with his own hand deliberately cut off the
upper lip of his enemy. Mortimer at his trial pleaded
Benefit of Clergy, but the Court held as this was only
a trespass and not a felony, the plea did not obtain. The
punishment was a fine of one hundred pounds.

Benefit of Clergy was the name for the privilege which
a clerk in holy orders had the right to claim of being
tried in an ecclesiastical court when charged with an
offence. It was later extended to peers and later still
to all persons who could read. It was a great advantage
to the clergy for it rendered them nearly exempt from
serious punishment. Gradually this privilege was reduced,
the graver crimes being withdrawn from Benefit, and it
was finally abolished, but not till the year 1841.

During the trial of the Duchess of Kingston for bigamy,
before the House of Peers in Westminster Hall, the Attorney
General made the following remarks in reference to
Benefit of Clergy and its applicability to women. "My
lords, this I take to be a clear proposition, that from the

beginning of time to this hour, clergy was never demand-
able by women. By the ancient law of the land this
privilege was so favourably used, that reading was
sufficient proof of clergy: and all were taken to be clerks,
who lay under no indisputable impediment to receive
orders. This rule is laid down in all the books. Several
statutes, nay the Provincial Constitution of 1531, adopt
the distinction thus made between persons in holy orders,
and other clerks, or lay clerks. But women were under
this indispensable impediment. They might be professed,
and become religious; but even a nun could not claim
this privilege. This was proved by the same books: and
lord Hale puts the case of manslaughter, where the husband
shall have his clergy, and the wife no privilege. The
statutes, which exempt women from judgement of death,
expressly recite, that they were not entitled to clergy;
and distinctly provide a new and different exemption."

The first statute which exempted women from capital
punishment for felony was passed in the reign of James I.
(21 James I, c. 6.) "Whereas, by the laws of this realm,
the benefit of clergy is not allowed to women convicted
of felony; by reason whereof many women do suffer death
for small causes; be it enacted by the authority of this
present parliament, that any woman being lawfully convicted by her confession, or by the verdict of twelve men,
of, or for the felonious taking of any money, goods, or
chattels above the value of twelve pence, and under the
value of ten shillings; or as accessory to any such offence;
the said offence being not burglary, nor robbery in or near
the highway, nor the felonious taking of any money, goods,
or chattels, from the person of any man or woman privily,
without his or their knowledge, but only such an offence as
in the like case a man might have his clergy, shall, for the
first offence be branded, and marked in the hand, upon
the brawn of the left thumb, with a hot burning iron,

having a roman T upon the said iron; the said mark to be made by the gaoler òpenly, in the Court, before the judge; and also to be further punished by imprisonment, whipping, stocking, or sending to the house of correction, in such sort, manner, and from, and for so long time (not exceeding the space of one whole year) as the judge, judges, or other justices, before whom she shall be convicted, or which shall have authority in the cause, shall, in their discretion, think meet according to the quality of the offence, and then to be delivered out of prison for that offence; any law, custom, or usage to the contrary notwithstanding.")

After a very long trial and many days of legal arguments, the Peers put the following question to the judges. "Whether a peeress, convicted by her peers of a clergyable felony, is entitled to the benefit of the statutes, so as to excuse her from capital punishment, without being burnt in the hand, or being liable to any imprisonment?" After hearing the opinion of the judges the Lord High Steward said: "Madam, the lords have considered of the prayer you have made, to which the benefit of the statutes, and the lords allow it to you. But, Madam, let me add that although very little punishment, or none, can now be inflicted, the feelings of your own conscience will supply that defect. And let me give you this information likewise, that you can never have the like benefit a second time, but another offence of the same kind will be capital. Madam, you are discharged, paying your fees."

Some cases of mutilation

Sir Edward Knevet was tried at Greenwich, in 1541, for striking a person within the King's Palace there. It happened a few months after the Statute of Henry VIII by which malicious striking in the palace where the King resides, so as to draw blood, is punishable not only with imprisonment for life and fine, but further with cutting off the right hand of the offender. He was sentenced to lose his right hand and the elaborate ceremony detailed was arranged. But Sir Henry having petitioned the King that he might lose his left hand instead of his right in order that he might still be able to fight for his sovereign, "The justices forthwith informed the King, who of his goodness, considering the gentle heart of the said Edmond, and the good report of lords and ladies, granted him pardon".

In 1573, a man named Birchet was executed for a murder committed in the Tower of London. Before the sentence was carried out, his right hand was cut off and nailed to the gallows.

When Felton was tried for the murder of the Duke of Buckingham, he pleaded guilty and was sentenced to death. He then offered the hand which had done the deed to be cut off, but the Court decided they could not inflict this further punishment on him. The King sent to the judges asking them to carry out the mutilation, but the Court answered, "that it could not be; for in all murders the judgement was the same unless when the Statute of 25 Ed. 3, did alter the nature of the offence, and upon a several indictment, as it was in Queen Elizabeth's time, when a felon at the bar flung a stone at the judge upon the bench, for which he was indicted, and his sentence was to have his hand cut off: which was accordingly done ".

In 1579, a pamphlet which offended the Queen was written by a man named Stubbs and sold by a bookseller, Page. They were indicted under an Act passed in the reign of Mary, for the protection of the Queen's husband. The title, "Queen's husband", was alleged by Elizabeth to cover her suitor the Duke of Alencon, against whom the pamphlet had been written. Lawyers gave their opinion that this was stretching the construction of the Act too far and one judge even resigned rather than be a party to any conviction, but the revengeful Queen obtained her desire and they were both found guilty. They were brought from the tower to the scaffold, and "their right hands were struck off and a cleaver driven through the wrist with a beetle." Page, as the bleeding stump was seared with a hot iron said proudly, "I have left there a true Englishman's hand". Stubbs waved his hat with his remaining hand and cried, "God save Queen Elizabeth", and fainted from loss of blood. It is remarkable how a man brutally punished by a cruel and callous woman should have felt any sentiments of loyalty at such a time.

The last case in which the question of cutting off the hand for rioting in the King's Court took place was in 1799, when the Earl of Thanet and others were tried at the Bar of the Court of King's Bench for a riot and other misdemeanours, committed at the Court at Maidstone during a trial there of certain prisoners. The Judges pointed out to the attorney-general that they could see no other sentence for this offence, if the prisoners were found guilty, than that of severing the hand, as it was a definite punishment fixed by Statute with which they had no power to interfere. On this the attorney-general withdrew the particular charge which entailed this punishment and proceeded on other counts of the indictment.

How terribly vindictive and brutal were these punishments of mutilation is well illustrated by the case of Alice Crithecreche, who was with others charged in 1203 with murder. Alice fled directly after the murder into Staffordshire with some of the goods of the murdered woman. She alleged that she had seen some men coming out of the house of the murdered woman and they had threatened her with death if she gave the alarm. She kept silence and they gave her the goods found on her. She was found guilty and sentenced to death. The penalty was commuted but both her eyes were plucked out.

Branding, too, was a very ancient punishment, dating back at least as far as the fourth century.

In the twelfth century, one of many sects which are always splitting off from established religion, known as the Paterines, appeared in England. They were ordered to do penance for their opinions, but refused. Their foreheads were seared with hot irons so that all might know that they had dared to assert the right of thinking for themselves. They were denied food and shelter, and perished from cold and starvation.

The branding iron consisted of a long wooden handle with an iron, shaped according to the letter, intended to be branded, M for malefactor, V for vagabond, etc. Iron hoops held the hand of the prisoner steady. As a rule the ball of the thumb was the place selected to mark. The custom of directing a prisoner to hold up his hand when he pleaded at the bar, was for the purpose of showing if he had been branded.

The branding of prisoners was carried out for many crimes. In 1619, Sarah Swanton made a false accusation against Lady Exeter, for which she was tried and convicted. She was told that if she persisted in denying her imposture, she was to be whipped and branded on the cheek with the letters FA, false accuser, and to be imprisoned for life.

The celebrated Statute of Labourers, which was passed in the reign of Edward VI, ordered a runaway servant to be branded on the breast with the letter V for vagabond, and adjudged him to be the slave of any purchaser for two years. His owner was to give him "bread, water, and small drink, and refuse meat, and cause him to work by beating, chaining or otherwise. If he absented himself for fourteen days during his two years of servitude, he was to be branded on the forehead with the letter S." In Elizabeth's time a vagabond above the age of fourteen years was to be severely whipped and burnt through the gristle of the right ear with a hot iron of one inch in compass. For brawling in churchyards the offender had one of his ears cut off, but if he had already lost both his ears, he had the letter F (fighter or fraymaker) branded on his cheek.

In 1698 it was enacted that in order to deter evil disposed persons from committing crimes, the branding should be done in a new way. Thieves were to be branded with the usual mark "in the most visible part of the left cheek, nearest the nose, which punishment shall be inflicted in open court, in the preesence of the judge who is directed and required to see the same strictly and effectually executed".

Branding was abolished in 1779 by Act of Parliament (19 Geo. III, c. 74).

CHAPTER XXI

MINOR CRUELTIES

A SHORT account of some punishments which, in comparison with those already described, may be called minor, though by present day standards they would be regarded as brutal and vindictive, is appended.

Among them are the pillory, the stocks, the finger pillory, the jougs, the ducking stool, and the branks or scold's bridle; these have all either been abolished by Act of Parliament (the pillory in 1837) or have died out of use.

The pillory consisted of a frame of wood erected on a post or pole, with moveable boards like those of the stocks. There were holes through which the head and hands of the offender were put. It was a common punishment for some minor offences, and was also part of the sentence for such crimes as seditious writings and other political crimes.

The stocks was an apparatus much used for the confinement of vagrants and petty offenders in different parts of Europe, and was retained until recently in country villages in this country. Many of them are still kept as interesting curiosities. It consisted of two heavy timbers, one of which could be raised and when lowered was held in place by a padlock. Notches in the timbers formed round holes when the two pieces of timber were closed and this held the legs of the offenders tightly in place.

Sometimes there were also holes for the hands and even the neck.

The jougs was an instrument formerly used in Scotland, consisting of an iron collar to go round the neck of the prisoner. This was then fastened by a chain to a wall or tree.

The branks or scold's bridle was an apparatus once used in England and Scotland for correcting nagging women. It consisted of a head piece enclosing the head of the offender, with a flat piece of iron to go in the mouth and press on the tongue.

The ducking-stool was a stool or chair in which common scolds were tied and plunged into water. They were of different forms, the most common consisting of an upright post with a transverse pivoted beam, on which the seat was fitted or from which it was suspended by a chain. It is mentioned in Doomsday survey and was in common use from the beginning of the fifteenth till the eighteenth century, and was actually used at Leominster as late as 1809.

The cucking-stool was a very similar instrument but this did not admit of ducking unless as was often the case it was conveyed by a cart to the waterside. It was used to place defaulting tradesmen and disorderly women in so that they might be hooted at and pelted by the crowd.

The finger pillory was an instrument on much the same plan as the ordinary pillory but smaller, and fitted for holding the fingers tight.

Some instances of the kind of offence which led to the use of these instruments and the method of their employment are given below.

In 1543, Dr. London, Warden of New College, in his overeagerness to convict some heretics, whose religious opinions did not coincide with those of the Government, blundered into giving false evidence. He was tried for this, convicted, and stripped of his dignities. He was compelled to ride through the streets of Windsor, Newbury, and Reading, with his face to the tail of a horse, and a paper on his head setting forth that he was a detected perjurer. In each town he was placed in a pillory so that the mob might have an opportunity of shouting at him and pelting him with filth. He was then put in the Fleet prison, where he died after a period of miserable existence.

When Lady Jane Gray was proclaimed Queen, a vintner's boy who expressed his disapproval paid for his rashness the next day. He was put in the pillory and nailed to it by both ears. These had to be cut off before he could be released.

In Edinburgh, in 1565, a priest said mass at Easter in a private house. He was denounced, captured, and at once tried before the Magistrates. He confessed and was then fastened by hands and feet to the market cross, where he stood for four hours. During this time he was pelted with thousands of eggs till he was rendered unconscious. He was eventually rescued by the Provost, who took him to the Tolbooth where he was made fast in irons.

A blackmailer, named Daniell, a servant of the Earl of Essex, threatened the Countess, after the execution of her husband, but she resisted his attempts and appealed at once to Cecil. The accused was brought before the Star Chamber and sentenced to pay two thousand pounds to the Countess, to be fined another thousand pounds, and to be imprisoned for life, and in addition, "to the end the said offences of the foresaid Daniell should not only be notifyed to the publique viewe, but to cause others to refrayne from committing of the like hereafter, it is likewise ordered and decreed that for the same his offences

he the said Daniell shall be sett upon the pillory, with
his eares thereunto nayled, with a paper on his head
inscribed with these words—For forgery, corrupte coseneges,
and other lewde practises".

The blasphemy laws in the seventeenth century were
very severe. A man named James Naylor was accused
of breaking the law on account of his opinions on various
matters of belief. He was sentenced to be sent in the
pillory in Palace Yard, and to be whipped thence by the
hangman to the Old Exchange. Two days later he was
to be put in the pillory at the Exchange and wear there
a paper cap setting forth his offence. At the Old Exchange
his tongue was to be bored through with a hot iron, and
his forehead branded with the letter B. He was afterwards to be sent to Bristol, ride through the town on
the bare back of a horse with his face to the tail, and to
be whipped publicly on the next market day. Finally
to complete this series of brutalities, he was to be put
to solitary confinement in the Bridewell in London with
no pens, ink, or paper. Perhaps in spite of all these
refinements of cruelty he was lucky. A hundred years
earlier he would have been burnt alive for this same
offence.

In the reign of Charles II, in 1680, Elizabeth Cellier
was charged with writing and publishing a libel; of this
offence she was convicted, and her punishment was as
follows:

She was fined £1,000 and committed to prison till the
fine was paid, and because "a pecuniary mulct is not
a sufficient recompense to justice which you have offended,
the Court doth likewise pronounce against you, that you
be put on the pillory three several days, in three several
public places: in the first place, in regard her braided
ware received its first impression and vent at her own
house, it is thought fit she stand (as near her own house

as conveniently can be) between the hours of twelve and one, for an hour's space, at the May-pole in the Strand, on the most notorious day; I think there is a market near that place, let it be on that day. At another time, that she stand in Covent Garden, on a public day the like space of time; a third time, that she stand at Charing-Cross on the most public day for the space of an hour. And in the next place, that she find sureties for her good behaviour during her life; and in every place where she shall stand on the pillory, some parcels of her books shall, in her own view, be burnt by the hands of the common hang-man and a Paper of the cause to be put upon the pillory."

In 1685 Titus Oates, one of the most unmitigated scoun-drels who has ever adorned the pages of history, was indicted for perjury before the Lord Chief Justice Sir George Jeffreys. The sentence pronounced on Oates was the following:

"Titus Oates, you are convicted upon two indictments for perjury, . . . one of the greatest offences that our law has cognizance of. . . . But your perjury had all the aggravations that can be thought of to heighten it. If a man kills another with the sword, and there be forethought malice in the case, he is to be hanged for it: but when a man shall draw innocent blood upon himself by a malicious, premeditated false oath, there is not only blood in the case, but like-wise perjury, corrupt malicious perjury. I know not how I can say, but the law is defective that such a one is not to be hanged. For, if we consider these dreadful effects which have followed upon your perjury, we must conclude our law defective: they are such, as no Christian heart can think of without bleeding for that innocent blood which was shed by your oath. . . . God be thanked, our eyes are now opened: and indeed we must have been incurably blind, if they had not been opened, first by the contradictions, improbabilities and impossibilities in your own testimony: but likewise by the positive, plain, direct and full proof of forty-seven witnesses to one point: against whom you had not one word to object, but they were papists and Roman Catholics, which is no objection at all: though at the same time it did appear that nine or ten of them were Protestants of the Church of England. That was all you had to say: you had not one word to justify yourself from that great and heinous perjury you were accused of. I hope I have not been thought a man of ill nature, and I confess, nothing has been so great a regret to me in my place and station as to give judgment and pronounce the sentence of law against my fellow creatures: but as to you, Mr. Oates, I cannot say my fellow Christian. Yet in this case, when I consider your offence, and the dismal effects that have followed upon it, I cannot say that I have any remorse in giving judgment upon you. And therefore having told you shortly my thoughts about your crime, and how readily I pronounce your sentence, I shall now declare the judgment of the Court upon you. And it is this: First the Court does order that for a fine, you pay one thousand marks upon each indictment.

"Secondly, that you be stript of all your Canonical Habits.

"Thirdly, the Court does award that you do stand upon the pillory and in the pillory, here before Westminster Hall gate, upon Monday next, for an hour's time, between the hours of ten and twelve, with a paper over your head (which you must first walk with round about to all the courts in Westminster Hall) declaring your crime. And that is upon the first indictment.

"Fourthly, on the second indictment, upon Tuesday, you shall stand upon and in the Pillory at the Royal

Exchange in London, for the space of an hour, between the hours of twelve and two, with the same inscription.

"You shall upon the next Wednesday be whipped from Aldgate to Newgate. Upon Friday, you shall be whipped from Newgate to Tyburn, by the hand of the common hangman.

"But Mr. Oates, we cannot but remember there were several particular times you swore false about: and therefore as annual commemorations, that it may be known to all persons as long as you live, we have taken special care of you for an annual punishment. Upon the 24th of April every year, as long as you live, you are to stand upon the pillory and in the pillory, at Tyburn, just opposite to the gallows, for the space of an hour between the hours of ten and twelve. You are to stand upon and in the Pillory here at Westminster Hall gate, every 9th of August, in every year, so long as you live. And that it may be known what we mean by it, 'tis to remember what he swore about Mr. Ireland's being in town between the 8th and 12th of August. You are to stand upon and in the Pillory at Charing Cross on the 10th of August every year during your life, between ten and twelve. The like over against the Temple Gate on the 11th. And upon the 2nd of September (which is another notorious time which you cannot but be remembered of) you are to stand upon and in the Pillory for the space of one hour between twelve and two, at the Royal Exchange: and all this you are to do every year during your life and to be committed close prisoner as long as you live. This I pronounce to be the judgment of the Court upon you, for your offences. And I must tell you plainly, if it had been in my power to have carried it further, I should not have been unwilling to have given judgment of death upon you, for I am sure you deserve it."

William Fuller, was tried at the Guildhall, London, "for a cheat and impostor", in the reign of Queen Anne in 1702. In the Annals of Queen Anne appears the following account. "June 23. William Fuller, that branded and infamous impostor, being by an order of the House of Lords, of the 19th of January, prosecuted for publishing two false and scandalous libels, the one entitled, 'Original Letters of the late King James, and others, to his greatest friends in England'; the other called, 'Twenty-six Depositions of Persons of Quality and Worth,' reflecting upon several members of both Houses of Parliament (particularly the earl of Nottingham), and being fully convicted thereof, was brought to the Queen's-bench bar, where sentence was pronounced upon him. That he should appear in all the courts of Westminster, with a paper, denoting his offence; that he should stand three times in the pillory, and afterwards be sent to the House of Correction in London, there to be whipped and continued to hard labour, until the 24th of October next, and that he should remain in custody, till he paid a fine of 1,000 marks. Pursuant to this sentence, Fuller stood three times in the pillory, and was most unmercifully handled by the mob at Charing-Cross and Temple-Bar, but was more favourably used before the Royal Exchange".

In 1750, Timothy Penredd, was found guilty of counterfeiting the seal of the Court of Queen's Bench, and of having forged and sealed some Queen's Bench writs and delivered them to the Sheriff of London in order to get two people arrested. The sentence on Penredd was that he should be put in the pillory on two successive market days in Cheapside; on the first day one of his ears was to be nailed to the pillory, in such a way that he should be compelled by his own movements to tear it off, and the same was to be carried out on the next occasion on the other ear.

Mr. Emlyn, writing in 1809, in the introduction to "State Trials", defines the ostensible objects of the pillory and protests against its misuse. "As to the Pillory, that is intended only to expose the Offender to shame and infamy, and to mark out to the public as a person not to be trusted, but to be shunned and avoided by all creditable and honest men; never did the law design that he should be exposed to the peltings of a mob, or to the assaults and injuries of a furious rabble, whereby the prisoner is so disguised as to defeat one main design of setting him there, which was, that he might be publicly known and observed. It is indeed a surprising neglect, that no effectual care has hitherto been taken to suppress these practices especially considering the fatal consequences which have sometimes ensued from them, even to the loss of the poor man's life. It is not sufficient that whoever injures him in this manner may be punished for so doing; for how is it possible that a man in his condition should observe who it is that does him the injury, or secure him if he did? He is at that time in the hands of justice, and justice ought to protect him; when a man is at liberty he is in many cases able to defend himself; but when he is in the custody of the law, and is thereby disabled from being his own defender, the law ought to be his security and defence against any injurious treatment. It cannot be pretended that this is altogether impracticable; experience shows us, how effectually it may be done, when the officers find an advantage by it, nor would there be any harm in it, if the officers were obliged by proper penalties to take the same care without money, which they are so well able to do with it."

In 1755, in the reign of George II, Stephen M'Daniel, John Berry, James Egan, and James Salmon were indicted and convicted for conspiracy and were sentenced to seven years' imprisonment and to be twice set in the pillory. They each stood once in the pillory and were so severely handled by the populace that it was with the utmost difficulty that one of the sheriffs and the keeper at Newgate prevented them being utterly destroyed. So great was the mob that the peace officers found it impossible to protect the prisoners from their fury. Egan and Salmon were put in the pillory at Smithfield. They were at once assaulted with showers of stones and oyster shells, and after half an hour it was found that Egan was dead and Salmon so dangerously wounded that it was thought he would not recover. In another case in 1732, two men, Dalton and Griffiths, were tried at the Old Bailey for the murder of John Waller in the pillory by pelting him with cauliflower stalks and other things, and found guilty. They were both hanged at Tyburn.

In 1777, John Horne was at the suit of the Attorney-General, proceeded against for a libel. The Trial was held in the court of King's Bench and during the course of the proceedings the Attorney-General said, "I stated in the third place to your lordships, the pillory to have been the usual punishment for this species of offence. I apprehend it to have been so in this case for above two hundred years before the time when prosecutions grew rank in the Star-chamber, and to those degrees which made that court properly to be abolished. The punishment of the pillory was inflicted, not only during the time such prosecutions were rank in the Star-chamber, but it also continued to be inflicted upon this sort of crime, and that by the best authority, after the time of the abolishing the Star-chamber, after the time of the Revolution, and while my lord chief justice Holt sat in this court. In looking over precedents for the sake of the other question, I observed that Mr. Tutchin (an author of some eminence in his day) was angry with Holt, the lord chief justice, for transferring, as he called it, the punishment of bakers to authors. That was upon a personal conceit which such an author as Tutchin thought himself entitled to entertain of the superior dignity of that character all along. He thought that the falsifying of weights and measures was a more mechanical employment than the forging of lies; and that it was less gentleman-like to rob men of their money than of their good name. But this is a little peculiarity which belongs to the little vanity which inspires an author. I trust therefore, when I speak of lord chief justice Holt, and of the time in which he lived, I speak (for all, but particularly for this) of as great an authority as ever sat in judgement upon any case whatever. His name was held high during his life, and has been held in reverence in all subsequent times. He deserved popularity, by doing that which was right upon great, trying, and important occasions. He obtained popularity, because he despised all other means of aiming at it, but that of doing right upon all occasions. From the temper of those times, from the vehemence and designs of that faction that opposed him, sir John Holt would have been reviled; if the revilers of that day had not observed in the greatness of his character, that it was impossible to reach him; and he has preserved a name which was highly honoured during his life, and which will live as long as the English constitution lives. Citing him, therefore, in support of this as a proper punishment to be inflicted upon this sort of offence, is giving, in my apprehension, the greatest authority for it." The plea of the Attorney-General failed and Horne was sentenced to fine and imprisonment and not to be put in the pillory.

In 1792, Patrick William Duffin and Thomas Lloyd were tried for a seditious libel. The information filed *ex officio* by the Attorney-General, stated that the two men were wicked, seditious, and ill-disposed persons, and greatly disaffected to the King and the government and constitution of this kingdom; and with force and arms did unlawfully and wickedly conspire, combine, confederate, and agree together to escape and go at large out of the Fleet prison; and to excite and stir up divers other prisoners to break open the said prison, and also to escape and go at large out of the said prison . . . afterward did unlawfully and wickedly, fix and put up . . . on the door of the chapel of the said prison . . . an infamous, seditious, and wicked libel . . . viz, This house (meaning the said prison) to let, peaceable possession will be given by the present tenants on or before the first day of January, 1793, being the first year of liberty in Great Britain.

They were convicted of the crime of seditious libel. The following appears in the Annual Register for 1793. "Lloyd, the attorney, who advertised the Fleet prison to let 'in the first year of English liberty' enjoyed an hour of notoriety on the pillory opposite the Royal Exchange. During the first quarter of an hour the engine was so loosely laced, that he simply looked through it at his comparative ease; an alteration was however made by order of the sheriff, that it should be shut close. The concourse of people was very great; but by the assistance of about two hundred constables, good order was preserved during the whole time." About twenty years later an Act (56 Geo. III, c. 138) was passed to abolish the punishment of the pillory except in certain cases (perjury and allied offences).

One of the most noted offenders who was put in the stocks was Perkin Warbeck. In 1497 he was sentenced to sit a whole day in the stocks at Westminster Hall, and the next at Cheapside, and on both occasions he had to read to the assembled mob a confession of his crime.   For further offences later he was hanged.

In 1528, a man named Dalaber, one of the early protestants, was questioned as to his knowledge of the whereabouts of another protestant for whom the authorities were searching. "At last when they could get nothing out of me whereby to accuse or hurt any man, or to know anything of that which they sought, they all three together brought me up long stairs, into a great chamber, over Master Commissary's chamber, wherein stood a great pair of very high stocks. Then Master Commissary asked me for my purse and girdle, and took away my money and my knives; and then they put my legs into the stocks, and so locked me fast in them, in which I sat, my feet being almost as high as my head; and so they departed, locking fast the door, and leaving me alone."

In 1530, in the reign of Henry VIII, an Act was passed dealing with vagrants. "The justice of the peace, high constable, or other officer, shall cause such idle person so to him brought, to be had to the next market town or other place, and there to be tied to the end of a cart, naked, and to be beaten with whips throughout the same town till his body be bloody by reason of such whipping." If caught begging once, then, he was whipped at the cart's tail: if caught a second time, his ear was slit or bored through with a hot iron: if caught a third time, thus proved to be a useless encumbrance, he was executed as a felon. And this for begging only.

Whipping was a frequent punishment at one time, for many crimes, e.g., stealing, drunkenness, rioting, and obtaining goods by false pretences. It was used for men and women. In 1791 an Act was passed forbidding its use on women, and for men it is now allowed only in cases of robbery with violence, and the prison medical officer must certify that the prisoner is physically fit to undergo the flogging. Boys can be ordered the birch or a whipping, but this is merely more or less of a domestic affair and entails no cruelty.

The floggings administered were of a very brutal nature. Men were whipped through the streets sometimes for two hundred yards, sometimes only in the market place, or at the gate of a town, sometimes even in private. The rule though was that men were flogged in public, women in private. When flogging in the army was legal, the punishment was often of a particularly brutal nature, men receiving hundreds of lashes until they were taken down from the triangle actually unconscious.

Cases in which flogging led to the death of the offender are recorded. In 1621, as Gondomar, the Spanish Ambassador in the time of James I, who was exceedingly unpopular with the people, was passing down Fenchurch Street in his litter, an impudent apprentice shouted after him, "There goes the devil in a dungcart." One of the servants of the ambassador turned to him, and said, "Sir, you shall see the Bridewell, ere long for your mirth". The apprentice promptly knocked the man down. The Lord Mayor was appealed to for punishment of the apprentice. Sorely against his will, the Lord Mayor, knowing the awe in which Gondomar was held by the feeble King, sentenced the boy to be whipped through the streets. That an Englishman should be flogged for insulting a Spaniard was intolerable to the London populace, whatever it might be to James. A crowd gathered, rioting occurred, and Gondomar once more complained to the Lord Mayor. He was told that the City could manage its own affairs, without any interference from him. The King was appealed to by Gondomar, and James at once went down in person to the Guildhall.

If such things were allowed, he said, he would put a garrison in the City and cancel its charter. The sentence was carried out and the boy died under the lash.

Judge Parry relates, in his delightfully humorous style, an account of one of the last cases in which sentence of ducking was passed though there is an instance recorded of its use one hundred years later. A Mrs. Foxley was indicted at Maidstone Quarter Sessions in 1702, in the reign of Queen Anne, for being a "common scold". She was found guilty and ordered to be ducked. Mrs. Foxley strongly objected and instructed her solicitors to move in arrest of judgment. The point which her lawyer made was that the prosecution had called· her by the wrong Latin name for scold in the indictment. The motion was heard in Trinity term, and Chief Justice Holt arrested judgment till Michaelmas. She was released on bail and then applied to the Attorney-General to quash the indictment. This entailed many hearings before the Court when long discussions as to whether she should have been indicted as *communis*, or *rixatrix*, or *calumniatrix*. After one judge had expressed doubt as to the legality of cold ducking, the Court decided that a common scold must be ducked by English law as long as you called her by the right name in the indictment. As the wrong Latin term had been used the conviction was quashed and Mrs. Foxley was released. In those days indictments were long and cumberous and the law insisted on absolute accuracy of terms and phrases. Since then an Indictments Act has been passed, which greatly simplifies matters.

A cruel form of punishment which must be almost unique is told of a Jew of Bristol, who in the reign of King John was found guilty of an attempt to defraud the King. He was sentenced to pay a fine of 10,000 marks (about 6,500 pounds). He protested that he had not so much money and could not possibly pay. He was told that he would lose a tooth every day till his jaws were edentulous unless the money was paid. For seven days a tooth was drawn and then the Jew, unable to stand the pain any longer, settled the fine.

CHAPTER XXII

WITCHCRAFT AND CRUELTY

VERY great and terrible cruelty was used against those suspected of witchcraft, in which there was an almost universal belief in the sixteenth and seventeenth centuries. It had always been regarded as an ecclesiastical crime, but it was not till 1541, in the reign of Henry VIII, that it was made a statutory offence. (33 Hen. VIII, c. 8.) This Act was repealed by Edward VI, but was re-enacted with slight variations by Elizabeth (5 Elizabeth c. 16). In 1603 a new and much more severe and searching Act was passed (1 James I, c. 11). It was of such a nature that a conviction could be obtained with the utmost ease. The invocation or conjuration of any evil or wicked spirit was a felony. To entertain, employ, feed, or reward such a spirit, to exhume any dead body, or any part of it —skin or bone—for purposes of enchantment or sorcery, to practise any witchcraft by which anyone should be killed, destroyed, wasted, pined, or lamed, was also felony, for which the punishment was death. Some minor forms of incantation rendered the persons guilty of them subject to the pillory. The ease with which convictions could be obtained under this Act is illustrated by the following. Seventeen witches were condemned to death on the evidence of one witness who afterwards confessed his fraud. Fortunately the judge had mercifully saved their lives by failing to inflict the death penalty.

The belief in witchcraft dates back to very ancient days. There are references to it in the Bible—the Romans regarded it as a crime, though they did not punish it with the severity of modern days, one year's penance for mild cases, seven years for those who were reputed to have killed their victims. For 1,500 years the reality of witchcraft endured and it was only in the eighteenth century that the superstition disappeared. There were laws in all countries to punish it, it was accepted by the clergy, by lawyers and judges, by scientists and by the most learned in the land, in spite of all their knowledge and experience. Tens of thousands perished; the acutest tortures, agonised and protracted, were experienced by the victims, and this without the least compassion from those who inflicted it. Most of those who suffered were of the poorest and most ignorant class, with no means of defending themselves. The Church, especially the reformed ministers in Scotland, put all its heart into the persecutions. Papal Bulls were issued as early as 1484 by Pope Innocent VIII, followed by others in the sixteenth century. Luther, Baxter, Wesley, all deeply religious men with the kindest of hearts, accepted the belief with all its cruel consequences. Luther for example said, "I would have no compassion on the witches. I would burn them all".

The laws in England were terrible in their harshness, but even so they were not so awful as those of continental nations. The Act of Henry VIII ordained that for the first conviction, witches who had not destroyed others by invoking evil spirits or incantations, were to be put in the pillory or imprisoned. The more serious offenders were hanged. In addition, the witches were treated with abominable cruelty. They were pricked all over to find the "insensible spot" which was looked on as a proof of witchcraft, they were thrown into the water to see if they would sink or swim, they were kept awake night after night in the hope that they would be driven to confess, and other methods of torture were used on them. James I passed another and more severe Act, soon after his accession. This subjected witches to death for a first offence even though they inflicted no injury on their neighbours. This Act was passed at a time when Coke was Attorney-General, Bacon a member of Parliament, and twelve Bishops sat on the Commission to which it was referred! James I was a confirmed and whole-hearted believer in witchcraft. On his return from a visit to Denmark, when his crossing back home was a stormy and rough one, a Dr. Fain was accused of being the author of the storm. Under the most terrible torture, he confessed his guilt, though he immediately afterwards retracted his confession. The bones of his leg were broken into small pieces in the boot. This was not enough. The King himself suggested a new device. "His nailes upon all his fingers were riven and pulled off with an instrument called in Scottish, a turkas, which in England we call a payre of pincers, and under everie nayle there was thrust in two needels over, even up to the head." Notwithstanding all this, "so deeply had the devil entered into his heart, that hee utterly denied all that which he had before avouched". He was burnt alive.

Instead of improving, matters grew much worse in the time of Cromwell. Probably during the short period of the Commonwealth more alleged witches perished in England than in all the times before and after. A regular panic spread through the country. Matthew Hopkins, a professional witch finder, selected Suffolk as the seat of his special activities. Sixty witches were hung in a year in this county. Among those on whom his enmity fell was an Anglican clergyman, aged 80, who for half a century had been minister of his church without a suggestion of wrong doing. The poor old man was kept awake for several nights running, "till he was weary of his life, and was scarce sensible of what he said or did". He was thrown into the water, condemned and hanged.

In the eighteenth century the belief declined and this decline was a fairly rapid one. There suddenly arose a most sceptical population which could no longer tolerate the ridiculous superstition of witchcraft. In England, in 1736, in Ireland, not till 1821, the laws on the subject were repealed, without difficulty or agitation.

In America, in the seventeenth century, persecutions for witchcraft were frequent and punishments severe. The Pilgrim Fathers brought the superstition with them from England, and at the time when this country was in sight of the end of this credulity, it flourished with great vigour in the new colonies, especially Massachusetts. Torture and floggings were freely used, many were executed, and one old man of eighty was even pressed to death. The Pilgrim Fathers, driven out of England by religious intolerance, unfortunately had not learnt the virtue of tolerance, and treated those who differed from them in religion and allied matters more bitterly and harshly than they themselves had been treated in England.

No one was exempt from the possibility of accusation.

One of the most distinguished sufferers was the Duchess of Gloucester. Her husband was next in succession to the imbecile youth, Henry VI. The Duke's chief opponent was Cardinal Beaufort, Bishop of Winchester. He resolved to strike a blow at the Duke, and accused the Duchess of witchcraft. The prelates who were to conduct the examination sat at St. Stephen's Chapel, at Westminster. They included Cardinal Beaufort and many Bishops, and the King himself was present. The Duchess was brought to the chapel and accused of having consorted with the

Witch of Eye and other sorcerers in making a waxen image of the King and melting it before the fire. Incantations had taken place, and as the waxen image lost its form the King was to sink slowly into the grave. She was, as in all these accusations, found guilty. She was actually induced to confess. She was made to walk through a jeering crowd in the streets of London, and imprisoned in the Isle of Man for the rest of her life.

The tortures which the poor wretched victims were made to endure were terrible. They were inflicted for the most part on old, feeble and half doting women. If the witch was obstinate, the first method of getting her to confess was by "waking" her. An iron bridle or hoop was bound across her face with four prongs, which were thrust into her mouth. It was fastened behind to the wall with a chain, in such a manner that the victim was unable to lie down. In this position she was kept for several days, while men were constantly with her to prevent her closing her eyes for a moment. Long pins were thrust into her body to discover the insensitive spot, and as in Scotland a witch was supposed never to confess whilst she could drink, excessive thirst was added to her tortures. If these measures were not sufficient, there were the penny-winkis, the boots, and the caschielawis. These instruments have already been referred to in a previous chapter.

The last of these, the caschielawis, an iron frame for the leg, which was from time to time heated over a brazier, was used on one man of whose torture there is a record for forty eight hours; another victim was in the same terrible instrument for eleven days and nights, his legs smashed in the boots for fourteen days, and the whole of the skin of his body flayed off.

As a rule the witch was strangled before she was burnt, but this merciful provision was not always carried out.

The Earl of Mar tells how, with a piercing yell, some women once broke, half burnt, from the slow fire which was consuming them, struggled for a few moments with the force of despair against the spectators, but were soon thrown back into the flames.

In foreign countries matters were if possible worse. 7,000 were burnt at Treves, 600 by one Bishop at Bamberg, 900 in one year in the bishopric of Wurtzberg, 400 in a single execution at Toulouse. At Nancy, Judge Remy boasted that he had executed 800 victims in sixteen years. These are specimens selected more or less at random from the enormous list of victims who suffered at the hands of the law for witchcraft at various times and in various places.

The last conviction for witchcraft in England was that of Jane Wenham at Hertford in 1712 but the prisoner was pardoned. In 1736 the Statute of James I was repealed and the crime of witchcraft ceased to exist in the eyes of the law, but anyone who pretended to practise it could be proceeded against as an impostor.

In Scotland a woman was burnt alive at the stake in 1722 (some authorities put it at 1727 but this is almost certainly a mistake). The last in Europe was in Switzerland as late as 1782.

Yet among the ignorant, cases of killing of witches have happened much later. In 1751, a man named Osborne and his wife Ruth lived at Tring, in Hertfordshire. They were reputed among their neighbours to be warlock and witch. One of those who disliked them paid the criers of the towns and villages around to give notice that on Monday next a man and woman were to be publicly ducked at Tring for their crimes. The witch and her husband took refuge in the workhouse. A great crowd collected, walls were pulled down and the two poor creatures were dragged to Marlston Mere. Each of them was tied up in a sheet and thrown into the Mere. The ringleader of the riot, Colley, waded into the water and turned them over and over with a stick. The woman died and Colley was convicted of murder and hanged.

In 1807, a beggar was seized, tortured and then burnt alive for sorcery by the populace of Mayenne. In 1850, a man and woman named Souberie were tried at Tarbes for having caused the death of a woman Bedouret. They said they believed her to be a witch, and that a priest had told them she was the cause of the illness of the female prisoner. They took Bedouret to a room and held her down in burning straw. They then placed red hot irons across her mouth, soon after which she died in agony. The prisoners had the very highest character. They exulted in the deed and declared they had only followed the highest ecclesiastical authority. The jury recommended them to mercy. They were sentenced to be imprisoned four months, and to pay twenty-five francs a year to the husband of their victim!

In *The Times* for September 24th, 1863, there is an account of an old man mobbed to death as a wizard in Essex.

In Howell's State Trials there are recorded many cases of witchcraft which came before the courts, from all over the country. The three Devonshire witches, Temperance Lloyd, Mary Trembles, and Susanna Edwards who were tried in 1682 was remarkable in that the poor wretched victims actually confessed the truth of the accusations of witchcraft against them. There are numerous instances of this kind of occurrence in the story of witchcraft. The victims were driven by torture and cruelty into such a mental state that they acknowledge the truth of the charges, either to escape further pain, or because their minds had actually become deranged, and they really believed they had committed the offences with which they were charged.

The latter condition can be seen in this account of the confession of the Devonshire witches.

The Substance of the LAST WORDS and CONFESSIONS of Susanna Edwards, Temperance Lloyd, and Mary Trembles, at the time and place of their execution; as fully as could be taken in a case liable to so much noise and confusion, as is usual on such occasions.

Mr. H.: Mary Trembles, what have you to say as to the crime you are now to die for?

Mary: I have spoken as much as I can speak already, and can speak no more.

H.: In what shape did the Devil come to you?

Mary: The Devil came to me once, I think, like a lion.

H.: Did he offer any violence to you?

Mary: No, not at all, but did frighten me, and did nothing to me; and I cried to God, and asked what he would have, and he vanished.

H.: Did he give thee any gift, or didst thou make him any promise?

Mary: No.

H.: Had he any of thy blood?

Mary: No.

H.: Did he come to make use of thy body in a carnal manner?

Mary: Never in my life.

H.: Have you a teat in your privy parts?

Mary: None. The Grand Inquest said it was sworn to them.

H.: Mary Trembles, was the Devil there with Susan when I was once in the prison with you, and under her coats? the other told me he was there, but is now fled; and that the Devil was in the way when I was going to Taunton with my son who is a minister. Thou speakest now as a dying woman, and as the Psalmist says, I will confess my iniquities and acknowledge all my sin. We find that Mary Magdalen had seven devils, but she came to Christ and obtained mercy: and if thou break thy league with the Devil, and make a covenant with God, thou mayest also obtain mercy. If thou hast anything to speak, speak thy mind.

Mary: I have spoke the very truth, and can speak no more. I would desire thay may come by me, and confess as I have done.

H.: Temperance Lloyd, have you made any contract with the Devil?

Temp.: No.

H.: Did he ever take any of thy blood?

Temp.: No.

H.: How did he appear to thee first or where in the street? in what shape?

Temp.: In woeful shape.

H.: Had he ever any carnal knowledge of thee?

Temp.: No, never.

H.: What did he do when he came to thee?

Temp.: He caused me to go and do harm.

H.: And did you go?

Temp.: I did hurt a woman sore against my conscience: he carried me up to her door, which was open; the woman's name was Mrs. Grace Thomas.

H.: What caused you to do her harm? what malice had you against her? did she do you any harm?

Temp.: No, she never did me any harm; but the Devil beat me about the head grievously because I would not kill her; but I did bruise her after this fashion (laying her two hands to her side).

H.: Did you bruise her till the blood came out of her mouth and nose?

Temp.: No.

H.: How many did you destroy and hurt?

Temp.: None but she.

H.: Did you know any mariners that you or your associates destroyed by overturning of ships and boats?

Temp.: No; I never hurt any ship, bark, or boat in my life.

H.: Was it you or Susan that did bewitch the children?

Temp.: I sold apples, and the child took an apple from me, and the mother took the apple from the child; for the which I was very angry; but the child died of the small pox.

H.: Do you know one Mr. Lutteril about these parts, or any of your confederates? did you or them bewitch his child?

Temp.: No.

H.: Temperance, how did you come in to hurt Mrs. Grace Thomas? did you pass through the key-hole of the door, or was the door open?

Temp.: The Devil did lead me up stairs, and the door was open; and this is all the hurt I did.

H.: How do you know it was the Devil?

Temp.: I knew it by his eyes.

H.: Had you no discourse or treaty with him?

Temp.: No; he said I should go along with him to destroy a woman, and I told him I would not; he said he would make me; and then the Devil beat me all about the head.

H.: Why had you not called upon God?

Temp.: He would not let me do it.

H.: You say you never hurted ships nor boats; did you never ride over an arm of the sea on a cow?

Temp.: No, no, master, it was she, meaning Susan.

When Temperance said it was Susan, she said she lied, and that she was the cause of her hanging to die; for she said when she was first brought to gaol, if that she was hanged, she would have me hanged too; she reported I should ride on a cow before her, which I never did.

H.: Susan, did you see the shape of a bullock? at the first time of your examination you said it was like a short black man, about the length of your arm.

Sus.: He was black, sir.

H.: Susan, had you any knowledge of the bewitching of Mr. Lutteril's child, or did you know a place called Tranton Burroughs?

Sus.: No.

H.: Are you willing to have any prayers?

Then Mr. H. prayed, whose prayer we could not take; and they sung part of the 40th Psalm, at the desire of Susanna Edwards; as she mounted the ladder, she said, the Lord Jesus speed me; though my sins be as red as scarlet, the Lord Jesus can make them as white as snow; the Lord help my soul. Then was executed.

Mary Trembles said, Lord Jesus receive my soul; Lord Jesus speed me; and then was also executed.

Temperance Lloyd said, Jesus Christ speed me well: Lord forgive all my sins; Lord Jesus Christ be merciful to my poor soul.

Mr. Sheriff: You are looked on as the woman who has debauched the other two: did you ever lie with the Devil.

Temp.: No.

Sh.: Did you not know of their coming to gaol?

Temp.: No.

Sh.: Have you anything to say to satisfy the world?

Temp.: I forgive them, as I desire the Lord Jesus Christ will forgive me. The greatest thing I did was to Mrs. Grace Thomas; and I desire I may be sensible of it, and that the Lord Jesus Christ may forgive me. The Devil met me in the street, and bid me kill her; and because I would not, he beat me about the head and back.

Sh.: In what shape or colour was he?

Temp.: In black, like a bullock.

Sh. : How do you know you did it? how went you in, through the key-hole or the door?

Temp. : At the door.

Sh. : Had you no discourse with the Devil?

Temp. : Never but this day six weeks.

Sh. : You were charged about twelve years since, and did you never see the Devil but this time?

Temp. : Yes, once before; I was going for brooms, and he came to me and said, this poor woman has a great burthen; and would help ease me of my burthen: and I said, the Lord had enabled me to carry it so far, and I hope I shall be able to carry it further.

Sh. : Did the Devil never promise you anything?

Temp. : No, never.

Sh. : Then you have served a very bad master, who gave you nothing. Well, consider you are just departing this world: do you believe there is a God?

Temp. : Yes.

Sh. : Do you believe in Jesus Christ?

Temp. : Yes; and I pray Jesus Christ to pardon all my sins. And so was executed.

It is difficult to believe that the above took place as part of the judicial proceedings in this trial.

A case in which a witch finder was himself convicted in 1703 is a welcome sign that the end of the legal recognition of witches was within sight. Richard Hathaway was tried at the Surrey Assizes as a cheat and imposter. He claimed that he had been bewitched by a woman, Sarah Morduck, and that as a result of this, he had been for ten weeks at a time unable to eat, he had vomited pins, and had become dumb and blind, and the only relief he got was when he scratched the witch. Morduck was in continual danger of her life. She was mobbed wherever she went. She obtained a warrant for the arrest of Hathaway, who was brought before Sir Thomas Lane, himself a firm believer in witches. He directed that Hathaway should again scratch her. This he did and was of course at once relieved of his symptoms. He recovered his appetite and ate greedily of bread and cheese. Lane was quite satisfied. But at the trial at the Assizes the jury had the good sense to convict him. Unfortunately the record of the case does not say what was the punishment meeted out to this impostor.

CHAPTER XXIII

THE CHURCH AND CRUELTY

In Tudor times political and religious matters became so intimately connected that it was difficult to separate them. It is not my intention to enter into this vexed question. Each side, Protestant and Catholic, claims that the host of executions which they carried out were for treason, and were demanded in the interests of the safety of the country. Burnings in the name of religion, for daring to hold opinions which did not happen to be in agreement with the views of the government of the day, were frequent and many. The maxim "Cujus regio, ejus religio" (he who rules the country may settle the religion) was definitely accepted.

Whether it were the Catholics under Mary, or the Protestants under Elizabeth, executing their opponents of the opposite religion, whether in the name of heresy, and the use of the stake and faggot, or in the name of treason, and the use of the rope and gibbet, there seems to be little to choose between the two. I do not propose to touch on the religious aspect, I merely mention that Mary in her five years burnt some 300 victims, Elizabeth in her forty-five years executed many hundreds, the number being impossible to exactly estimate.

These religious persecutions were even worse abroad. As an example, in France in 1546, under Francis I, some 4,000 poor wretched human beings, old men, women and children, were hunted from the glens of Languedoc and the valley of the Loire, and put to death.

The church adopted the Roman law with all its cruelties, except that it was heresy instead of treason which was the crime specially aimed at. But until the time of the inquisition, the use of torture by the church was of a fairly mild nature. But when this was in full sway, the cruelty was appalling. How it was possible for Torquemada whose terrible atrocities even now make the world shudder, to carry out these bloodthirsty and brutal tortures in the name of religion is difficult for the ordinary mind to understand.

Froude expresses this attitude of religion and the Church in his usual delightful diction.

"In secular convulsions the natural distress at the sight of human suffering is seldom entirely extinguished. In the great spiritual struggle of the sixteenth century, religion made humanity a crime, and the most horrible atrocities were sanctified by the belief that they were approved by Heaven. The fathers of the church at Trent had enjoined the extirpation of heresy, and the evil army of priests thundered the accursed message from every pulpit which they were allowed to enter, or breathed it with yet more fatal potency in the confessional. Nor were the other side slow in learning the lesson of hatred. The Lutheran and the Anglican, hovering between the two extremes, might attempt forbearance, but as the persecuting spirit grew among the Catholic, European Protestantism assumed a stronger and a sterner type. The Catholic on the authority of the Church made war upon *spiritual* rebellion. The Protestant believed himself commissioned like the Israelites to extinguish the worshipper of images. 'No mercy to the heretics' was the watchword of the

Inquisition; 'the idolaters shall die' was the answering thunder of the disciple of Calvin; and as the death-wrestle spread from land to land, each party strove to outbid the other for Heaven's favour by the ruthlessness with which they carried out its imagined behests."

The Inquisition, which was the very worst example of the intolerance and cruelty of the Church, was established in 1480, for the detection and suppression of heresy. It started its activities in Seville and during its first year over 2,000 victims were roasted alive in that neighbour-hood. Shortly after its foundation a Dominican father, Thomas of Torquemada, became its head and the cruelties for which he was responsible are beyond imagination.

The method of procedure of the "Holy Office" was terrifying and unfair to the accused from its very com-mencement. When a suspected person was first denounced to the Inquisition a preliminary enquiry was opened and its results given to the court. If, as was almost invariably the case, it was thought proper to proceed, further enquiries were made and the results put before "the qualifiers of the Holy Office". When they were satisfied of the guilt of the accused party (and it required very little to bring them to this frame of mind) he was at once taken to the secret prison of the "Office", and here he was allowed no communication with his friends and advisers. He was entirely isolated from the world. Next there followed "first audiences". The officials did all in their power to get a confession, so that the accused might be ranked as a penitent and trust to the "mercy" of the Inquisitors. If he refused to acknowledge his guilt, he was tortured to extract a confession. The most awful forms of cruelty were employed and authentic writers declare that "none of the descriptions of them can be accused of exaggera-tion". After the torture was over, the accused was brought before the court again, and then for the first time, he was told of what he was accused. Finally in the great majority of examples the prisoner was found guilty and sentence pronounced. He was ordered to be burnt alive at the *auto-da-fe*, dressed in a sanbenito, or condemned man's robe. This was carried out by the secular authority, for of course the Church could shed no blood.

The Inquisition, though Spain was the chief centre of its activities, spread to the Netherlands, Portugal, France, and Italy. It was finally abolished early in the nineteenth century, after being responsible for over 30,000 executions, mostly by burning, and untold thousands of cases of horrible cruelties. The last victims were in 1826, when a Jew was burnt, and a Quaker schoolmaster hanged in Spain.

Among the methods of torture employed was that of gradually pouring water drop by drop on a particular spot of the body, *the tormento de toca*, or pouring water into a gauze bag in the throat, which gradually forced the gauze into the stomach, and the *pendola*, or swinging pendulum, so graphically described in one of the stories of Edgar Poe.

Even after death the Inquisitors could not let their victims rest in peace. A man, De Dominis, who held "heretical opinions" went from England to Rome, where he was handed over by the Pope to the Inquisition. He was imprisoned and died. After his death, his body was burnt as a punishment. This same outrage was perpetrated on the bodies of immense numbers of other victims of the vengeance of the Inquisition.

In the early part of the reign of Mary before the fires of Smithfield had really started on their wholesale slaughter, an attempt was made to pass an Act of Parliament preventing the putting to death of persons for their religious opinions. The bill did not pass, but the peers, anxious to relieve the mind of the Queen and to assure her that her victims would not escape, told her that even if there were an Act of Parliament forbidding the burning of heretics, the common law existed independent of Statute and the common law allowed the burning of a heretic. This may have been of comfort to a bloodthirsty mind like that of Mary, but it was bad law.

In May, 1550, that is after the Statute for the punishment of heresy by death had been repealed, Joan Bocher, a Kentish woman, who had remained in prison where she had been put by Somerset's heresy commission, was sent to the stake. The judges actually allowed the traditions of common law, which for generations had regarded the burning of a heretic as the right and proper custom, to override Statute law, whereas all legal authorities are agreed that Common Law which has been defined as "a general immemorial usage not inconsistent with any Statute, especially if it be the result of evident necessity, and withal tendeth to the public safety", is superseded and over-ridden by Statute Law.

The execution of John Hooper, Bishop of Gloucester, is typical of the many hundreds who were burnt in the reign of Queen Mary. "When he came to the place where he should die, he smilingly beheld the stake, which was near to the great elm-tree over against the college of priests, where he had been wont to preach. The place round about the house, and the boughs of the trees, were filled with spectators; and in the chamber over the gate stood the priests of the college. Then he kneeled down. . . . While at his prayer a box was brought and laid before him upon a stool, with his pardon from the Queen if he would recant. At the sight of this he cried, "If you love my soul, away with it". The box being taken away, the lord Chandos said, "Seeing there is no remedy, dispatch him quickly". Hooper replied, "Good, my lord; I trust your lordship will give me leave to make an end of my prayers".

When he had risen from his last devotions in this world, he prepared himself for the stake, and put off his host's gown, and delivered it to the sheriffs, requiring them to see it restored unto the owner, and put off the rest of his apparel, unto his doublet and hose, wherein he would have burned. But the sheriffs would not permit that, unto whose pleasure he very obediently submitted himself, and his doublet, hose, and waistcoat were taken off. Thus being in his shirt, he took a point from his hose himself, and trussed his shirt between his legs, where he had a pound of gunpowder in a bladder, and under each arm the like quantity delivered him by the guard.

So desiring the people to say the Lord's Prayer with him, and to pray for him, he went up to the stake; when he was at it, three irons made to bind him thereto were brought—one for his neck, another for his middle, and the third for his legs. But he refusing them, said, "You need not thus to trouble yourselves. I doubt my God will give me strength sufficient to abide the extremity of the fire without bands; notwithstanding, suspecting the frailty and weakness of the flesh, but having assured confidence in God's strength, I am content to do as you shall think good."

Then the hoop of iron prepared for his middle was brought, which being somewhat too short, he shrank and pressed in his body with his hand, until it fastened; but when they offered to have bound his neck and legs with the other hoops, he refused them saying, "I am well assured I shall not trouble you". Being now ready, he looked around on all the people, of whom he might well be seen, for he was both tall, and stood also upon a high stool, and beheld that in every corner there was nothing to be seen but weeping and sorrowful people. Then lifting up his hands and eyes to heaven, he prayed in silence. By and by, he that was appointed to make the

fire came to him and asked his forgiveness. . . . Command
was now given that the fire should be kindled. But because
there were not fewer green faggots than two horses could
carry, it did not kindle speedily, but was some time before
it took the reeds upon the faggots. At length it burnt
about him; but the wind having full strength in that
place, it blew the flame from him, so that he was in a
manner little more than touched by the fire. Endeavours
were then made to increase the flame, and then the bladders
of gunpowder exploded, but did him little good, being
so laced, and the wind having such power. In this fire
he prayed with a loud voice. "Lord Jesus, have mercy
upon me! Lord Jesus, have mercy upon me! Lord
Jesus, receive my spirit!" And these were the last words
he was heard to utter. Yet he struck his breast with his
hands, until by the renewing of the fire his strength was
gone, and his hands stuck fast in striking the iron upon
his breast. So immediately, bowing forward, he yielded
up his spirit. Thus lingering were his last sufferings.
He was nearly three quarters of an hour or more in the
fire, as a lamb, patiently bearing the extremity thereof,
neither moving forwards, backwards, nor to any side;
but he died as quietly as a child in his bed.

Latimer and Ridley when sent to the stake, had bags
of gunpowder round their necks. This was for the purpose
of lessening the sufferings of prisoners and of hastening
their death. It was quite frequently used when the executioner was merciful or could be bribed. Latimer died
at once, Ridley, who was almost covered with faggots,
by his brother-in-law died more slowly for unfortunately
the heaping up of the wood checked the progress of the
flames. His legs were consumed before the vital parts
were touched. The bystanders opened out the pile and
then fortunately the gunpowder exploded and put an
end to his sufferings.

In 1532, during the ministry of Wolsey, Thomas Bilney, one of the reformers who preached against the practices of the clergy, was sentenced to be burnt. At his execution, the officers put the reeds and faggots about his body and set fire to the first. This made great flames which disfigured his face: he held up his hands and struck his breast crying, "Jesus", and "Credo", but the flames were blown away from him several times, the wind being very high, till at length the wood took fire, the flames became stronger and life became extinct. As his body shrunk up, it leaned on the chain, till one of the officers struck out the staple with his halberd when the body fell down and was consumed by the fire.

Roger Clarke is another example. When the fire was lighted the wood would not burn for it was green; his sufferings were dreadful as he was choked by the smoke. In addition he was put in a pitch barrel, which burnt and added to his agony. One of the bystanders in pity struck the ring about his neck, and then with blows on the head forced the poor writhing body into the flames where it was soon consumed.

The wonderful endurance and courage of a woman burnt alive is illustrated by the execution of Mrs. Joyce Lewes. "When she was tied to the stake with the chain, she showed such a cheerfulness that it passed man's reason, being so well coloured in her face, and being so patient, that the most part of them that had honest hearts did lament and even with tears bewail the tyranny of the papists. When the fire was set upon her, she neither struggled nor stirred, but only lifted up her hands towards heaven, being dead very speedily; for the under-sheriff, at the request of her friends, had provided such stuff by the which she was suddenly despatched out of this miserable world."

The following example of wholesale executions for

unorthodox religious beliefs is from Stow's Chronicle. "The five and twentieth day of May were, in St. Paul's church, London, examined nineteen men and six women, born in Holland whose opinions were (here follows a list of their unorthodox views). Fourteen of them were condemned; a man and a woman were burnt at Smithfield. The remaining twelve were scattered among other towns, there to be burnt."

The trial and execution of John Fisher, Bishop of Rochester, and of Sir Thomas More in 1535, are instances of men of the very highest standing and intellect whose lives were taken for their religious opinions. The proceedings of the trial of the former are thus shortly given in the official record. "Thursday after the feast of St. Barnabas, John Fisher was brought to the bar by Sir William Kingston, Constable of the Tower. Pleads not guilty. Venure awarded. Verdict—guilty. Judgement as usual in cases of treason."

He was allowed five days before death. He was over eighty years old. When the day of execution arrived he insisted on dressing himself very carefully as if for some important function. He was able to walk the short distance to Tower Hill, though with difficulty on account of his feeble old age. On the scaffold he chanted the *Te Deum* and then after a brief interval of prayer he laid his head on the block, and the axe descended and he was no more. Thus ended one of the saddest of the many sad spectacles which have been witnessed on this tragic spot.

The execution of Sir Thomas More followed. He was accused of the same offence as Fisher. The High Commission sat at Westminster to try the most illustrious prisoner who had ever appeared before them. He was as in practically the case of every accused person at this time before this Court, convicted and sentenced to death. On the morning of his execution, "about nine of the clock he was brought by the Lieutenant out of the Tower, his beard being long, which fashion he had never before used, his face pale and lean, carrying in his hands a red cross, casting his eyes often towards heaven ". The scaffold was not very firm and shook as he ascended. "See me safe up. For my coming down I can shift for myself." The executioner begged his forgiveness. More kissed him. "Thou art to do me the greatest benefit that I can receive. Pluck up thy spirit, man, and be not afraid to do thine office. My neck is very short. Take heed therefore that thou strike not awry for saving of thine honesty." The executioner offered to tie his eyes. "I will cover them myself," he said; and binding them with a cloth which he had brought with him, he knelt and laid his head upon the block. The executioner was about to strike the fatal blow, when he asked for a short delay. He moved aside his beard. "Pity that thou should be cut," he mused, "that has not committed treason." With these last words, he passed from this world.

In the time of Henry VIII, in 1537, The Pilgrimage of Grace, a rising of the people, half political, half religious, took place, and after its suppression large numbers of those concerned were arrested. Among them were the Abbot of Barlings, one of his monks, and ten others who were alleged to have been concerned in the murder of the chancellor. They were hung on gibbets in various parts of the country as a warning to others. Many more also suffered death. Darcy, who begged that all his body might be buried together (a request which was actually granted), Lady Bulmer, who was burnt alive as she was a woman, and many others, rich and poor were executed, one of the many examples of wholesale slaughter which occurred in this reign, during which no less than 72,000 people suffered death as a punishment for their various crimes real or imaginary.

Forest, the late Prior of the Observants' Convent at Greenwich, denied the King's supremacy, and this was, according to the law of the Church in 1538, heresy. He was naturally condemned to death. Latimer was selected to preach on the occasion of the execution. The preparations were made with horrible completeness. A gallows was erected over the stake, from which the poor victim was suspended in chains. When all was ready Forest was brought out to listen to the sermon of Latimer. When he had finished, Latimer turned to the convicted man and asked him whether he wished to live or die. "I will die. Do your worst upon me. Seven years ago you durst not, for your life, have preached such words as these; and now, if an angel from heaven should come down and teach me any other doctrine than that which I learnt as a child, I would not believe him. Take me; cut me to pieces, joint from joint. Burn, hang, do what you will, I will be true henceforth to my faith." He was put in the cage, slung into the air, and the fire lighted, and all was soon over. Latimer himself was later burnt alive.

In Scotland early in the sixteenth century, Archbishop Beaton, determined to extirpate heresy, rumours of which reached his ears. Patrick Hamilton, nephew of the Earl of Arran was one of the first to suffer. He was arrested and convicted of Lutheranism, and brought out to be burnt in front of the old college of St. Andrews. He gave his servant his gown, coat, and bonnet. "They will not profit in the fire. They will profit thee; I have no more to give now but the example of my death. Think well on that. It seems to be dreadful; but it is the gate of eternal life." A fisherman named David Straiton was called on to pay tithe of all he caught. If the priests would rob him, he said, they might come and fetch their tithe from whence he got it. Every tenth fish he flung back into the sea. He was excommunicated for disrespect, and afterwards burnt alive. Forret, the Vicar of Dolor, another victim, was tied to the stake awaiting the kindling of the fire. "Will ye say as we say," asked the abbot of him, "and keep your mind to yourself and save yourself?" "I thank your lordship," he answered, "you are a friend to my body but not to my soul. Before I deny a word which I have spoken, you shall see this body of mine blow away with the wind in ashes." To give him a last chance of recanting they burnt another victim in front of his face but Forret held out to the last and perished in the flames.

George Wishart, a Cambridge University man, with a high reputation began to preach in Scotland in 1545. He became very popular. Cardinal Beaton, who looked upon him as a troublesome heretic, commissioned a priest to stab him. This was quite the correct thing for a prelate to order in these times. The plot failed, but his enemies had him arrested and conveyed to the fatal Sea Tower of St. Andrews. He was tried and his heresy easily proved. But the very holy men who had attempted to stab him, though they could and did convict him, did not sentence him to death. They washed their hands of him and handed him over to the secular power. The lay people, more fair and merciful than the Church, hesitated to burn him. The Cardinal in accordance with his usual disgraceful conduct, procured his further trial by a court of his own. A stake and gallows were erected under the windows of the Castle, where the two Archbishops were to sit in state to hear the case. As an attempt to rescue was anticipated, the Castle was strongly guarded. "After this, Mr. Wishart was led to the fire, with a rope about his neck, and a chain of iron about his middle; and when that he came to the fire, he sat down upon his knees and rose up again, and thrice he said these words: 'Oh, thou Saviour of the world, have mercy on me. Father of Heaven, I commend my spirit into thy holy hands.' He then spoke a few words to the people and then last of all to the hangman that was to be his tormentor, sat upon his knees and said, 'Sir I pray you forgive me, for I am not guilty of your death'; to whom he answered, 'Come hither to me'; and he kissed his cheek and said, 'Lo, here is a token that I forgive thee. Do thy office'. And then he was put on a gibbet and hanged, and then burnt to powder."

Cardinal Beaton did not live long after this last brutal act. The avengers of Wishart tracked him to his Palace at St. Andrews and Beaton, finding they had obtained admittance, fled to his room and barricaded himself in. They were not long in finding him. The tramp of steps sounded along the gallery. He was ordered to open the door. "Who calls?" he cried. When he found as he expected that vengeance had caught him, he cried out to know if his life could be spared. The door was burnt down, armed men rushed through the smoke, and found their trembling victim standing before them. "I am a priest! I am a priest! ye will not slay me," he called. He was stabbed to death by his pursuers. The alarm bell rang, and the provost and townspeople clamoured to bring out the Cardinal. "Incontinent, they brought out the Cardinal to the wall dead in a pair of sheets and hung him over the wall by the tane arm and the tane foot, and bade the people see their god." A fitting end to such a man. The multitude departed, without any regret for the deed. "Because the weather was hot," says Knox, "and his funeral could not be suddenly prepared, it was thought best to bestow enough of great salt upon him, a coffin of lead, and a corner in the bottom of the Sea Tower, to await what exequies his bretheren the bishops would bestow upon him."

The last heretic burnt in England was in the reign of James I, in 1612, and in Scotland in 1697, but for a very long period after this women were burnt alive for high or petty treason. This was not so rare an event as might be thought. Rarely did a year pass without the murder of a husband by a wife or of a master by his female servant and both these crimes were petty treason. As late as 1782, Rebecca Downing was burnt alive for poisoning her master, and in 1789, a woman was burnt for coining at Newcastle. This was the last execution by this method in our country.

CHAPTER XXIV

THE TRIAL AND TORTURE OF DR. SPREULL

THIS case was one of those which occurred during the persecution of the Presbyterians in Scotland during the reign of Charles II, after the battle of Bothwell Brig. At this time Scotland was governed from Edinburgh by her own Privy Council, which was for all practical purposes under no control from the Scottish Parliament. The Council was notorious for its constant resort to torture, which as we have seen, was abolished in England some forty years previously.

The attempt to force the Presbyterian Clergy to conform to certain religious tests gave rise to the resistance of the Covenanters. The Pentland Rising of 1666 was followed twelve years later by the more serious rebellion which began with the murder of Archbishop Sharp, continued with the defeat of Claverhouse by the Covenanters at Drumclog Moss, and terminated with their destruction at Bothwell Brig in 1679.

In 1681, John Spreull and Robert Ferguson were indicted at Edinburgh for treason and rebellion. The accusation was: "That the saids John Spreull and Robert Ferguson, having shaken off all fear of God, respect and regard to his majesties authoritie and lawes, had presumed to committ and is guilty of . . . having most cruellie kiled and murdered his grace the late archbishop of St. Andrews, they to escape justice and involve others in their guilt, fled into the westerne shyres and there joined in armes . . . their accomplices, under the command of Robert Hamilton, brother to the laird of ,Prestoun; who to the number of three-score and upwards, went to the burgh of Rutherglen and that upon the twenty-ninth day of May, 1679, after reading acts of their own coining, most treasoniblie and wickedlie burnt several acts of parliament, asserting his majesties prerogatives and establishing the governmentt of the church, drowned out bone-fyres sett on in com-memoration of that day, and thereafter they and their accomplices did most treasoniblie waylay a small partie of his mejesties forces under the command of the laird of Claverhouse at Loudonhill, and did most cruellie murder and kill severall of them, and being assembled and convocat to the number of two or three thousand men at arms . . . did most treasonabley attack a small partie of his majesties forces . . . and still continuing in their rebellious armes they did swell and growe to the number of ten or twelve thousand, . . . did take boldness upon them to issue proclamations and print declarations bearing the treasonable grounds of their rebellion . . . proudly and insolently boasting of their treasonable armes, in which they and ther accomplices did most treasonible continue, until the twentie-second day of the said month of June, 1679, that his majesties forces did attacque and assault them at Bothwell-Bridge, wher by God's blessing on his majesties armes, ther numerous and rebellious army was dissipat, routed and vanquished."

Mr. Walter Pringle, one of the counsel for the defence at once raised the point that his client having been subjected to torture by order of the Scottish Privy Council, and having maintained his innocence whilst under torture, was entitled to release. The King's advocate argued that it would be a miscarriage of justice to release a man simply because he was obstinate under torture. The most he could claim in law was that he should not be tried on questions for which he was tortured, and that Spreull was indicted for other matters than those for which he had been subjected to the boots. His denial during torture could not acquit him, because those who had maltreated him had not been authorised to ask him those particular questions. After long and complicated legal arguments, the Judges ordered the trial to proceed.

Among the witnesses called for the prosecution were John Layng, surgeon, who said he met Spreull at Hamiltoun in June, in order to transact some business with him. This was eight days before the battle of Bothwell Brig. Layng was asked if any conversation concerning the rebellion or the rebels took place, to which he replied that nothing passed between them on the subject nor did he see Spreull in the company of any of the rebels.

David Caldwell deponed that he thought he saw John Spreull riding in arms near Hamiltoun on the Friday before the defeat of the rebels at Bothwell, but he would not go further than to say he thought the prisoner was the man.

James Hamiltoun said he saw Spreull riding through Hamiltoun by himself with a sword about him, four or five days before the battle but he was alone, no one speaking to him although Hamiltoun was full of rebels.

James Miller said he saw a man called John Spreull very like the prisoner riding a grey horse in June, 1679 on Hamiltoun Muir. He would not swear prisoner was the man.

John Spreull, a writer of Glasgow, said he was with about twenty or thirty rebels, when he met the prisoner John Spreull four or five days before Bothwell, on horseback. He himself used two horses at the time of the rebellion, one grey, one brown. He did not see him in the company of the rebels. He himself had a periwig of the colour of his own hair, the prisoner had no periwig at all.

George Peirs, of Glasgow, said he saw a man whom he was told was John Spreull riding in Hamiltoun on a bay horse, with a velvet cape. He was riding alone. He did not know if it was the prisoner or another man with the same name.

An alleged confession was put in but this was at once denied by counsel for the accused. The verdict of the jury was one of "not guilty". After the very feeble evidence adduced by the prosecution no other verdict seems to have been possible even in a prosecution by the Scottish Privy Council.

But so vindictive were the Government that the Lords of the Privy Council ordered him to be detained in prison in order that they might have him tried on further counts. He was brought before them and fined 9,000 marks for refusing to make any statement about his attendance at conventicles, and he was ordered to be sent to the Isle of Bass till he paid it. Here he remained in prison for six years when he was released by order of the Council after the receipt of a letter from the King.

A fuller account which deals more especially with the application of the torture to Spreull follows, written by a contemporary writer, and quoted in Vol. X of Howell's *State Trials*.

"On June 13th, 1681, John Spreull was tried at the Criminal Court at Edinburgh, and probation led against him, who deponed they saw one called John Spreull at Bothwell bridge, but they knew not if the pannel was he, there being another of that same name present in the court (who confessed his being at Bothwell bridge, and had taken the benefit of the indemnity), to whom all the tokens and descriptions they gave agreed more than to the pannel, as the colour of his horse, his having a cap and not a hat, a black peruke, etc. The assize, upon this, cleansed and assolized him; notwithstanding whereof the king's advocate procured an order, from the privy council, to detain him still in prison, till he got a new indictment, which was the 3d, to wit, for treasonable expressions uttered by him before the council, such as refusing to call Bothwell bridge a rebellion, or the assassinating and killing the archbishop a murder; which last is no treason, though it be a very perverse opinion.

"On the 14th June, the king's advocate having complained to the king's council that the witnesses led against Spreull had prevaricated and deponed falsely, at least did conceal their knowledge; it was moved by my lord Haddo and approven by the king's advocate, that witnesses in such a case might be tortured when they vary, as well as the parties. This is indeed agreeable to the R. law but does not suit the genius of our nation, which looks upon the torture of the boots as a barbarous remedy; and yet of late it hath been frequently used among us. I think, however, these witnesses deserve to be punished, yet the assizes should not look upon the testimonies of such witnesses as a full probation, not being spontaneous and voluntary, where they are either threatened with the boots, or tortured.

"After all this, on the 14th July, 1681, Spreull is brought before the privy council, and fined in 9,000 marks, for refusing to depone anent his presence at conventicles, the same being referred to his oath conform to the 2nd act of Parl. 1670; and he was ordained to be sent to the Bass till he paid it.

"I shall send this section with an account of the process against John Spreull, apothecary in Glasgow, who was before the Justiciary June this year, and give it at some length, both because it was after torture, and made no little noise; and I have distinct and attested accounts

of it, and he continued more than six years a close prisoner
after torture. This gentleman is still alive after all his
sore sufferings, and I know his modesty will not allow
me to give that character of him which he deserves, and
therefore I shall only relate his sufferings as they stand
in the public records, intermixing some other hints which
I have well vouched.

"Mr. Spreull's troubles began very soon after Pentland.
His father, John Spreull, merchant in Paisly, was fined
by Middleton, although he had suffered for his refusing
the tender: he paid the one half of his fine, and being
prosecuted for the other, or rather his refusing the declaration, he was forced, with many other worthy persons,
to abscond. When general Dalziel came, as we have
heard, to Kilmarnock 1667, a party of soldiers were sent
to Paisly and took Mr. Spreull, whose suffering I am
now relating prisoner, merely because he would not discover where his father was. At that time, after many
terrible threatenings of being shot to death, roasted at
a fire, and the like, and some short confinement, he was
dismissed.

"In the year 1677, he was, with Aikenhead and many
other gentlemen, cited before a court at Glasgow, of
which some account has been already given. Finding
that severity was designed against all that compeared,
Mr. Spreull absented, and was with several other worthy
persons denounced and intercommuned, though nothing
was laid to their charge but non-conformity.

"This obliged him to quit his house and shop, and
go abroad, sometimes to Holland, France, and Ireland,
and merchandize. He was in Ireland with his uncle,
Mr. James Alexander, in May, 1679, and came over to
Scotland after the scuffle at Drumclog in June, and went
to his house at Crawford's-dyke, where understanding
the conduct of the west country army, he had no freedom

to join them, though his own brother, James Spreull, and two cousins, John Spreull, writer, and John Spreull, merchant in Glasgow, were with them in arms. His business obliged him to be with some in that army, but he never joined them.

"After the defeat at Bothwell he absconded again, however his wife and family was turned out of his house and shop, and all the moveables secured. Within a little he retired to Holland, and stayed there some time, where hearing of the continued persecution in Scotland, and growing divisions among the sufferers, he came home 1680, with a design to bring his wife and family to Rotterdam.

"When lurking at Edinburgh, November 12th, a severe search was made for Mr. Cargil and his followers, and Mr. Spreull was apprehended by major Johnstoun when in his bed, and his goods he had brought from Holland seized by the party, though none of them were prohibited. He was carried first to the general, and then to the guard at the Abbay, where Mr. Skene and Archibald Stuart were prisoners; with whom he was carried up to the Tolbooth next day about nine of the clock, when the council was convened.

"By the council registers we have seen he was examined, November 13th, but his answers are not insert, and therefore I shall give the substance of what passed as far as Mr. Spreull remembers. He was interrogated, were you at the killing of the archbishop? *Ans.* I was in Ireland at that time.—*Quest.* Was it murder? *Ans.* I know not, but by hearsay, that he is dead, and cannot judge other men's actions upon hearsay. I am no judge, but in my discretive judgement I would not have done it, and cannot approve it.—He was again urged; but do you not think it was murder? *Ans.* Excuse me from going any further, I scruple to condemn what I cannot approve, seeing that there may be a righteous judgement of God, where there is a sinful hand of man, and I may admire and adore the one when I tremble at the other.—*Quest.* Were you at Drumclog? *Ans.* I was at Dublin then.— *Quest.* Did you know nothing of the rebels rising in arms when in design? *Ans.* No; the first time I heard of it was in coming from Dublin to Belfast on my way home, when I heard that Claverhouse was resisted by the country people at Drumclog.—*Quest.* Was not that rebellion? *Ans.* I think not; for I own the freedom of preaching the gospel, and I hear, what they did was only in self defence.—*Quest.* Were you at Bothwell with the rebels? *Ans.* After my return from Ireland I was at Hamiltoun seeking in money, and clearing counts with my customers, so I went through part of the west country army, and spoke with some there, since the king's high-way was as free to me as to other men; but I neither joined them as commander, trooper, nor soldier.—*Quest.* Was that rising rebellion? *Ans.* I will not call it rebellion. I think it was a providential necessity put on them for their own safety, after Drumclog. This confession of his he was urged to subscribe, but absolutely refused it. By the Registers, I find, 'Mr. Spreull before the council, November 15th, confesseth he was in company with Mr. Cargil in Edinburgh, but will not discover in what house,' and adds, 'That there was nothing 'twixt them but salutation'.

"Mr. Spreull having come from Ireland in the time of Bothwell, and having just now come from Holland, and owning he had been in company with Mr. Cargil, the managers were of opinion, that he could give them more information; and now being got into the inhumane way of putting people to the torture, and A. Sturat being examined this way, November 15th, that same day the council pass the following Act: 'The lords of his majesty's privy council having good reason to believe, that there is a principle of murdering his majesty, and those under him, for doing his majesty service, and a design of subverting the government of church and state, entertained and carried on by the fanatics, and particularly by Mr. Donald Cargil, Mr. Robert Macwaird, and others their complices, and that John Spreull and Robert Hamilton have been in accession thereunto, ordain them to be subject to the torture, upon such interrogatories as relate to questions regarding the rebellion'.

"I find no report in the council books, because nothing was expiscate by torture, which was not before acknowledged. Indeed there was nothing in this plot and murdering design, but imaginary fears, and therefore I shall, from other papers, give some account of this torture, the questions proposed, and answers given by Mr. Spreull, as far as his memory could serve him afterwards to write down.

"The lord Haltoun was preses of this committee, and the duke of York, and many others were present. The preses told Mr. Spreull, that if he would not make a more ample confession than he had done, and sign it, he behoved to underly the torture. Mr. Spreull said, he had been very ingenuous before the council, and would go no further; that they could not subject him to torture according to law; but if they would go on, he protested that his torture was without, yea, against all law; that what was extorted from him under the torture, against himself or any others, he would resile from it, and it ought not to militate against him or any others; and yet he declared his hopes, God would not leave him so far, as to accuse himself or others in the extremity of pain. Then the hangman put his foot in the instrument called the boot, and, at every query put to him, gave five strokes or thereby upon the wedges. The queries were, Whether he knew anything of a plot to blow up the Abbey and duke of York? who was in the plot, and where Mr. Cargil was, and if he would subscribe his confession before the council? To these he declared his absolute and utter ignorance, and adhered to his refusing to subscribe. When nothing could be expiscate by this, they ordered the old boot to be brought, alleging the new one used by the hangman was not so good as the old one, and accordingly it was brought, and he underwent the torture a second time, and adhered to what he had before said. General Dalziel complained at the second torture, that the hangman did not strike strongly enough upon the wedges: he said, he struck with all his strength, and offered the general the mall to do it himself. Mr. Spreull was very firm, and wonderfully supported, to his own feeling in body and spirit, during the torture. When it was over, he was carried to prison on a soldier's back, where he was refused the benefit of a surgeon; but the Lord blessed so the means he himself used, that in a little time he recovered pretty well. That same day his wife came to Edinburgh, but by no means could she be allowed access to him, to help him, after his torture. . . . And so Mr. Spreull was sent back again to prison. . . . Upon the 14th of July, I find Mr. Spreull and Wm. Lin, writer in Edinburgh, brought before the privy council, for being present at field conventicles; and they are found guilty of hearing Presbyterian ministers preach, when some of the hearers were without doors. . . . Mr. Spreull was out of the kingdom at the times libelled as to conventicles; and each of them is fined five hundred pounds sterling, and sent to the Bass. Mr. Spreull lay six years in the Bass, and, from his long continuation in that place, he has yet the compellation of Bass John Spreull, whereof he needs not be ashamed. . . . In May, 1687, an order is granted to liberate Mr. Spreull. Favours were now shown to the prisoners, and after near seven years imprisonment, Mr.

Spreull sent a Petition to the Council. On May 13th, the council granted the following act of liberation. 'The lords of his Majesty's privy council having considered an address made on behalf of John Spreull, apothecary in Glasgow, now prisoner in the Isle of the Bass, supplicating for liberty, in regard of his majesty's late gracious proclamation, do hereby give order and warrant to Charles Maitland, Lieutenant Governor of the Isle of the Bass, to set the said John Spreull at liberty, he having . . . to appear before the council once in June next, under the penalty of £1,000 Scots money, in case of failie.'

"When this Order comes to the Bass, Mr. Spreull was unwilling to take his liberty upon any terms that to him appeared inconsistent with the truth he was suffering for; and he apprehended this order involved him in an approbation of the proclamation specified, which he was far from approving. So much he signified to the governor of the Bass, and continuing sometime in prison, till a letter came over requiring the governor to set open doors to him, and tell him he was at liberty to go or stay as he pleased. Whereupon after so long imprisonment, he chose to come out under a protestation against what he took to be wrong in the orders and proclamation, and went over to Edinburgh, and waited on the councillors, thanked them for allowing him liberty, and verbally renewed his protest against the proclamation and orders. Thus ended the long tract of suffering this good man was under."

CHAPTER XXV

THE TRIAL OF THE SUFFOLK WITCHES

THE trial of the Suffolk Witches is one of the very many similar cases met with in the sixteenth and seventeenth centuries, when the highest and most learned in the land were steeped in superstition, and only too ready to accept evidence which to us seems simply ludicrous. The trial was held at Bury St. Edmond's, in Suffolk, in 1665, before Sir Matthew Hale, Lord Chief Baron of the Court of Exchequer. Rose Cullender and Amy Duny, widows, of Leystoff, were charged with bewitching Elizabeth and Ann Durent, Jane Bocking, Susan Chandler, William Durent, and Elizabeth and Deborah Pacy. The prisoners pleaded not guilty.

The following account is taken mainly from Howell's *State Trials*. "Three of the persons above named, viz., Anne Durent, Susan Chandler, and Elizabeth Pacy were brought to Bury to the Assizes, and were in a reasonable good condition; but that morning they came into the hall to give instructions for the drawing of their bills of indictment, the three persons fell into strange and violent fits, shrieking out in a most sad manner, so that they could not in any wise give any instructions in the court who were the cause of their distemper. And although they did after some certain space recover out of their fits, yet they were every one of them struck dumb, so that none of them could speak, neither at the time, nor during the Assizes, until the conviction of the supposed witches.

"Dorothy Durent was the mother of William Durent, an infant. She swore that on the 10th of March, 1669, she left her son William, who was then sucking, in charge of Amy Duny whilst she went away from home, giving her a penny for her trouble. She laid a great charge on Amy not to suckle the child, and on being asked why she did this, she explained that Amy had long gone under the reputation of a witch. Nevertheless, when she came back Amy told her that she had given the child suck; Whereupon the deponent was very angry with the said Amy for the same; at which the said Amy was much discontented, and used many high expressions and threatening speeches towards her; telling her, that she had as good to have done otherwise than to have found fault with her, and so departed out of her house; and that very night her son fell into strange fits of swooning and was held in such terrible manner, that she was much affrighted therewith, and so continued for divers weeks. And the said examinant further said that she being exceedingly troubled at her child's distemper, did go to a certain person named Dr. Jacob who lived at Yarmouth, who had the reputation in the country to help children that were bewitched, who advised her to hang up the child's blanket in the chimney-corner all day, and at night when she put the child to bed, to put it into the said blanket, and if she found anything in it, she should not be afraid, but throw it into the fire."

She carried out these directions and at night when she took the blanket down a great toad fell out which ran up and down the hearth. The toad was thrown into he fire. It made a horrible noise and suddenly exploded and was seen no more. The next day a relation of Amy Duny came and told the witness that the said Amy was in a bad condition having her face all scorched. She went to see her and found her with her face, legs, and thighs scorched and burnt. She asked her how she got burnt and Amy Duny replied that she had witness to thank for it and she would live to see some of her children dead and herself on crutches. After the burning of the toad, her child completely recovered. Later, her daughter Elizabeth, aged ten, was taken ill and she went to the chemist for something for it. When she came back she found Amy Duny at the house. She turned her out of doors. "You need not be so angry, for your child will not live long," said Amy. The child died two days later. She believed that the child died because she was bewitched. After the death of the child, witness was taken with a lameness in both legs and had had to use crutches ever since.

(This woman had used her crutches for three years. Directly the jury brought in their verdict, her lameness disappeared, and she was able to go home without them.)

"As concerning Elizabeth and Deborah Pacy, the first of the age of eleven years, the other of the age of nine years or thereabouts; as to the elder, she was brought into the court at the time of the instructions given to draw up the Indictments, and afterwards at the time of trial of the said prisoners, but could not speak one word all the time, and for the most part she remained as one wholly senseless, as one in a deep sleep, and could move no part of her body, and all the motion of life that appeared in her was, that as she lay upon cushions in the court upon her back, her stomach and belly, by the drawing of her breath, would arise to a great height; and after the said Elizabeth had lain a long time on the table in the court, she came a little to herself and sat up, but could neither see nor speak, but was sensible of what was said to her, and after a while she laid her head on the bar of the court with a cushion under it, and her hand and her apron upon that, and there she lay a good space of time; and by the direction of the judge, Amy Duny was privately brought to Elizabeth Pacy, and she touched her hand; whereupon the child without so much as seeing her, for her eyes were closed all the while, suddenly leaped up, and catched Amy Duny by the hand, and afterwards by the face; and with her nails scratched her till blood came, and would by no means leave her till she was taken from her."

Samuel Pacy, a merchant of Leystoff, "a man who carried himself with much soberness during the trial, from whom proceeded no words either of passion or malice though his children were so greatly afflicted," said his daughter, Deborah, was afflicted with fits, that Dr. Feavor, a doctor of physic, could not understand what was the cause of these fits, and that he believed the girl was bewitched by Amy Duny. In their fits they would cry out, "There stands Amy Duny or Rose Cullender". They used to bring up pins in their fits. Later he sent the children to the house of Margaret Arnold, his sister, to see if a change would do them good.

Margaret Arnold gave no credit to what was related to her when the children came, "conceiving that possibly the children might use some deceit in putting pins in their mouths themselves"; so she took all the pins out of their clothes but in spite of this they vomited up at least thirty pins in her presence.

Many other witnesses gave similar ridiculous evidence. "This was the sum and substance of the evidence which was given against the prisoners concerning the bewitching of the children before mentioned. At the hearing of this evidence there were divers known persons as Mr. Serjeant Keeling . . . present. Mr. Serjeant Keeling seemed much unsatisfied with it, and thought it not sufficient to convict the prisoners; for admitting that the children were in truth bewitched, yet said he, it can never be applied to the prisoners, upon the imagination only of the parties afflicted; for if that might be allowed no person whatsoever can be in safety, for perhaps they might fancy another person, who might altogether be innocent in such matters."

The celebrated Sir Thomas Browne, of Norwich, the author of *Religio Medici* gave evidence that in his opinion the children were bewitched. "In Denmark there had been lately a great discovery of witches, who used the very same way of afflicting persons, by conveying pins into them. . . . His opinion was, That the devil . . . did work upon the bodies of men and women . . . to stir up, and excite such humours super-abounding in their bodies to a great excess, whereby he did in an extraordinary manner afflict them with such distempers as their bodies were most subject to . . . these swooning fits were natural, and nothing else, but only heightened to a great extent by the subtlety of the devil, co-operating with these which we term witches, at whose instance he doth these villainies."

Some experiments were made in court to test the truth of the children's fits. It was observed that when they were in the midst of their fits, "to all men's apprehension wholly deprived of all sense and understanding, closing their fists in such manner, as that the strongest man in court could not force them open; yet by the least touch of one of these supposed witches, Rose Cullender by name, they would suddenly shriek out opening their hands, which accident would not happen by the touch of any other person."

Some unbelieving person in court suggested that the children might be malingering. "And there ought not to be any stress put upon this to convict the parties, for the children might counterfeit this their distemper, and perceiving what was done to them they might in such manner suddenly alter the motion and gesture of their bodies, on purpose to induce persons to believe that they were not natural, but wrought strangely by the touch of the prisoners. Wherefore to avoid this scruple it was privately desired by the judge, that the Lord Cornwallis, Sir Edmund Bacon, and Mr. Serjeant Keeling, and some other gentlemen there in court, would attend one of the distempered persons in the further part of the Hall, whilst she was in her fits, and then to send for one of the witches, to try what would then happen, which they did accordingly; and Amy Duny was conveyed from the bar to the maid; they put an apron before her eyes, and then one other person touched her hand, which produced the same effect as the touch of the witch did in the Court. Whereupon the gentlemen returned, openly protesting that they did believe the whole transaction of this business was a mere imposture. This put the Court and all persons into a stand. But at length Mr. Pacy did declare, that possibly the maid might be deceived by a suspicion that the witch touched her when she did not." Many in Court agreed with this saying it was not possible for anyone, much less children, to simulate fits as these children had, especially without the fact being discovered by their parents. Moreover it was urged, was it possible that so many had conspired together "to do an act of this nature whereby no benefit or advantage could redound to any of the parties, but a guilty conscience for perjuring themselves in taking the lives of two poor simple women away, and there appears no malice in the case."

Sir Matthew Hale, who has been described as one of the greatest Judges we have had, charged the jury. He said he would not review the evidence for that they had all heard. They had two things to determine. First, had the children been bewitched. Secondly, whether the prisoners at the bar were guilty of it? That there were such creatures as witches he had no doubt. Firstly, the scriptures said as much. Secondly, the wisdom of all nations had made laws against such persons, which showed their belief in such a crime. "And such hath been the judgement of this kingdom, as appears by that act of parliament which hath provided punishments proportionable to the quality of the offence. And desired them, strictly to observe their evidence; and desired the great God of heaven to direct their hearts in this weighty thing they had in hand. For to condemn the innocent, and to let the guilty go free, were both an abomination to the Lord."

The jury after a deliberation of half an hour, found a verdict of guilty on all counts.

The next day it was found that all the children had recovered from their ailments within half an hour of the finding of the verdict. The judge and all the court were fully satisfied, and the prisoners were sentenced to be hanged, which sentence was duly carried out on March 17th. "They confessed nothing."

There are many features of interest in this case—the real and earnest belief in the reality of witchcraft by the judge, Sir Matthew Hale, one of our greatest and most learned judges, by Sir Thomas Browne, one of the best known doctors and scientists of the age, the author of *Religio Medici*, and by the parents of the children affected, who without any feelings of spite or revenge, gave their evidence in the full and genuine belief that their children had been bewitched. In spite of the fact that the nature of the attacks was clearly demonstrated in the Court, the wretched women were condemned and hanged, to the satisfaction of the judicial authorities concerned.

CHAPTER XXVI

THE TRIAL OF SIR THOMAS PICTON

THE trial of Sir Thomas Picton, sometime Governor and Commander in Chief of the Island of Trinidad, for causing torture to be inflicted on Luisa Calderon, a free Mulata. This trial which commenced in 1804 and lasted till 1812, and even then was never actually completed as the narrative will show.

The case for the prosecution was as follows: In 1797, as the result of the destruction in turn of the fleets of France, Spain and Holland, the island of Trinidad was surrendered to Sir Ralph Abercrombie and became the possession of the English. He entered into an agreement with the conquered allowing them the continuation of their own laws. In December, 1801, Luisa Calderon was ten or eleven years of age. At this early age she lived with a man Pedro Ruiz as his mistress. In that climate women matured early and motherhood at twelve was not an unusual event. Whilst she was living with Ruiz she engaged in an intrigue with a man, Carlos Gonzales. Gonzales robbed Ruiz of money, and for this offence he was arrested. Luisa was also suspected and she too was taken into custody. She denied having had anything to do with the matter. The magistrate felt his powers were at an end and he applied to General Picton, who had been appointed Governor of the island, for advice. The General sent him a note with these words. "Inflict the torture

upon Luisa Calderon." This order was at once carried
out. The girl was informed that if she did not confess,
she would be subjected to the torture, and that under
this process she might loose her limbs or her life. If she
confessed, there would be no torture. While her mind
was in a state of fear and dread from this threat, two or
three negresses who were to be tortured for witchcraft,
were put into her cell to further terrify her. She persisted
in her innocence. A punishment which had improperly been
called picketing, after the military punishment of this
name, but which in fact was not picketing but real torture,
was administered. In the military punishment the soldier
stood on a picket or piece of sharp wood, but he had a
means of resting on the inside of his arm to take off the
weight of his body on the picket. Luisa had one hand
and foot lashed together, her other great toe was lodged
on a sharp piece of wood, and she was then suspended by
a pulley by her free wrist. The punishment was repeated
with the other hand and foot bound together.

Mr. Garrow, who prosecuted, first addressed himself
to the lawfulness of torture. "He was to be told, that
though the highest authority in this country could not
practice this on the humblest individual, yet that by the
laws of Spain, it could be perpetrated in the island of
Trinidad. He would venture to assert that if it were
written in characters impossible to be misunderstood,
that if it were the acknowledged law of Trinidad, it could
be no justification of a British governor. . . . The
governor ought to have been aware that the torture was
not known in England; and that it never would be, never
could be tolerated in this country.

"The trial by rack was utterly unknown to the law of
England, though once, when the Dukes of Essex and
Suffolk, and other ministers of Henry VI had laid a design
to introduce the civil law into this kingdom, as the rule of

government, for the beginning thereof they erected a
rack for torture, which was called in derision the Duke
of Exeter's daughter, and still remained in the Tower of
London, where it was occasionally used as an engine of
state, not of law, more than once in the reign of Queen
Elizabeth. But when, upon the assassination of Villiers,
Duke of Buckingham, by Felton, it was proposed in the
privy council to put the assassin to the rack, in order to
discover his accomplices, the judges, being consulted,
declared unanimously, to their own honour, and the honour
of the English law, that no such proceeding was allowable
by the laws of England."

It is remarkable that a well-known lawyer such as Mr.
Garrow, afterwards created a Baron of the Exchequer,
should have quoted these few instances of torture as if
they were unusual, when as all history must have taught
him they took place by the hundreds. "The rack seldom
stood idle in the reign of Queen Elizabeth."

"But what were they to say to this man, who, so far
from having found torture in practice under the former
governors, had attached to himself all the infamy of having
invented this instrument of cruelty? Like the Duke of
Exeter's daughter, it never had existed until the defendant
cursed the island with its production."

Luisa Calderon was then called. She looked about
eighteen, though actually not more than fourteen. She
was a good looking Mulatto girl, slender and graceful.
She said she had been arrested on suspicion of theft and
taken before Governor Picton, who told her that if she did
not confess, the hangman would have to deal with her.
She was taken to the room where the torture was prepared.
Her left hand was tied up to the ceiling by a rope, with
a pulley; her right hand and foot were tied together behind
her, while the end of her left foot rested on the wooden
spike. A negro pulled the rope up. She was kept on the

spike three quarters of an hour and the next day over twenty minutes. She fainted each time before she was taken down, and she was then put into irons, called the grillos, which were long pieces of iron with two rings for the feet, fastened to the wall, and thus she was kept for eight months. The torture caused her very bad pain, her wrists and ankles were much swollen, and showed the marks to the present day.

Don Rafael Shandoz, an alguazil in the island, said he saw Luisa directly after she had been tortured. The place where she was later confined was a garret with sloping sides, and the grillos were so placed that she could not raise herself up during the eight months of her imprisonment. She had no lawyer and no doctor. He had never known torture inflicted on the island before. There had been no instrument for the purpose. The first he saw was in the barracks. Luisa was discharged after her eight months of imprisonment.

The order for the application of the torture in the following words, "Applicase la question a Luisa Calderon" was then proved to be in the handwriting of Picton.

Don Juan Montes said torture was unknown in the island before the advent of Governor Picton. It was introduced after the conquest of the island and was then practised by order of the defendant.

Mr. Dallas, counsel for Sir Thomas, based his defence on three main points. (1) By the law of Spain, in the present instance, torture was directed; he was bound to administer the law. (2) The order for torture was not maliciously issued. (3) If it were unlawful, yet issued by mistake, it was a complete answer to the charge. He contended that the law of Spain as it existed in Trinidad was more merciful than the law of England and of some of our own islands.

Mr. Gloucester, the Attorney-General of the Island, deposed that the law books of Trinidad not only permitted torture in certain cases, including that particular case before the jury. Among the books he referred to was the Recopilacion de Leyes. Mr. Garrow was allowed to call rebutting evidence. Don Padro de Vargass was an advocate in the Spanish law-courts in the colonies. He had resided in five or six of the West Indian islands in the pursuit of his profession, and according to his knowledge of the Book of Recapitulations, by which the laws were administered, there was nothing contained in it to justify the infliction of torture nor was torture to his knowledge ever resorted to. There was a law of Old Castile of the year 1260, which justified the torture in certain cases, but he never understood it extended to the West Indies, and it was so much abhorred in Spain that it was either repealed or had fallen into disuse. (He appears to have forgotten the brutalities and torture of the Inquisition, just as Mr. Garrow had forgotten the Tudor atrocities.)

Lord Ellenborough in his summing up said that for all practical purposes the only point to which the jury need direct their attention was this, What was the law by which the island of Trinidad was governed at the period at which it was captured by Britain? They must consider whether the law as it existed authorised personal torture to be inflicted. By the indulgence of this country the existing law was to continue. What was the existing law? The jury would see that it did not necessarily follow because Trinidad was a colony of Old Spain, that it must therefore in every part have the laws of Old Spain. It did not form any part of the original country but had been annexed to it, on what terms there was no positive evidence. It did not appear that either the schedule peculiar to this island, or the recapitulation, embraced the criminal law, or made any mention of torture. So, if the torture did subsist in this island, it must be on the authority of law books read to the jury. It had been ascertained that authorities on the island had never known torture to be practised in Trinidad. It was therefore for the jury to say in the absence of all positive proof on the subject whether the law of Spain was so fully and completely established in Trinidad as to make torture a part of the law of the island. Without going through the authorities, he thought the jury might take it that torture was allowed by the laws of Old Spain. It was too much to say that the discontinuance of a practice could repeal a law, but they had to determine whether they were convinced that torture had ever been part of the law of Trinidad, and also whether they were convinced that it was part of the law when the island was captured.

The jury found that there was no such law existing in the island of Trinidad as that of torture, at the time of the surrender of that island to the British. They found General Picton guilty.

Mr. Dallas moved for a new trial on the following grounds:

(1) The infamous character of the girl who was a prostitute and thief.

(2) That Governor Picton, who condemned her to torture, fully believed that torture was allowed and that in this belief he was supported by reference to the written legal authorities.

(3) That the Governor had shown no malice or disposition to tyranny.

(4) That one of the principal witnesses had brought forward the "Recopilacion des Leyes des Indes", expressly compiled for the Spanish colonies, which did not authorise torture but when that code was silent upon criminal cases,

recourse was always to be had to the laws of Old Spain, and that these laws sanctioned torture, and that this applied to the present case.

The new trial was granted and the jury then found the following facts: "That, by the law of Spain, torture existed in the island of Trinidad at the time of the cession of that island to Great Britain; and that no malice existed in the mind of the defendant against Luisa Calderon independent of the illegality of the act". A special verdict was drawn up on these findings of the jury, a verdict which took 8,000 words to express itself. Lord Ellenborough announced that the court would consider the special verdict and give judgment later.

No further proceedings took place till two years afterwards when the court ordered the defendant's recognizances to be respited till further orders. It was generally believed in legal circles that had judgment been given it would have been against General Picton on the legal points, but that the punishment would have been so slight that it would have been clear that the court regarded his crime as a minor one.

In July, 1809, whilst the prosecution was still going on, General Picton was appointed to the command of a brigade, at the attack on Walcheren. In 1810 he held a similar command under Sir Arthur Wellesley, in Portugal, and was soon after nominated to the command of the celebrated third division. After the battle of Vittoria, he returned to England on account of ill-health, was elected to Parliament for Pembroke, and made a Knight of the Bath. The unanimous thanks of the House of Commons were given to him for his military services. He returned to the front, and was killed at the battle of Waterloo, "gloriously leading his division to a charge of bayonets, by which one of the most serious attacks made by the enemy upon our position was defeated." (Duke of Wellington's despatch after the battle of Waterloo.) There is a monument to Sir Thomas Picton in St. Paul's Cathedral.

It is evident that on account of his great services, and also of the fact that his conduct in Trinidad was not regarded as of a serious nature by the authorities, the proceedings against him were deliberately allowed to lapse.

CHAPTER XXVII

TRIAL BY BATTLE

PROCEEDINGS in the Court of Chivalry on an appeal of high treason, by Donald Lord Rea, against Mr. David Ramsey, in 1631.

Donald Lord Rea, a Scottish highlander, had accused David Ramsey on designs of treason against the King and kingdom, which Ramsey denied and on account of this they were "admitted the Trial by Combatte, the manner being as followeth."

"The prefixt for trial was the 28th of November, 1631, before Robert, earl of Lindsey, lord high-chamberlain of England, and now *pro tempore* deputed lord high constable of England. . . . The place was the Painted Chamber at Westminster; at the upper end thereof a bench was erected four feet high for the constable, and marshal, and lords-assistants. Under them seats about a square table, filled with the heralds of arms, and serjeants at arms, and other officers of the court. Directly under the upper bench sate the registrar, doctor Dethick, and over against him doctor Duck, the king's advocate for the marshall's court. Behind him at the bar were the two pews for the appellant and the defendant.

"At eight a clock comes the earl marshall . . . and all took place in their degrees.

"The earl marshall rises, makes obedience to the constable, and passing forward meets sir William Seager, king of heralds, and both of them present to the constable his commission, which he received with his hat off; and delivered it to the register to reade, in effect:

" 'That his majesty being informed by Donnold lord Rea, how David Ramsey esq. had plotted, and was privy under divers Treasons and Conspiracies against his royal person, government, and kingdoms. In the search whereof the king had used all ways and means for the discovery of the truth; the one of them accusing, the other denying, and so no certain security in his own person and his subjects; therefore he doth authorise the said Robert Bartie, earl of Lindsey, lord high constable, for to call unto him, Thomas earl of Arundel, earl marshall, and with him such other peers, sheriffs, and officers, as he thinks fit, to hold a marshall's court, for sifting the truth between the said parties, &c.' Then the king of heralds delivers to the constable, his silver verge or staff, half a yard in length, headed with a crown of gold. Then the earl marshall delivered a key to the herald, to fetch in the Appellant ushered in by the herald, and accompanied with his sureties. . . . He was apparelled in black velvet trimmed with silver buttons, his sword in a silver imbroidered belt, in his order of a Scottish baronet, about his neck and so with reverence entered into his pew. His counsel, doctor Reeves standing by. . . . The Defendant was alike ushered in by another herald. His sureties were the lord Roxborough and lord Abercorn. . . . His apparel scarlet, over-laced with silver . . . but unarmed without a sword. After his reverence to the court, he faced the Appellant, who like sterned a countenance at him.

"After O yes! the earl Marshal told them the effect of the commission, and the power of this court, which was not of any strange nature, but legal and justifiable as any other trial in Westminster-hall; and that there had been no more nor other trials of this kind of late, we were to attribute it to God's goodness, the justice of the king, and loyalty of the subject, with the providence of state, and wished that there might be no more in time to come; and that to expect any combate, this court he hoped would prevent it by the discovery of the light, and so 'magna est veritas, et prevalebit.'

"He referred the further proceedings unto Dr. Duck, the king's advocate, who spoke thus in effect:

" 'That the king's majesty had committed the trial of the business to your grace my lord high constable, the earl marshal, and this court, which course was warrantable by the laws of other nations, and also by our own, who have used the same manner of trial—That our law admitted sundry proofs for Treason, which in other matters it did not; that all subjects were bound to discover treasons; and cited two ancient civilians, Hieronymus and Tiberius, who gave their reasons for this kind of trial. And he mentioned sundry records of our own chronicles, as the duke of Norfolk combatting against the duke of Hartford in Henry 4, his time; Jo. Ely and William Scroop against Ballamon at Bordeaux, the king being there; the lord Morley impeached Montague, earl of Salisbury; and that Thomas of Walsingham and Thomas of Woodstock in their learned writings, expressed sundry precedents for this manner of proceeding; wishing the court in God's name to go on to the trial, and the Appellant to give in his evidence.'

"Then the Appellant came up upon the table, to whom the earl Marshal delivered the petition, which he had the day before exhibited to the king. And the Defendant being also called up, the petition was read, which was in effect, that he having accused Ramsey of treason, and also Meldram his kinsman, and of confederacy, against whom captain Nothwick was witness, therefore had desired, that the court would proceed against Meldram first.

"But he was told by the court, that their cases differing, the Appellant was ordered to deliver in his Charge against the Defendant, which he did, in writing by bill, containing sundry particulars, viz:

"That in May last, in the Low-Countries, Ramsey complained to him against the court of England. That the matters of church and state was so out of frame we must tend to a change, if not desolation. That therefore he had abandoned the kingdom, to live where now he was. . . . That afterwards at Amsterdam, Ramsey with Alexander Hamilton solicited him the lord Rea to be true to them, and to be of their counsel, though as yet they dare not reveal too much of Hamilton's secrets, but if he repaired to England, he would entrust him with letters. . . .

"He added, That if Ramsey would deny it, he was a villian and a traitour, which he would make good, And therewith cast down his glove.

"Ramsey denied all, and said, Rea was a liar, a barbarous villian, and threw down his glove, protesting, to gar him dy for it, if he had had him in place for that purpose.

"Rea was temperate without any passion, but smiling, replied, Mr. Ramsey, we will not contend here. Answer to my bill.

"Ramsey in general acknowledged all the particular circumstances of time and place alleged by Rea, and the discourse to that affect; but concluded, that no treason was intended or uttered, and craved counsel to answer, which was granted. . . .

"Then the Lord Constable taking the Appeal in his hands, and folding it up, put it into the glove, which the lord Rea had cast forth in the court for a pawn in this behalf; and held the Bill and glove in his right hand, and in his left the Answer and glove or pawn of David Ramsey; and then joining the Bill and Answer, and the gloves, and folding them together, he, with the earl Marshal, adjudged a Duel between the parties under this form of words:

"'In the name of God the Father the Son and the Holy-Ghost, the Holy and most blessed Trinity, who is one, and the only God and Judge of Battels; we, as his vice-gerents under the most excellent prince in Christ our Lord and king, by whom we are deputed to do this, do admit you the aforesaid Donald lord Rey, the party challenging, and you the aforesaid David Ramsey, the defendant, to a duel, upon every accusation contained in this bill, and the answer to the same; and we assign unto you the 12th day of the month of April next following, between sun and sun, in the fields called Tuttle-fields, in or near Westminster, in the presence of our lord the king, to do and perform your parts to the utmost of your power respectively. And we will and enjoyn you the aforesaid lord Rea the challenger, to be in the aforesaid fields, and within the list there, between 7 and 9 of the clock in the forenoon of the aforesaid day. And we enjoyn you the aforesaid David Ramsey the defendant to be in the fields in the aforesaid list between 9 and 11 of the clock in the forenoon of the said day, upon peril attending you respectively in that behalf.'

"After a good deal of argument the court decided the dimension of the weapons allowed. 'A long sword, four foot and a half in length, hilt and all; in breadth two inches. Short sword, a yard and four inches in length, hilt and all; in breadth two inches. Pike, fifteen foot in length, head and all. Dagger, nineteen inches in length, hilt and all; in breadth an inch. The weapons not to exceed this proportion; but the parties might abate of this length and breadth if they thought fit.'

" On the the 10th of April, Rea and Ramsey appeared again before the court, sitting in the counsel chamber at Whitehall; at which time the lord high constable and the earl Marshal signified to the parties, that it was the king's pleasure, for certain just and urgent causes, to prorogue the day of combat, from the 12th of April to the 17th of May; and they prorogued the same accordingly."

Later the king decided that he would allow no combat and sent both the Appellant and the Defendant to the Tower till such time as he thought it would be safe to release them.

"On the 8th of May this year (1632), a period was put to the great trial in the court of honour. . . . However, take his majesty's thoughts of it, as expressed in this letter to the marquess.

"'James; Since you went I have not written to you of Mackey's business, because I neither desire to prophesy nor write half news; but now seeing (by the grace of God) what shall be the end of it, I have thought fit to be the first advertiser of it to you. I doubt not but you have heard, that (after long seeking of proofs for clearing the business as much as could be, and formalities which could not be eschewed) the combat was awarded, day set, weapons appointed; but having seen and considered all that can be said on either side, as likewise the carriage of both the men, upon mature deliberation I have resolved not to suffer them to fight. Because, first for Mackay, he hath failed so much in his circumstantial probations, especially concerning Muschamp, upon whom he built as a chief witness, that nobody now is any way satisfied with his accusations. Then for David Ramsey, though we cannot condemn him for that that is not, yet he hath so much, and so often offended by his violent tongue, that we can no way think him innocent, though not that way guilty whereof he is accused; wherefore I have commanded the court shall be dismissed, and combat discharged, with a declaration to this purpose, that though upon want of good proof the combat was necessarily awarded, yet upon the whole matter I am fully satisfied that there was no such treason as Mackay had fancied. And for David Ramsey, though we must clear him of that treason in particular, yet not so far in the general, but that he might give occasion enough by his tongue of great accusation, if it had been rightly placed, as by —his foolish presumptious carriage did appear.—This is the substance, and so short, that it is rather a direction how to believe others, than a narration itself; one of my chief ends being that you may so know David Ramsey, that you may not have to do with such a pest as he is, suspecting he may seek to insinuate himself to you upon this occasion. Wherefore I must desire you, as you love me, to have nothing to do with him.—To conclude now: I dare say that you shall have no dishonour in this business; and for myself, I am not ashamed that herein I have showed myself to be, Your faithful friend, and loving cousin, CHARLES R. London, May 8, 1632.'"

There are many cases recorded in Tudor times in which there were trials of "Wager of Battel", but in all of them for some reason or other, either because the judicial pronouncement was against them or because after trial and permission given, one of the parties repented and failed to appear, there is no case in which the actual combat took place during this period.

An interesting account of the old procedure is given by an antiquarian, named Verstagan, in a book entitled, *A Restitution of decaied intellegence, in antiquities concerning the most noble and renowned English nation,* speaks thus: "In the triall by single combat or camp-fight, the accuser was with the perill of his owne bodie to prove the accused guiltie, and by offering him his glove, to challenge him to his triall; the which the other must either accept of, or else acknowledge himself culpable of the crime whereof he was accused. If it were a crime deserving death, then was the camp-fight for life and death, and either on horse-backe or foot. If the offence deserved imprisonment, and not death, then was the camp-fight accomplished when the one had subdued the other, by making him to yield, or unable to defend himselfe, and so bee taken prisoner. The accused had the liberty to choose another in his stead, but the accuser must performe it in his owne person, and with equalitie of weapons. No women were admitted to behold it, nor men children under the age of thirteene yeares. The priests that were spectators, did silently pray that the victory might fall unto the guiltlesse. And if the fight were for life or death, a beere stood ready to carry away the dead bodie of him that should bee slaine. None of the people might crie, scrike out, make any noise, or give any signe whatsoever. This was so strictly and severely punished at Hall in Swevia (a place appointed for camp-fight) that the executioner stood beside the judges, ready with an axe to cut off the right hand and left foot of the partie so offending. Hee that (being wounded) did yield himselfe, was at the mercie of the other, to be killed, or to be let live. If he were slaine, then was he carried away, and honourably buried; and he that slue him reputed more honourable than before. But if being overcome he were left alive, then was he by sentence of the judges declared utterly void of all honest reputation, and never to ride on horseback nor carrie arms."

BIBLIOGRAPHY

BIBLIOGRAPHY

ANDREWS. *Bygone Punishments.*

BACON. *Novum Organum.*
BELLOC. *History of England.*
BLACKSTONE. *Commentary on the Laws of England.*
BOLINGBROKE. *History of England.*
BOUVIER. *Law Dictionary.*
BRADLAUGH. *Labour and Law.*
BRAY. *Boy Labour and Apprenticeship.*
BRYAN. *Round about Harley Street.*

CALVERT. *Capital Punishment.*
COBBETT. *State Trials.*
CHAMBERLIN. *Private Character of Queen Elizabeth.*
CREIGHTON. *The Age of Elizabeth.*

Encyclopædia Brittanica.

FOXE. *Book of Martyrs.*
FROUDE. *History of England.*

GARDINER. *History of England.*
GARDINER. *History of the Great Civil War.*
GARNIER. *Annals of the British Peasantry.*
GOLDWIN SMITH. *The United Kingdom.*
GROTE. *History of Greece.*

HAGGARD. *The Lame, the Halt, the Blind.*
HALLAM. *Constitutional History of England.*
HALLAM. *Europe during the Middle Ages.*
HARMSWORTH. *Encyclopædia.*
HARMSWORTH. *History of the World.*
HOWELL. *The Conflicts of Capital and Labour.*

HOWELL.　*State Trials.*
HUME.　*Commentary on the Law of Scotland.*

JARDINE.　*The Use of Torture.*
JEVONS.　*The State in Relation to Labour.*

LAWRENCE.　*History of Capital Punishment.*
LECKY.　*Rise and Influence of Rationalism in Europe.*
LINGARD.　*History of England.*

MACAULAY.　*Essay on Lord Bacon.*
McKECHNIE.　*Magna Carta.*
MEYER.　*England and the Catholic Church under Elizabeth.*
MONTAIGNE.　*Essays.*

NEWDIGATE.　*Our Martyrs.*

PARRY, SIR EDWARD.　*The Bloody Assize.*
PARRY, SIR EDWARD.　*Drama and the Law.*
PARRY, L. A.　*Criminal Abortion.*
PARRY, L. A.　*Famous Medical Trials.*
PELHAM.　*Chronicles of Crime.*
Penny Cyclopædia.
PIKE.　*History of Crime in England.*
POLLARD.　*Political History of England.*

ROGERS, THOROLD.　*Six Centuries of Work and Wages.*
ROGERS, THOROLD.　*The Economic Interpretation of History.*

SALZMANN.　*English Industries of the Middle Ages.*
SEEBOHM.　*Era of the Protestant Revolution.*
SMITH, SIR T.　*Commonwealth of England.*
Statutes of England.
STEPHEN.　*State Trials.*
STEPHENS.　*Commentaries on the Laws of England.*
STUBBS.　*Select Charters.*
STRACHEY.　*Elizabeth and Essex.*

TASWELL-LANGMEAD.　*English Constitutional History.*
TOUT.　*Political History of England.*
TREVELYAN.　*History of England.*

WALKER.　*The Wages Question.*
WINGFIELD-STRATFORD.　*History of British Civilisation.*

INDEX

Act of Settlement, 2
Act of Supremacy, 13
Alban, Saint, 146
amputation, 105, 110, 154-5,
  161, 164. *See also* mutilation
Anne, Queen, 68, 169, 176
Archer, John, 28, 60, 62
Askew, Anne, 43-4
assassination
  of Buckingham, 11, 59
  of Lennox, 85
  plots of against Elizabeth I,
  34, 40, 61, 123

Bacon, Francis, 39-40, 57, 58,
  180
Bailey, Charles, 52-3
Bainham, James, 148
Balfour, Alison, 63-4
Balthazar. *See* Gérard, Balthazar
barbed hooks, 104
Bass, Isle of, 208, 214, 215
Baxter, Richard, 179
Bayle, Pierre, 29
Beaton, David Cardinal, 141,
  201, 202-3
Beaufort, Henry Cardinal, 181
Beccaria, Cesare, 29-30
beheading
  after death, 55, 107-9, 120,
  122
  display of heads after, 42,
  107, 108, 136

on Drake's voyage, 134-5
instruments used for, 137-9
notables executed by, 130-6,
  199
privilege of, 129
procedure of, 129, 130-1
Bell, John, 15
Benefit of Clergy, 155
Bill of Rights (William III), 2
Bilney, Thomas, 198
Blackstone, Sir William, 152
blasphemy laws, 165
boiling, death by, 142, 144-5
Boleyn, Anne, 130, 132-3
Bolingbroke, Henry St. John
  Viscount, 14
Bonner, Edmund, 43, 148, 149
boots, the
  description of, 78
  use of, 182
  victims of torture by, 64-7,
  71, 207, 213
Boys, William, 140
Brambre, Sir Nicholas, 117
branding
  abolition of, 161
  instances of, 8, 10-11, 160,
  165
  marks of, 8, 156-7, 160-1, 165
  of vagrants, 174
  of women, 156-7
branks, 162, 163
Breed, John, 110
brodequin, 81-2

Browne, Sir Thomas, 220, 222
Bryan, Cyril P., 124, 126
Burghley, William Cecil Lord,
    36-7, 46, 53
burial alive, 105
Burnet, Gilbert, 71-2, 78
burning
    by Catholics, 106
    executions by, 198-9
    heresy punished with, 146-9,
        150-1, 194-8, 201-2, 204
    human sacrifice by, 146
    and Inquisition, 193-4
    Roman practice of, 104
    treason punished with, 149-52
    witchcraft punished with,
        179, 180, 183
Byrnes of Wicklow, 75

Calderon, Luisa, 224-7, 229,
    230
Calvin, John, 193
Campion, Edmund, 37, 49, 61,
    62
Carlisle, Harclay Earl of, 109
Carstairs, William, 65-7
cashilaws (or caspitaws), 64, 78,
    79-80, 182
castration, 105, 122, 123, 124
Cecil, Sir Robert, 34, 46, 164
Cellier, Elizabeth, 60-2, 165-6
"chains, the," 109
Charles I
    beheading of, 130
    and law, 2, 8, 14
    and torture, 28, 56, 61
Charles II, 109
Charles III, King of Spain, 29
Charron, 29
children
    cruelty to, 20-2
    Employment Commission for,
        17
    executions of, 15, 148, 152

    labour conditions of, 16-19
    torture of, 64
Chovet, Abraham, 126-7
Clarke, Roger, 198
Coke, Sir Thomas, 3, 27
common law
    and heretics, 195
    misuse of, 28
    and prerogative courts, 4, 5,
        13-14, 36
    torture forbidden by, 1, 2-3,
        29, 47-8, 50, 58, 59, 61
    unification of begun, 27
    and witchcraft, 183
"common scold," 163, 176
"confirmatio cartarum," 2
Cook, James, 112
courts
    of Chancery, 4
    of Chivalry, 232
    of Commission of Ecclesiasti-
        cal Causes, 14
    of Common Pleas, 7
    Consistory, 57
    Council of the North, 3, 7
    Council of Wales and the
        Marches, 3, 7
    Ecclesiastical of the Bishop of
        Bath and Wells, 57
    of High Commission, 3, 7,
        13-14, 57
    of Inquisition (Scottish), 72
    of King's Bench, 7, 95, 159
    at Maidstone, 15, 159, 176
    Prerogative, 3, 4-14, 32, 36,
        58-9
    of Queen's Bench, 169
    Star Chamber, 3, 4-12, 13,
        14, 171
Covenanters, 205
Cowper, Spencer, 94-5
Cranmer, Thomas, 147, 148-9, 150
Criminal Law Amendment Act
    of 1861, 113

Crithecreche, Alice, 159-60
Cromwell, Oliver, 109, 120, 180
Cromwell, Thomas, 132
crucifixion, 104
cruelty
  to animals, 23-5
  to children, 20-2
cucking-stool, 163

Dalaber (early Protestant), 174
disembowelment
  Blackstone on, 152
  description of, 107
  instances of, 109, 119, 120,
    123-4
dissection
  after death, 111, 114, 115
  punishment of, 107, 109, 122
Dorset, Edward Sackville Earl
  of, 10-11
Doughty (sailor), 134
Douglas, Mammy, 125-6
Drake, Sir Francis, 134
drawing, 85, 108, 109
drowning, 104, 105, 140, 141-2
drowning pits, 140
ducking-stool, 41, 162, 163, 176
duel. See trial, by battle
Duffin, Patrick William, 172-3
Durant, John, 102-3

Earlstone, Gordon of, 71
Edward I, Statutes of, 2
Edward III, 2, 97
Edward VI, 178
Edwards, Susanna, 184-5, 188
Elizabeth I
  and law, 13-14, 41, 158-9,
    161, 178
  and torture, 36-9, 45-52, 62,
    77, 226
  and treason, 39-40, 73-4, 106,
    120-4, 191
  and Weston fabrication, 61

Elizabeth and Essex (Strachey),
  40
Encyclopaedists, 29
Essex, Robert Devereux Earl of,
    34-5, 39, 40, 134, 164
estrapade, 153

Factory Acts, 18-19
Fawkes, Guy, 54-5, 62
Felton, John, 59-60
Ferguson, Robert, 205
Ferrers, Lawrence Earl, 114
finger pillory, 162, 163
Fisher, Clement, 45
Fisher, John, 130, 142, 143,
    147, 199
Fitzherbert, Thomas, 39
flogging
  in the army, 175
  death from, 175
  knotted cords used for, 86
  leaden balls used for, 104
  and witches, 181
  See also whipping
Floyd, Edward, 31
Forest, Prior, 147-8, 201
Foster, George, 127-8
Foxley, Mrs., 176
Francis I, King of France, 153
Frederick II, King of Prussia, 30
Froude, James Anthony, 47-8,
    49-51, 51-2, 192-3
Fuller, William, 169

galvanism, 127-8
Gardiner, Samuel Rawson, 58
Garnet, Henry, 55-6
Gaunt, Elizabeth, 149-50
Gavan, John, 89-92
George II, Statute of, 110-11
Gérard, Balthazar, 86
gibbet and gibbeting, 41, 109-10,
    112, 116, 124, 200
Gibbet Marsh, 110

Gloucester, Eleanor Duchess of, 181-2
Gondomar (Spanish ambassador), 175
Gordon (highwayman), 126-7
Great Charter. *See* Magna Carta
Grey, Lady Jane, 130, 131-2
grillos, 227
gunpowder, in execution by burning, 152-3, 196-7

habeas corpus, 2, 7
Hale, Sir Matthew, 220
Hamilton, Patrick, 201-2
Halifax Gibbet, 137-9
Halifax and its Gibbet Law (Midgley), extract from, 138
Hall, James, 111
hanging
  for anarchy, 142
  beheading after, 107-9
  ceremony of, 112-15
  for heresy, 141
  for murder, 111, 115-16
  after "pressing," 101
  by Protestants, 106
  survival after, 126-8
  for treason, 60, 75, 106, 116-24
  at Tyburn, 100, 124-6, 171
  witches condemned to, 179, 180-1
  of women, 152
hanging in chains, 60, 109-12, 116, 147
Hathaway, Richard, 189-90
Hayes, Catherine, 151
Haywarde, Sir John, 39-40
Henesey, Dr., 125-6
Henry I, 105
Henry II, Pipe Roll of, 27, 32
Henry III, 2
Henry IV, 2
Henry V, 2

Henry VI, 2, 181, 225
Henry VII, 4
Henry VIII
  and Anne Boleyn, 132-3
  and boiling alive, 142-4
  and law, 154, 157-8
  and Pilgrimage of Grace, 200
  and torture, 36, 77
  and treason, 106
  and vagrants, 174
  and witches, 179
Henry III, King of France, 40
Henry IV, King of France, 81
heresy
  duty of Catholics to eliminate, 51
  last burning in Britain for, 150-1
  John London's eagerness to convict for, 163-4
  persecutions for, 192-3
  punishment for in Europe, 191-2, 193-4
  punishment for in Scotland, 141
  punishment for under Tudors, 147-9, 191, 194-5
  treason confused with, 106
Hill, John, 92
History of England (Bolingbroke), extract from, 14
History of England (Gardiner), extract from, 58
History of My Own Time [sic] (Burnet), extracts from, 71-2, 78
History of Sandwich (Boys), extract from, 140
Histrio-mastix, or a Scourge for Stage Players, 9-10
Holinshed's *Chronicle*, extract from, 137-8
Holt, Sir John, 171-2
Hooper, John, 195-7

Hopkins, Matthew, 180
House of Commons Journal,
    extracts from, 86, 109
Howard, Catherine, 130
Howell, Thomas Bayly. *See*
    State Trials
Hudson, William, 9
Huntingdon, Waltheof Earl of, 129
Hurley (priest), 73-4

Innocent VIII, 79
Inquisition, 29, 50, 192-3, 228
iron bridle, 182
iron gauntlets, 77
Isle of Bass, 208, 214, 215

James I, 54, 150-1, 175, 180
James II, 14, 129, 150
Jardine, David, 43
Jeffreys, Sir George, 6-7, 149,
    150, 166
Jesuits
    persecution of, 50, 55, 120
    plots of assassination by, 120-1
    torture of, 47-9, 51, 77-8
    trial of, 89-91
John, King, 1
jougs, 162, 163
Judgment of Penance, 98
jury. *See* trial, by jury

Knevet, Sir Edward, 157-8
Knox, John, 203

Lamb, Robert, 141
Lambert, Sir Daniel, 112
Lateran Council, 89
Latimer, Hugh, 147, 201
Laud, William, 130
law
    common. *See* common law
    of Ireland, 33, 73
    martial, 74
    of Rome, 192

of Scotland, 33, 63
Statute, 33, 178, 195
of Trinidad, 224, 227, 288-9
Ledmond, Patrick, 127
Lee, Sir William, 111
legislation
    and death penalty, 16, 113,
        152, 156-7
    humanitarian, 16, 18-19
    penalties fixed through, 97,
        110-11, 143, 146, 157, 159,
        160-1, 174
    punishments abolished
        through, 89, 102, 103, 112,
        145, 162, 173, 174, 193
    rights guaranteed through, 2
    witchcraft affected by, 178,
        179, 180, 181, 183
Leighton, Alexander, 8-9
Leopold, Duke of Tuscany, 30
Lewes, Joyce, 198
libel, 10-11, 57, 60-2, 165, 169,
    214. *See also* seditious libel
Lisle, Dame Alice, 6-7, 129, 130
Little Ease, 31, 80
Lloyd, Temperance, 184-5,
    186-7, 188-9
Lloyd, Thomas, 172-3
Loftus, Adam, 73-4
London, Dr. John, 163-4
London Bridge, 42, 108, 109,
    119
Long Parliament, 7
Lopez, Ruy, 122-3
Lovat, Simon Fraser Lord, 129
Luther, Martin, 179

Magna Carta, 1, 4, 32
Maidstone, Court at, 15, 159,
    176
manacles, 52, 58
Marise (pirate), 108
Mary I, 36, 44, 46, 50, 191,
    194-5

Mary, Queen of Scots, 52, 121, 130, 133-4
mercy at executions, 60, 108, 124, 152-3, 182, 197
Midgley, Dr. Samuel, 138
Monke, William, 56-7
Monmouth, James Scott Duke of, 6, 135, 149
Montaigne, Michel Eyquem de, 29, 34
Montesquieu, Charles de Secondat Baron de, 29
Morduck, Sarah, 189-90
More, Sir Thomas, 130, 147, 148, 199-200
Mortimer, Guy, 155
Morton, James Douglas Earl of, 139, 142
Muir, James, 68
Murphy, Christian, 152
muteness. See refusal to plead
mutilation
    ancient practice of, 104, 154
    early records of, 154
    instances of, 10-11, 155, 157-60
    procedure of, 154-5
    protest against, 12
    sentencing of vagrants to, 174
    Star Chamber sentences for, 8-9
    See also amputation

National Society for Prevention of Cruelty to Children, 20-2
Neile, Richard, 150-1
Nevil, Edmund, 121
Norfolk, Thomas Howard Duke of, 46, 130
Normans, 1, 3, 27, 91, 105
Norton, Christopher and Thomas, 118-19

Oates, Titus, 166-8

Page (bookseller), 158-9
Pain, Henry Nevill, 68-71
"pains, the," 51, 59. See also rack
Pandulph (papal legate), 1
parboiling, 119
Parry, Dr. William, 120-2
Paterines, 160
Peacham, Edward, 57-9
"peine forte et dure," 98-103
pendola, 194
Penn, William, 150
Penny, Rev. Dr., 111
Penredd, Timothy, 169
Pentland Rising of 1666, 205
perjury, 166-7, 173
Petition of Right, 2
Philip II, King of Spain, 40
picketing, 225, 226-7
Picton, Sir Thomas, 224-31
Pike, Luke Owen, 97
Pilgrim Fathers, 181
Pilgrimage of Grace, 200
pilliwinks (or pinniewinks), 78, 79, 182
pillory
    abolition of, 173
    crowd at, 164, 171
    mutilations at, 8-9, 11, 164, 169
    objectives of, 170
    use of for minor offences, 41, 162, 164-8
    and witchcraft, 178-9
pincers, red-hot, 34, 50, 84, 86
piquet, 80
pitch and feathers, 105
poisoning, 99, 142-5
politics
    religion confused with, 49-51, 106, 120, 191-2
    Star Chamber in, 4-5
Praunce (witness), 60-2
press, torture of, 98-103, 181

prisons
    Bridewell, 52
    Fleet, 30, 164, 173
    House of Correction, 169
    Mont Orgueil (Jersey), 11
    Newgate, 43, 113, 119, 125,
        126-7, 168, 171
    Sea Tower of St. Andrews,
        202-3
    See also Tower of London
Privy Council of England
    powers of, 7, 14, 36, 57, 62
    records of, 44-6
    and Star Chamber, 4-5
Privy Council of Ireland, 73, 75
Privy Council of Scotland, 33,
        63-4, 66-70, 79, 205-6,
        208-9, 212
Prynne, William, 9-11
punishment
    annual, 168
    capital for minor offences,
        15-16
    determined by crime, 9, 15,
        141, 142, 146
    House of Commons' feeling
        on, 30-1
    in Middle Ages, 41
    ordered by Star Chamber, 5,
        7, 8-9
    of women, 140, 151-3, 155-7,
        163, 174, 204

quartering, 107, 108, 109, 119,
        122, 123
Queen's Husband (Stubb), 158

rack
    abolition of, 30, 60
    cases of torture on, 34, 43-7,
        48-9, 51-3, 56
    in England, 36, 61, 76, 225-6
    in Europe, 29
    in Ireland, 33, 73, 75

selection for, 48
    use of for extracting confes-
        sions, 28, 41
Raleigh, Sir Walter, 130-1
Ramsay, Sir John, 68
Ramsey, David, 232-8
Ravaillac, Francis, 81-5
Rea, Donald Lord, 232-7
Reading on the use of Torture in
        the Criminal Law of England
        (Jardine), 43
rebellions, 108, 149, 200, 205
recreancy, 91-2
refusal to plead, 97, 98, 101,
        103
religion
    ancient practices of, 146
    and clergy, 8, 28, 55, 56
    and Inquisition, 29
    persecution for, 37-8, 160,
        202, 205
    politics confused with, 49-51,
        106, 120, 191-2
    and prerogative courts, 3,
        13-14
    and witchcraft, 178, 179
    See also burning; heresy
Richard I, 105
Richard II, 2
Ridley, Nicholas, 197
rights, guaranteed by law, 1-3
Romans, 104-5, 179
Rosewell, Thomas, 106
Roundabout Harley Street
        (Bryan), 124, 126-8
Rouse, Richard, 143-4, 145
Royal Society for the Preven-
        tion of Cruelty to Animals,
        23-5
Rygeway, Cecilia, 98

Salisbury, John de Montague
        Earl of, 234
Sautre, William, 147

Savage (pretended conspirator), 11-12
scavenger's daughter, 77, 79, 80
scold's bridle, 162, 163
scottish maiden, 139
seditious libel, 37, 169, 172-3
serpents, sack of, 104
Sherwood, Thomas, 47
Smith, George, 16-17
Smithfield
  boiling at, 144
  burning at, 44, 146, 147-8, 194, 199
  pillory at, 171
Smyth, Thomas, 46
Social Science Association, 16-17
Somerset, Edward Seymour Duke of, 130
Southwell, Robert, 39
Spence, William, 64-5, 78
Spencer, Barbara, 151
Spiggot, Thomas, 102
Spreull, Dr. John, 205-15
Squires (soldier), 34-5
State Trials (Howell), 6, 170, 184, 208-15, 216
Statute of Labourers, 160-1
Stirk, Helen, 141
stocks, 157, 162-3, 173, 174
stoning, 104, 151
Story, Dr. John, 46
Strachey, Lytton, 40
Strafford, Thomas Wentworth Earl of, 135-6
Straiton, David, 201-2
Strangeways, Major George, 100-1
strangulation as act of mercy, 113, 152, 182
Stuarts, 3, 7, 28, 54, 62, 150
Stubbs, John, 158-9
Suffolk Witches, 216-23
Sundercombe, Miles, 120
superstition, 101-2, 179, 181, 216. See also witchcraft

Tacitus, 40
tar and feathers, 105
teeth, extraction of, as torture, 176-7
Temple Bar, 108, 136
Thornton, Abraham, 95
Throckmorton, Sir Nicholas, 6
Throgmorton, Francis, 51-2
throwing from a height, 104
thumbikins, 64, 65, 67, 68, 78-9
thumbs, tying and twisting of, 102-3
thumbscrew, 67, 79, 80. See also thumbikins; pilliwinks
Topcliff, Richard, 37-8, 39
tormento de toca, 194
Torquemada, Thomas of, 192, 193
torture
  abolition of, 29-30, 32-5, 68
  ancient practices of, 26, 28, 104-5
  art of, 29
  chambers of preserved, 80
  defense of, 36-7
  denial of charge during, 206-7
  evidence gained from, 27, 41, 47, 59-63
  exemptions from, 26, 28, 42-3
  for extraction of confessions, 26, 34-5, 46-7, 51-3, 55, 58-9, 60, 63, 65, 66, 81-4, 105, 184-5, 193
  House of Commons debate on, 31
  and law, 1-3, 27, 29, 32-3, 47-8, 50, 58-9, 61
  medieval practices of, 28-9
  outside England, 80-7
  warrant for, 26, 33, 44, 56, 62, 63
  See also law

Tower of London
  conditions in, 47, 48, 52
  heads displayed at, 136
  as museum, 76, 80
  prisoners in, 43, 46, 54, 57, 59, 114, 118-22, 132-3, 148-9
  and rack, 39, 45, 51-2, 53, 75
Tracey, William, 150
tracheotomy, 127-8
treason
  accusations of not proven, 56, 232-8
  actions considered as, 106
  Gaunt convicted of, 149-50
  Hayward suspected of, 39-40
  penalties for, 42, 107-9, 130-6, 144-5, 151, 204. *See also* burning; hanging
  petty, 111, 151-2, 204
  poisoning deemed, 144
  reasons for prosecution for, 36-7, 40, 50
  and rebellion, 60, 106, 205-6
  and religion, 106, 191-2
  torture for confessions of, 34-5, 42, 46-9, 51-2, 54, 57-8, 74
  trials for, 106-7
Treatise on the Star Chamber (Hudson), extract from, 9
Trembles, Mary, 184-6, 188
Tresilian, Sir Robert, 116-18
trial, methods of
  by battle, 91-5, 236-9
  by compurgation, 96
  by jury, 5-7, 97, 107, 218, 222, 229-30
  by ordeal, 88-91, 97, 105
Tudors
  executions under, 118-19
  and heretics, 147
  prerogative courts of, 4, 7
  prisons under, 52

torture under, 3, 28, 36, 42, 44, 54, 105-6
and trial by battle, 238-9
Tyburn
  brutal punishment at, 120
  burning at, 151-2
  Charles II's revenge at, 109
  hangings at, 15, 100, 124-6, 171
  pillory at, 168
  route to, 9, 114, 119
"Tyburn pew-openers," 125-6

Voltaire, 29

Wager of Battle. *See* trial, by battle
"waking," 182
Wallop, Sir Henry, 73-4
Walpole, Horace, 108
Warbeck, Perkin, 173-4
Wenham, Jane, 183
Wesley, John, 179
Weston, Richard, 95-100
Weston, Sir Richard, baron of exchequer, 60-2
wheel, the, 85
whipping
  in conjunction with branding, 8, 157, 160, 161, 165
  crimes punishable by, 156-7, 165, 174-5
  instances of, 8, 148, 165, 169
  under Tudors, 38, 161, 174
  of women, 157, 160, 174
  See also flogging
White, Nicolas, 15
Whitgift, John, 13
Wightman, Edward, 150-1
William I, 27, 88, 91, 105, 129
William I of Orange, 40
Wishart, George, 202-3
witch finder, 180, 189
witchcraft, 33, 63, 78, 141, 178-90, 225
witches, trials of, 184-9, 216-23

PATTERSON SMITH SERIES IN
CRIMINOLOGY, LAW ENFORCEMENT, AND SOCIAL PROBLEMS

1. *Lewis: *The Development of American Prisons and Prison Customs, 1776–1845*
2. Carpenter: *Reformatory Prison Discipline*
3. Brace: *The Dangerous Classes of New York*
4. *Dix: *Remarks on Prisons and Prison Discipline in the United States*
5. Bruce *et al.*: *The Workings of the Indeterminate-Sentence Law and the Parole System in Illinois*
6. *Wickersham Commission: *Complete Reports, Including the Mooney-Billings Report*. 14 vols.
7. Livingston: *Complete Works on Criminal Jurisprudence*. 2 vols.
8. Cleveland Foundation: *Criminal Justice in Cleveland*
9. Illinois Association for Criminal Justice: *The Illinois Crime Survey*
10. Missouri Association for Criminal Justice: *The Missouri Crime Survey*
11. Aschaffenburg: *Crime and Its Repression*
12. Garofalo: *Criminology*
13. Gross: *Criminal Psychology*
14. Lombroso: *Crime, Its Causes and Remedies*
15. Saleilles: *The Individualization of Punishment*
16. Tarde: *Penal Philosophy*
17. McKelvey: *American Prisons*
18. Sanders: *Negro Child Welfare in North Carolina*
19. Pike: *A History of Crime in England*. 2 vols.
20. Herring: *Welfare Work in Mill Villages*
21. Barnes: *The Evolution of Penology in Pennsylvania*
22. Puckett: *Folk Beliefs of the Southern Negro*
23. Fernald *et al.*: *A Study of Women Delinquents in New York State*
24. Wines: *The State of Prisons and of Child-Saving Institutions*
25. *Raper: *The Tragedy of Lynching*
26. Thomas: *The Unadjusted Girl*
27. Jorns: *The Quakers as Pioneers in Social Work*
28. Owings: *Women Police*
29. Woolston: *Prostitution in the United States*
30. Flexner: *Prostitution in Europe*
31. Kelso: *The History of Public Poor Relief in Massachusetts, 1820–1920*
32. Spivak: *Georgia Nigger*
33. Earle: *Curious Punishments of Bygone Days*
34. Bonger: *Race and Crime*
35. Fishman: *Crucibles of Crime*
36. Brearley: *Homicide in the United States*
37. *Graper: *American Police Administration*
38. Hichborn: *"The System"*
39. Steiner & Brown: *The North Carolina Chain Gang*
40. Cherrington: *The Evolution of Prohibition in the United States of America*
41. Colquhoun: *A Treatise on the Commerce and Police of the River Thames*
42. Colquhoun: *A Treatise on the Police of the Metropolis*
43. Abrahamsen: *Crime and the Human Mind*
44. Schneider: *The History of Public Welfare in New York State, 1609–1866*
45. Schneider & Deutsch: *The History of Public Welfare in New York State, 1867–1940*
46. Crapsey: *The Nether Side of New York*
47. Young: *Social Treatment in Probation and Delinquency*
48. Quinn: *Gambling and Gambling Devices*
49. McCord & McCord: *Origins of Crime*
50. Worthington & Topping: *Specialized Courts Dealing with Sex Delinquency*
51. Asbury: *Sucker's Progress*
52. Kneeland: *Commercialized Prostitution in New York City*

* new material added

PATTERSON SMITH SERIES IN
CRIMINOLOGY, LAW ENFORCEMENT, AND SOCIAL PROBLEMS

53. *Fosdick: *American Police Systems*
54. *Fosdick: *European Police Systems*
55. *Shay: *Judge Lynch: His First Hundred Years*
56. Barnes: *The Repression of Crime*
57. †Cable: *The Silent South*
58. Kammerer: *The Unmarried Mother*
59. Doshay: *The Boy Sex Offender and His Later Career*
60. Spaulding: *An Experimental Study of Psychopathic Delinquent Women*
61. Brockway: *Fifty Years of Prison Service*
62. Lawes: *Man's Judgment of Death*
63. Healy & Healy: *Pathological Lying, Accusation, and Swindling*
64. Smith: *The State Police*
65. Adams: *Interracial Marriage in Hawaii*
66. *Halpern: *A Decade of Probation*
67. Tappan: *Delinquent Girls in Court*
68. Alexander & Healy: *Roots of Crime*
69. *Healy & Bronner: *Delinquents and Criminals*
70. Cutler: *Lynch-Law*
71. Gillin: *Taming the Criminal*
72. Osborne: *Within Prison Walls*
73. Ashton: *The History of Gambling in England*
74. Whitlock: *On the Enforcement of Law in Cities*
75. Goldberg: *Child Offenders*
76. *Cressey: *The Taxi-Dance Hall*
77. Riis: *The Battle with the Slum*
78. Larson: *Lying and Its Detection*
79. Comstock: *Frauds Exposed*
80. Carpenter: *Our Convicts.* 2 vols. in one
81. †Horn: *Invisible Empire: The Story of the Ku Klux Klan, 1866–1871*
82. Faris et al.: *Intelligent Philanthropy*
83. Robinson: *History and Organization of Criminal Statistics in the U. S.*
84. Reckless: *Vice in Chicago*
85. Healy: *The Individual Delinquent*
86. *Bogen: *Jewish Philanthropy*
87. *Clinard: *The Black Market: A Study of White Collar Crime*
88. Healy: *Mental Conflicts and Misconduct*
89. Citizens' Police Committee: *Chicago Police Problems*
90. *Clay: *The Prison Chaplain*
91. *Peirce: *A Half Century with Juvenile Delinquents*
92. *Richmond: *Friendly Visiting Among the Poor*
93. Brasol: *Elements of Crime*
94. Strong: *Public Welfare Administration in Canada*
95. Beard: *Juvenile Probation*
96. Steinmetz: *The Gaming Table.* 2 vols.
97. *Crawford: *Report on the Penitentiaries of the United States*
98. *Kuhlman: *A Guide to Material on Crime and Criminal Justice*
99. Culver: *Bibliography of Crime and Criminal Justice, 1927–1931*
100. Culver: *Bibliography of Crime and Criminal Justice, 1932–1937*
101. Tompkins: *Administration of Criminal Justice, 1938–1948*
102. Tompkins: *Administration of Criminal Justice, 1949–1956*
103. Cumming: *Bibliography Dealing with Crime and Cognate Subjects*
104. *Addams et al.: *Philanthropy and Social Progress*
105. *Powell: *The American Siberia*
106. *Carpenter: *Reformatory Schools*
107. *Carpenter: *Juvenile Delinquents*
108. *Montague: *Sixty Years in Waifdom*

* new material added   † new edition, revised or enlarged

PATTERSON SMITH SERIES IN
CRIMINOLOGY, LAW ENFORCEMENT, AND SOCIAL PROBLEMS

109. *Mannheim: *Juvenile Delinquency in an English Middletown*
110. Semmes: *Crime and Punishment in Early Maryland*
111. *National Conference of Charities & Correction: *History of Child Saving in the United States*
112. ‡Barnes: *The Story of Punishment*
113. Phillipson: *Three Criminal Law Reformers*
114. *Drähms: *The Criminal*
115. *Terry & Pellens: *The Opium Problem*
116. *Ewing: *The Morality of Punishment*
117. ‡Mannheim: *Group Problems in Crime and Punishment*
118. *Michael & Adler: *Crime, Law and Social Science*
119. *Lee: *A History of Police in England*
120. ‡Schafer: *Compensation and Restitution to Victims of Crime*
121. †Mannheim: *Pioneers in Criminology*
122. Goebel & Naughton: *Law Enforcement in Colonial New York*
123. *Savage: *Police Records and Recollections*
124. Ives: *A History of Penal Methods*
125. *Bernard (ed.): *Americanization Studies.* 10 vols.:
    Thompson: *Schooling of the Immigrant*
    Daniels: *America via the Neighborhood*
    Thomas: *Old World Traits Transplanted*
    Speek: *A Stake in the Land*
    Davis: *Immigrant Health and the Community*
    Breckinridge: *New Homes for Old*
    Park: *The Immigrant Press and Its Control*
    Gavit: *Americans by Choice*
    Claghorn: *The Immigrant's Day in Court*
    Leiserson: *Adjusting Immigrant and Industry*
126. *Dai: *Opium Addiction in Chicago*
127. *Costello: *Our Police Protectors*
128. *Wade: *A Treatise on the Police and Crimes of the Metropolis*
129. *Robison: *Can Delinquency Be Measured?*
130. *Augustus: *John Augustus, First Probation Officer*
131. *Vollmer: *The Police and Modern Society*
132. Jessel & Horr: *Bibliographies of Works on Playing Cards and Gaming*
133. *Walling: *Recollections of a New York Chief of Police;* & Kaufmann: *Supplement on the Denver Police*
134. *Lombroso-Ferrero: *Criminal Man*
135. *Howard: *Prisons and Lazarettos.* 2 vols.:
    The State of the Prisons in England and Wales
    An Account of the Principal Lazarettos in Europe
136. *Fitzgerald: *Chronicles of Bow Street Police-Office.* 2 vols. in one
137. *Goring: *The English Convict*
138. Ribton-Turner: *A History of Vagrants and Vagrancy*
139. *Smith: *Justice and the Poor*
140. *Willard: *Tramping with Tramps*
141. *Fuld: *Police Administration*
142. *Booth: *In Darkest England and the Way Out*
143. *Darrow: *Crime, Its Cause and Treatment*
144. *Henderson (ed.): *Correction and Prevention.* 4 vols.:
    Henderson (ed.): *Prison Reform;* & Smith: *Criminal Law in the U. S.*
    Henderson (ed.): *Penal and Reformatory Institutions*
    Henderson: *Preventive Agencies and Methods*
    Hart: *Preventive Treatment of Neglected Children*
145. *Carpenter: *The Life and Work of Mary Carpenter*
146. *Proal: *Political Crime*

* new material added   † new edition, revised or enlarged

PATTERSON SMITH SERIES IN
CRIMINOLOGY, LAW ENFORCEMENT, AND SOCIAL PROBLEMS

147. *von Hentig: *Punishment*
148. *Darrow: *Resist Not Evil*
149. Grünhut: *Penal Reform*
150. *Guthrie: *Seed-Time and Harvest of Ragged Schools*
151. *Sprogle: *The Philadelphia Police*
152. †Blumer & Hauser: *Movies, Delinquency, and Crime*
153. *Calvert: *Capital Punishment in the Twentieth Century & The Death Penalty Enquiry*
154. *Pinkerton: *Thirty Years a Detective*
155. *Prison Discipline Society [Boston] Reports 1826–1854.* 6 vols.
156. *Woods (ed.) : *The City Wilderness*
157. *Woods (ed.) : *Americans in Process*
158. *Woods: *The Neighborhood in Nation-Building*
159. Powers & Witmer: *An Experiment in the Prevention of Delinquency*
160. *Andrews: *Bygone Punishments*
161. *Debs: *Walls and Bars*
162. *Hill: *Children of the State*
163. Stewart: *The Philanthropic Work of Josephine Shaw Lowell*
164. *Flinn: *History of the Chicago Police*
165. *Constabulary Force Commissioners: *First Report*
166. *Eldridge & Watts: *Our Rival the Rascal*
167. *Oppenheimer: *The Rationale of Punishment*
168. *Fenner: *Raising the Veil*
169. *Hill: *Suggestions for the Repression of Crime*
170. *Bleackley: *The Hangmen of England*
171. *Altgeld: *Complete Works*
172. *Watson: *The Charity Organization Movement in the United States*
173. *Woods et al.: *The Poor in Great Cities*
174. *Sampson: *Rationale of Crime*
175. *Folsom: *Our Police [Baltimore]*
176. Schmidt: *A Hangman's Diary*
177. *Osborne: *Society and Prisons*
178. *Sutton: *The New York Tombs*
179. *Morrison: *Juvenile Offenders*
180. *Parry: *The History of Torture in England*
181. Henderson: *Modern Methods of Charity*
182. Larned: *The Life and Work of William Pryor Letchworth*
183. *Coleman: *Humane Society Leaders in America*
184. *Duke: *Celebrated Criminal Cases of America*
185. *George: *The Junior Republic*
186. *Hackwood: *The Good Old Times*
187. *Fry & Cresswell: *Memoir of the Life of Elizabeth Fry.* 2 vols. in one
188. *McAdoo: *Guarding a Great City*
189. *Gray: *Prison Discipline in America*
190. *Robinson: *Should Prisoners Work?*
191. *Mayo: *Justice to All*
192. *Winter: *The New York State Reformatory in Elmira*
193. *Green: *Gambling Exposed*
194. *Woods: *Policeman and Public*
195. *Johnson: *Adventures in Social Welfare*
196. *Wines & Dwight: *Report on the Prisons and Reformatories of the United States and Canada*
197. *Salt: *The Flogging Craze*
198. *MacDonald: *Abnormal Man*
199. *Shalloo: *Private Police*
200. *Ellis: *The Criminal*

* new material added   † new edition, revised or enlarged